REPORTS FROM THE CLASSROOM

CASES FOR REFLECTION

Sarah Huyvaert
Eastern Michigan University

Allyn and Bacon
Boston London Toronto Sydney Tokyo Singapore

Reports from the Classroom: Cases for Reflection is dedicated to all the conscientious teachers who never give up in spite of the challenging situations they face day to day and year to year. This book demonstrates that teachers are professionals who are willing to share their insights and reflections in order to advance the field of education.

Editor-in-Chief, Education: Nancy Forsyth
Series Editor: Virginia Lanigan
Editorial Assistant: Nicole DePalma
Marketing Manager: Ellen Mann
Cover Administrator: Suzanne Harbison
Composition Buyer: Linda Cox
Manufacturing Buyer: Megan Cochran
Production Coordinator: Eleanor Sabini
Editorial-Production Service: TKM Productions

Copyright © 1995 by Allyn and Bacon
A Division of Simon & Schuster, Inc.
160 Gould Street
Needham Heights, Massachusetts 02194

Library of Congress Cataloging-in-Publication Data

Huyvaert, Sarah H., 1946–
    Reports from the classroom : cases for reflection / Sarah
Huyvaert.
        p. cm.
    Includes bibliographical references.
    ISBN 0-205-15514-6
    1. Teachers—United States—Case studies. 2. Teaching—Case
studies. 3. Classroom management—United States—Case studies.
I. Title.
LB1775.2.H89 1995
371.1'00973—dc20   94-9514
                                                                      CIP

Printed in the United States of America
10 9 8 7 6 5 4 3 2 1   99 98 97 96 95 94

Contents

Preface

Reports from the Classroom: Cases for Reflection is composed of a collection of case reports written by classroom teachers. Case reports differ from case studies. Case studies are usually written by a third party and the central focus of the case is someone other than the author of the study. It is the responsibility of the case study writer to present the case as impartially as possible. A case report, on the other hand, presents the issues from only one perspective—that of the author. The case reports in this book were written by classroom teachers who present the events from their own perspectives.

In compiling the book, case reports were solicited from over 150 teachers across the nation. Each case that was received was reviewed by the author and a second reader to determine if it was appropriate for a book on challenges or dilemmas in teaching. The number of case reports was narrowed to 50, and teachers who were taking graduate courses in education were asked to read and rate the cases. Each report was reviewed by at least five teachers and was rated on the importance of the issues discussed and the relevance of the issues to other teachers. From these 50 case reports, the 32 that received the highest ratings were selected for inclusion in this book. It is important to note that every case in the book was written by a *practicing teacher* who was reflecting on an *actual event*. The classroom experience of the teachers ranges from 1 year to over 30 years. The incidents involve students from small rural schools, middle-size suburban schools, and large metropolitan schools and examine events from kindergarten through high school.

Many of the reports in this book are followed by commentaries from professional educators. The group of commentators is comprised of teachers, administrators, and professors of education from across the United States. Each was asked to read specific case reports and to respond to the questions posed by the author. They were also asked to include any observations or concerns that they might have about the incident. These comments are included along with the case reports. Additional cases, without commentary, also have been included. This was done to allow readers to construct their own responses to the case writers' questions without a preconceived notion of how others interpret the cases.

The task of dividing the cases into sections that addressed similar problems proved to be difficult because the cases are based on actual experiences and they do not always fall into well-defined categories.

However, after careful analysis, seven themes did emerge: Disruptive Children and Antisocial Behaviors; Dealing with Parents; Placement of Students; Curricular and Instructional Decisions; Professional Interactions: Teacher to Teacher; Children in Crisis; and Evaluation of Students. The divisions are arbitrary, and several of the cases could have been placed in more than one group. In addition, other categories and groupings could easily have been formulated.

The strength of this book lies in the fact that the case reports were written by classroom teachers, were selected based on the judgment of classroom teachers, and were evaluated by professional educators across the nation. The case reports provided in this book have no "right answers," but rather reflect the complexity of the classroom and the need for teachers to be aware of the consequences of their actions.

Acknowledgments

Contributors of Case Reports

I greatly appreciate the generosity of those teachers who took time away from their busy schedules to write the incidents. The following is a partial list of the teachers who contributed case reports:

Dianna Armstrong	Jane Goerge	Lois Oldfield
Victoria Borgman	Beth Gryniewicz	Elizabeth Pascoe
Ted Braciak	Jeri Hart	Betty Polley
Lori Broughton	John Hester	Peter Roop
Thomas Craig	Donna Hicks	Karen Seibert
Christine Curvin	Sondra Johnson	Charles Swadling
Sharon Doran	Robin Klein	James Teevens
Sylvia Edwards	Laura Lewis	Mary Thallemer
Marilyn Emery	Jacquelinea McGowan	Annette Theiss
Sharon Emery	Mary McGrath	Mike Waters
Beth Feiten	Kelly Moss	Julie Wilson
Lisa Fett	Dawn Murrell	Corinne Widmayer

Respondents to the Cases

The following educators generously lent their expertise to this project. Each person is a dedicated professional who took time away from his or her busy schedule to respond to the case reports. Their help and advice are greatly appreciated.

Dennis C. Black has taught composition and literature for 25 years in a suburban setting, the last 20 of which have been in the Hazelwood School District in St. Louis County, Missouri. Black firmly believes that reading and writing about the human condition is an integral part of preparing students for life. He graduated in 1964 with a B.S. in education from Southeast Missouri State University, where he majored in English and history. He received his master's degree in English and education from the University of Missouri in St. Louis and has completed an additional 45 hours of graduate work.

Nicholas Byrne is a fifth-grade teacher at Tenakill School in Closter, New Jersey. He began his 25-year teaching career as a special education teacher. Since that time, he has taught grades 3 through 5, including students with social and emotional problems and students who are gifted and talented. Byrne is a recipient of President Bush's Thousand Points of Lights program; the Take Pride in America Award: the To Give and Learn Award honoring outstanding teacher-directed student community service, which was given by IBM in association with

U.S. News and World Report; and the New Jersey School Board's School Leader Award.

Jan Collins-Eaglin received a joint doctorate in psychology and education from the University of Michigan. Currently an assistant professor of educational psychology in the Department of Teacher Education at Eastern Michigan University, Collins-Eaglin has served as research coordinator for the University of Michigan, where she organized and administered faculty research projects dealing with psychological issues such as motivation, identity formation, and adolescent development; developed a field placement program for 350 undergraduate students in the Department of Human Services; advised and monitored students' activities at local human service agencies; and conducted training sessions for Hospice of Washtenaw volunteers on interpersonal techniques for working with dying patients.

Sandra E. Cornwell is a fourth-grade teacher at Deer Creek-Mackinaw Middle School in Deer Creek, Illinois. She has 23 years of classroom experience and has taught kindergarten, second grade, and fourth grade. Cornwell has served as president of the Illinois Valley Reading Council and is a member of the Illinois Reading Council. She is presently working on incorporating literature, art, and music with the social studies curriculum. She has several "theme days" a year that offer cross-curriculum activities for the entire day.

Billie Hughes has her Ph.D. in educational technology, a master's degree in library science, and a bachelor's degree in education. She has served as a faculty member in the school of education at Texas A&M University and Western Oregon State College. In her present role as a faculty member at Phoenix College, she is involved in outcomes assessment and evaluation. She is currently the evaluation and research coordinator of the Urban Partnership's Project (Phoenix Think Tank), which is charged with implementing systemic change throughout the Phoenix urban schools. She chaired the Maricopa Community College's Commission on Outcomes Assessment. Hughes is noted for her work on classroom research and has delivered numerous presentations on this topic at colleges across the country.

Sarah Huyvaert is an associate professor of teacher education at Eastern Michigan University, where she teaches both graduate and undergraduate courses in educational psychology, educational technology, and curriculum and instruction. Among the courses she teaches are Principles of Classroom Learning, Issues in Elementary Education, Psychology of the Adult Learner, Instructional Systems Design, and Technology of Instruction. Huyvaert holds a master's degree in elementary education and a doctorate in instructional systems technology from Indiana University. She has 10 years' teaching experience at the elementary level in both traditional and open classrooms programs.

Barbara Lowenthal is a professor of special education at Northeastern Illinois University, where she serves as the practicum supervisor and seminar instructor in early childhood and special education. She also teaches courses in early childhood special education diagnosis, assessment, and intervention. Lowenthal has published numerous articles dealing with interagency collaboration, training of early childhood regular and special educators, ecological assessment, and techniques for family assessment. She has also served as director of the Intergeneration Program and co-director of the Parent Effectiveness Grant and the Birth to Six Children with Special Needs Grant.

Judith Spitler-McKee is a professor of early childhood education and educational psychology at Eastern Michigan University. She is active in many professional associations at the local, state, and national levels and spends a great deal of her time working with professionals in the field. McKee holds an Ed.D. from Teacher's College, Columbia University. Her publications include *Annual Editions of Early Childhood Education* from 1976 through 1991; *Play: Work Partner of Growth* (1986); and *The Developing Kindergarten: Programs, Children, and Teachers* (1990).

Nancy Meadows is director of guidance at Wadsworth High School in Wadsworth, Ohio. She has a Ph.D. in counselor education and supervision from Kent State University and has served as a counselor at Wadsworth High School for the last 20 years. Meadows is a member of the American School Counselors Association and the Ohio School Counselor Associations. In January 1993, *The School Counselor* published an article by Meadows entitled "The Teacher Guidance Handbook."

Pat Olive is principal at Edgewater Elementary School in Edgewater, Colorado. She has a master's degree in special education, was a classroom teacher for 15 years, and has been an elementary principal for 4 years. Her current school is a nongraded, multiage (kindergarten through sixth grade), Chapter 1 school with a population of 450.

Patti Ritchey is the department chair for English, foreign languages, speech, and journalism in a department of 34 teachers in a seventh- through twelfth-grade school of more than 1,800 students. She has taught journalism and English for 16 years at West High School in Hazelwood, Missouri, has supervised the department's Writing Center, has acted as faculty advisor to the school's yearbooks and newspaper, and has state teaching certifications in French, English, and journalism instruction.

Tracy Robinson is an assistant professor of counselor education at North Carolina State University in Raleigh, North Carolina. She received B.A. degrees in psychology and communication arts from Azusa Pacific University in Azusa, California. She earned both her master's degree and doctorate in human development from Harvard University. Robinson has served as the director of research for the Quality Education for Minorities Project at Massachusetts Institute of Technology. She has also served as director of counseling and testing at Johnson C. Smith University. Her areas of research include teachers' and counselors' perspectives on race, gender, and culture; the intersections of gender, race, culture, and class in psychosocial identity formation; and African American adolescents and skin color.

Robert E. Rubinstein teaches language and performing arts at Roosevelt Middle School in Eugene, Oregon. He is a recipient of the Oregon Education Association's Noel Connal Instructional and Professional Development Award. Rubinstein has written over 100 articles and his books include *Hints for Teaching Success in Middle School, Who Wants to Be a Hero!* and *When Sirens Scream.* Rubinstein is the founder and director of the nationally known Troupe of Tellers, which consists of sixth- through eighth-grade students who travel to other schools to perform. Since 1969, these troupes have performed for over 70,000 students. The Tellers have conducted workshops for teachers and for the Oregon Young Writers, and have performed for the Oregon International Reading Association's Conference, the Oregon Library State Conference, and the National Storytelling Conference.

Charline Socci has 18 years of teaching experience at the elementary level. She has taught grades 1 through 6 and has been with the Fairfax County Public Schools in Virginia for 16 years. Currently, she is a fourth-grade teacher at Hutchison Elementary School in Herndon, Virginia.

Additional Acknowledgments

In addition to the contributors and respondents listed elsewhere in this book, I wish to express my appreciation to the many people who helped make this book possible. It would be impossible to list all of those who offered their support and encouragement, but I do especially want to thank the individuals who helped to select the case reports that have been included in the book; my graduate students in the Principles of Classroom Learning course who read and reacted to the case reports; and Virginia Lanigan, my editor at Allyn and Bacon, who seemed to have all the answers. I also would like to thank the reviewers selected by Allyn and Bacon: Gregory Bryant, Towson State University; Dawna Lisa Buchanan-Berrigan, Shawnee State University; Douglas D. Hatch, University of South Florida; Michael John Horvath, Bradley University; Anne C. Troutman, Memphis State University; and John R. Zelazek, Central Missouri State University.

Heather Yost, a graduate student in the teacher education program at Eastern Michigan University, deserves special thanks. Not only did Heather read and react to the case reports but she also spent many hours in the library looking for references that would assist the reader in analyzing and evaluating the case reports.

Finally, I would like to thank my husband, Tom. I can only begin to list the many things that he did to help make this book a reality. From helping to compile the list of possible contributors, to giving up numerous Sunday afternoons to look for misspelled words or misplaced commas, to taking calls and answering questions from various contributors, he was always there when I needed him. Without his support and encouragement, this book would never have been completed.

It is the hope of everyone who has contributed that this book will be of value both to teachers and prospective teachers. Together we can make a difference in education and hence in the quality of life of our students.

Introduction

Teachers are continually making critical decisions that may seriously affect the students in their classrooms. Many of these decisions, although significant, become almost a routine part of the teaching day. However, even the most experienced teachers will occasionally encounter a situation that leaves them in a quandary and, although they handle the episode to the best of their ability, they often have a nagging feeling that there must have been a better way to deal with the incident.

As a teacher, when you take the time to reflect on the dilemmas in your classroom—pondering what went right, what went wrong, and what still bothers you about the situation—you will find that you are better able to handle the next dilemma that you face. Likewise, when you are able to discuss your concerns with other educators in a rational, nonthreatening manner, you become increasingly astute at handling some of the more perplexing conditions that you face in the classroom. The more experience you gain in the classroom, the easier your decision making will become.

The case reports in this book provide you with an opportunity to practice the skills involved in critical and reflective thinking (analysis, evaluation, synthesis) and to further develop your problem-solving ability.

The book is divided into eight sections. The cases within any given section may include case reports from elementary, middle, and high school or from only one or two of these areas. Even in the sections that include only one or two school levels, there are cases that deal with critical issues that can be translated across grade levels. For instance, in Section 3, Placement of Students, all of the cases were written by elementary teachers. However, the issues of whether to promote a student who lacks the academic skills for advancement but who will be socially harmed if retained ("Social Promotion versus Retention: Is It Really a Question of Self-Esteem versus Achievement?") and whether a student who is disruptive and gifted should be placed in a program for students who are gifted and talented or a program for students who are emotionally impaired ("Bright and Disruptive: Should One Concentrate on the Gift or the Wrapping?") are applicable at almost all grade levels. Likewise, in some sections, all the cases are written by middle or high school teachers. However, the issues of getting students to cooperate ("Cooperation through No Fault of My Own—Or How to Succeed without Really Trying") and of establishing standards ("Student Needs versus School Logistics") are definitely appropriate issues for the elementary teacher to address.

How to Use This Book

As you read each of the cases, think about how you would have reacted if you had been in the teacher's position. The following steps may prove helpful:

1. Read the case report and jot down your observations and note any questions you might have about the situation.
2. Think about how you would answer the questions posed by the author of the case report.
3. See if you can determine the key elements of the problem. Can you identify what the teacher did to make a bad situation better? What did the teacher do that may have made the situation worse?
4. Identify other problem-solving techniques the teacher might have used.
5. Decide on the advice you would give the teacher.
6. If the case report is followed by respondents' comments, determine if the respondents identify the same key elements that you did. Did they offer some techniques that you hadn't thought of or that were unfamiliar to you? Did you come up with some techniques that the consultants didn't mention? If you did, do you still believe that your suggestions are valid? Do you agree with one of the consultants more than the others?
7. For those cases that contain no commentary, write a commentary of your own.

8. Now see if you can answer the discussion questions at the end of the case report.
9. Share your answers with a fellow student and see how closely your answers agree.
10. Finally, review the "Questions, Exercises, and Activities" that relate to the section's overall theme. For further study, refer to the "Suggested Readings" at the end of the section.

As you read each case, remember that you are not looking for a "right" or "wrong" answer. Instead, you should be assessing your own ability to analyze a classroom situation, evaluating the effectiveness of a particular problem-solving technique, and taking what you know about teaching and learning in an *academic* sense and applying it to a real-life problem.

SECTION 1

DISRUPTIVE CHILDREN AND ANTISOCIAL BEHAVIORS

This section contains case reports on disruptive children and the dilemmas that they created for their teachers. The first case, "Teacher Action Leads to Student Reaction: Two Negatives Don't Make a Positive," deals with a seventh-grade girl whose behavior is often unpredictable and erratic. The case addresses an incident in which the teacher's behavior, rather than helping improve a poor situation, served to make it worse. Although the teacher learned from the incident, she still has concerns about the way she handled the situation. In the second case, "Abuse or Excuse?" a high school student loses her temper and begins swearing during class. When her teacher threatens to call the girl's parents, the girl begs the teacher to reconsider, claiming that her father abuses her. The teacher made a decision but she is still wondering if she did the right thing. "Suspension: Bridge from Misbehavior to Appropriate Behavior?" the third and final case in this section, involves a fourth-grade student who also uses profanity in the classroom. The teacher questions the wisdom of how the situation was handled and questions the role that the school should play in the moral development of children.

In all three cases, you will find that a bad situation escalated into a worse situation. You will also notice that the parents become involved on some level or another. As you review each case, take some time to analyze what the teacher did to make the situation better or worse and what strategies he or she used to deal with the student's misconduct. See if you can evaluate what effects both the student's *and* teacher's behavior had on the other children in the classroom. Examine the similarities and differences among the situations and then compare and contrast (1) the techniques the teachers used; (2) the roles played by other adults (parents, administrators, other teachers); (3) the ways in which the classroom environment may have helped or hurt the containment of the situation; and (4) the responses of the commentators.

Professional educators have reviewed the first two cases and their comments are included at the conclusion of each of the case reports. As you read the commentaries, decide if the respondents agree with one another and if you agree with them. From your readings, discussions with professional educators, and personal observations and experiences, develop your own commentary for the third case report.

As you read the case reports, it will not be unusual for you to feel as if something is missing—as if you're not getting the whole story. Remember—the cases present only the teachers' interpretations of what has happened, and your feeling that there must be more to the story is probably accurate. Although you are reading what the *teacher* believes to be the important aspects of the case, you are provided with enough data to analyze the situation, critically evaluate the issues, and synthesize the information to form a credible response to the questions.

Teacher Action Leads to Student Reaction: Two Negatives Don't Make a Positive

Background

This incident occurred in my sixth-hour, seventh-grade life science class. The class consisted of 31 students—8 of whom were girls and 23 of whom were boys. As a group, they were very intelligent but they tended to act very immaturely. Most of the students were generally "charged up" from being in gym class during the previous hour. Students at the school were grouped into sections and each section had all of the same classes together during the course of the day. The only times the students weren't together were during gym class and during their electives.

By the time the students got to sixth hour, I never knew what type of behavior to expect from them. Some days everyone would be getting along fine but other days they would be angry and fighting with one another. It often seemed that by the time they reached my class their anger and frustrations had been pushed to the limit and they were about to come to blows.

One particular girl, Kristine, was very loud and physically aggressive toward most of the boys in the class. If a boy said anything to her, and if he was close enough, her normal response was to punch the boy. This was not just a jab in the arm, but a punch in the middle of the back that was hard enough that the blow could be heard from several feet away. If Kristine was not close enough to punch the boy, she would respond verbally and very loudly.

It seemed as though I was constantly talking to her and threatening to send her to the office for hitting other students. One time I did actually send her to the office for this behavior. In addition, I changed her seating assignment several times, spoke with her constantly about her behavior, and made her write sentences in response to her verbal outbursts.

Even though there were 34 seats in the room, there weren't enough seats to separate the students who couldn't or wouldn't work next to each other. At first, I thought it was just my inexperience that made me so frustrated with this group. After speaking to the other teachers, I realized that it wasn't my lack of experience that was causing the problem, but that this was a unique and challenging combination of students.

Incident

One day, as I approached my classroom, I noticed that Kristine was having another confrontation with one of the boys. Just as I entered the room and began arranging my materials, I heard Kristine yell at the boy. As I looked up, I saw Kristine hit the boy hard in the middle of his back. She hit him so hard that I heard the hollow thud of her fist on his back.

I yelled at her to sit down. All of the students hurried to their seats since this was such unusual behavior for me. I began to lecture her in front of all of the other students. I must admit that I was angry and very frustrated because I had just spoken to her the day before about such incidents. I was also scared that she might hurt one of the boys if she kept up this behavior. I reminded her that students were not allowed to hit other students, and I told her how tired I was of having to remind her of the inappropriateness of her behavior. I said that it was unfair for her to hit the boys the way she did, especially since they were not allowed to hit a girl. I then asked her how she would like it if every boy who had been hit by her hit her back just as hard as she had hit them. As soon as these words left my mouth, I knew I had made a mistake. Every boy who was sitting anywhere near her got up and hit her. I immediately ordered them back to their seats and discussed the inappropriateness of what had just taken place. I punished all those involved.

At the end of the hour, as Kristine left school, she told her mother of the incident. Before I could even get down to the office to report the situation, her mother had called the principal. The principal called me into the office and I was unable to defend my actions and reactions. He could see that I was upset by the incident, but he still reprimanded me severely.

Discussion

Luckily, Kristine was not injured in this incident, but she was just as shook-up as I was. I know I used the power of suggestion very poorly as an example and that this problem stemmed, in part, from my own anger and frustration. Needless to say, if I learned nothing else that year, I did learn not to give poor examples or to ask questions of a student in front of the entire class unless I wanted the students to take me literally. Also, in the future I will immediately remove the student from the classroom for such behavior and take care of the matter on an individual basis.

One thing that really bothered me about this situation was the way the principal treated me. He could see that I was upset and that I knew I had made a mistake, yet he really bawled me out. He was upset because he had to find out about the incident from a parent. He told me that I should have informed him immediately and not waited until after Kristine's mother had spoken to him. I tried to explain that I had planned on going to the office right after school, but I had to wait until all the students left my class. But he just didn't seem to hear me.

I knew the situation needed to be dealt with, so I spoke with one of the counselors who is very good with the students. She offered to come into my class to do a personal communication exercise designed to help students get along better. When my principal heard about this, he seemed to be put at ease and told me that he thought I had gained a new perspective and understanding of this class and that he was pleased.

Questions

1. What should a teacher do to stifle verbally and physically abusive behavior toward the opposite sex?
2. I was really frustrated with Kristine even before this happened and I know I let my temper get the better of me. Is there something I can do to prevent this from happening in the future?
3. How does a teacher get a class to work together, cooperate, and respect each other when they refuse to do so?
4. I was feeling bad about the situation to begin with, so why did the principal have to reprimand me?
5. Is it ever okay to leave a disruptive group of students alone or would that make a bad situation worse?

Response of Robert E. Rubinstein, Teacher

The background material indicates there are some general group dynamics happening with this class. When a class is together all day, day after day, the students can soon become bored with one another. This generally occurs with any group of people—children or adults. Typically, some members do well at most tasks, some members do well at only some of the tasks, and others don't do well on any of the tasks. Those individuals who are difficult to get along with or who cause trouble are well known. The class's cliques probably remain the same throughout the year. By sixth period, not only are the students tired but also the teacher is tired. Both feel on edge—and the teacher has to be aware of this.

In this country we have one of the few education systems that demand that kids, with all their energy and questions, rush from one 40-minute period to another with just 3 or 4 minutes passing time. There's no time to consider what's been learned because they have to readjust quickly to another subject area that has nothing to do with the previous one. Most countries realize that young people—indeed, people in general—don't learn well with a system of 40-minute disconnected periods throughout the day. Teachers also don't teach as effectively in such a system. Most other cultures allow students time to go to the restroom, to socialize, to ask the teacher questions after class, and to release some of the tension and energy caused by being forced to sit for 40 minutes. Socializing should be an important part of the school day— that's how students learn to deal with others, and that's an important part of life.

Studies show that the average attention span of a person under 14 years old is 10 minutes and that for a person over age 14 it is 20 minutes. Yet, students are expected to sit in class for 40 minutes and read silently, listen to a lecture, or do worksheets—and then teachers wonder why they have behavior problems. I can't sit in a university class for an hour without losing attention or becoming restless—often because the teacher and material are boring and tedious. If I, as an adult, can't do this, how could I expect a young teenager with all that energy to sit still and not create problems?

Tasks need to be varied during a class period. During the school day, more focus must be placed on giving these young people an outlet within classes for organized physical activities where they can move around. Perhaps it's worth taking the first five minutes of this class to allow the students to vent their day's frustrations. This could be done in writing and kept confidential, unless, of course, the students choose to share their frustrations. However, their comments should never be corrected or re-marked on by the teacher or the other students. This "frustration shar-ing" might be done orally if the teacher can create a secure atmosphere in which all students listen with respect. In addition, to break up the cliques and foster new relationships, the teacher might purposely keep rotating or rearranging groups of students who work together or sit next to each other.

What did the teacher know about Kristine? The moment she real-ized that Kristine had behavior problems, the teacher and/or counselor should have collected information about Kristine, including:

- How does she work with other teachers in other classes?
- How has she worked and behaved in school in the past?
- Have there been any changes this year, and why?
- What is her home life and her life, in general, like outside of school?
- Are there any special concerns or problems?

It's not simply a matter of "making a student behave" by punishing the student. That's negative, forced discipline, not self-discipline. A teacher must take the time to find out the cause of this behavior or it will occur again and again.

The teacher might give Kristine, if not all the students in this class, a personal "like/dislike" sheet or a sheet with other types of questions to complete. The students should know that this information will be kept confidential. These questions should allow for responses about life goals and interests, as well as responses about the students' feelings about school, an assessment of personal strengths and weaknesses, and how the students want to improve. Although individual answers would not be revealed, the teacher could discuss general results with the students and allow them to offer their views.

In this case, the teacher constantly threatens to send Kristine to the office but doesn't. The teacher talks *at* her about behavior, yells *at* her and the class, and makes her write as punishment. No communication is really occurring when the teacher behaves this way. Repeated threats without action show vacillation on the part of the teacher and the students don't believe the threats after a while. When someone is yelled *at* or talked *at* rather than *with*, the first human responses are self-defense and escape. The student is too busy protecting himself or herself to listen. Making a student write as a punishment only helps make writing a negative experience in the student's mind. Why would teachers want to do that?

In general, I would have used a simple one-two response to Kristine's behavior. She would understand that I would give only one warning and with the very next incident she would have to leave the room. There would be no arguments and no lectures, but simply: "Kristine, it's time for you to leave. We'll talk later." I would have an agreement with the counselor or an administrator so that Kristine would go to one of them if sent from the room. I would also quickly jot down the time and specific reason for her departure. While Kristine is in the office, I might have her write (uncensored by me) about the following: Why did you act this way? What are the results of this type of behavior choice? What other behavior choices could you have made and with what likely results? Then, Kristine and I could sit down together to discuss what she had written. The focus should be on the behavior, not the student.

The teacher might also create a personal, daily behavioral goal sheet with Kristine. Together they would agree on which behaviors Kristine will improve. At the end of the day, or maybe a week, the teacher and Kristine would then list the good behaviors she displayed (even if it's merely getting to class on time) as well as those behaviors that still need improvement. Plenty of praise should be given to Kristine for what she's done well. In general, all students should be encouraged to recognize and praise themselves for what they do well. (This might be another way to begin this class period.)

When the hitting incident occurred, Kristine should have been sent immediately to the office without any yelling, lecturing, or anger on the teacher's part. (Remember—Kristine doesn't make the teacher angry or cause the teacher to behave that way; the teacher chooses to respond that way.) All that needs to be said is: "Kristine, that behavior's unacceptable. Please go to the office now. We'll talk later about this." Then, by intercom, the teacher should notify the office that Kristine has been sent there.

The incident where the boys hit Kristine was the teacher's fault. Punishing the whole class for something the teacher initiated isn't fair. Taking the time, though, for a class discussion about what happened would be in order. If the teacher can't handle such a discussion, then the counselor or someone else with expertise should be asked to lead one. After the incident occurred, the teacher should have sent word to the principal, sent for the principal, or sent a note to the office.

Naturally, Kristine's mother would be upset that a teacher helped instigate such abuse of her daughter, no matter what happened prior to the incident. Hopefully, the teacher would immediately take the initiative to arrange a parent-teacher meeting, and include other teachers and/or administrators who have experience with Kristine. Kristine should be present and the teacher might even have her run the meeting.

Response of
Tracy Robinson, Professor

Given the alarming statistics concerning the likelihood of assault on women, it's a good thing that the aggressive young woman in this study knows how to physically protect herself. However, her behavior is inappropriate when used to inflict physical harm on someone who is not physically attacking her.

Kristine obviously has energy that needs to be rerouted and relabeled. Important questions for the teacher to ask include:

- Why does the student behave as she does? (There has to be a reason since behavior does not occur in a vacuum.)
- Might there be physical abuse in her home?
- Is she hungry for attention?
- Why is she so angry?
- What is the school's policy concerning students who physically endanger other students?
- Am I adequately trained to resolve classroom conflict?
- Do I have adequate control over my classroom?

Teachers are human and will make mistakes. Where appropriate, when adults can admit their mistakes to their students, a teachable moment is made available from which all can learn and develop. The counseling staff should have been called on immediately to assist this teacher.

Concluding Questions and Activities

1. What do you believe are the key elements of the problem? Did the consultants identify the same key elements that you did?
2. What did the teacher do to make the situation better?
3. What did she do that may have made the situation worse?
4. What other problem-solving techniques might the teacher have used? What advice would you give the teacher?
5. Did the consultants offer some techniques that you had not thought of or that were unfamiliar to you? Did you come up with some techniques that the consultants didn't mention? If you did, do you still believe that your suggestions are valid?
6. Do you agree with one of the consultants more than the other? What, if anything, does this say about your philosophy of education?
7. Mr. Rubinstein suggested that the students begin the class period by sharing their frustrations, either in writing or orally. Do you think this will work? Might there be some dangers in doing this? If so, what are they, and how might you handle them if they arose?
8. It is obvious that the teacher made several mistakes, including losing her temper and not immediately reporting the incident to the office. She realized her mistakes and took steps to correct them. Do you think that her actions following the incident will correct the situation?
9. Do the teacher's questions and comments convince you that she really will handle the situation better the next time around?

Does she demonstrate that she understands the true problem or does the problem run deeper than she acknowledges? What makes you think so?

10. Both consultants recommended that the teacher seek additional information about Kristine. Develop a plan that the teacher could use to get this information. Include the types of questions she should ask, a list of people she should consult, and a way to identify the kinds of existing data she might examine.

11. Mr. Rubinstein noted that the United States has one of the few educational systems where students move from one 40-minute period to another. Explore how the school day is structured in other countries. You can do this by consulting some of the sources that follow and/or by interviewing international students on your campus. Once you have collected your data, write an opinion paper that either supports or refutes Rubinstein's position.

Suggested Readings

Anderson, L. M., & Prawat, R. S. (1983). Responsibility in the classroom: A synthesis of research on teaching self-control. *Educational Leadership, 40*(7), 62–66.

Ben-Peretz, M., & Bromme, R. (1990). *The nature of time in schools: Theoretical concepts, practitioner perceptions.* New York: Teachers College Press.

Canter, L. (1979). Taking charge of student behavior. *National Elementary Principal, 58*(40), 33–36, 41.

Creton, H. A., Wubbels, T., & Hooymayers, H. P. (1989). Escalated disorderly situations in the classroom and the improvement of these situations. *Teaching & Teacher Education, 5*(3), 205–215.

Diamond, S. C. (1992). Resolving teacher-student conflict: A different path. *The Clearing House, 65*(3), 141–143.

Dubelle, S. T., & Hoffman, C. M. (1987). When an attention seeker gets under your skin. *Principal, 66*(4), 28–30.

Eitzen, D. S. (1992). Problem students: The sociocultural roots. *Phi Delta Kappan, 73*(8), 584–588, 590.

Lumpkin, J. (1991). Rocky Roxanne. *Learning, 19*(6), 58–60.

Miller, E. (1992, March/April). Breaking the tyranny of the schedule. *Harvard Education Letter,* 6–8.

Pasch, M., Sparks-Langer, G., Gardner, T. G., Starko, A. J., & Moody, C. D. (1991). *Teaching as decision making: Instructional practices for the successful teacher* (pp. 308–317). New York: Longman.

Stevenson, H. W. (1992, December). Learning from Asian schools. *Scientific American*, 70–76.

Stevenson, H. W., & Stigler, J. W. (1992). The organization of schooling. In H. W. Stevenson & J. W. Stigler (Eds.), *The Learning Gap* (pp. 130–155). New York: Summit Books.

Abuse or Excuse?

Background

It's sadly ironic that her name was Harmony. Never before, or since, have I observed anyone in such a state of disharmony. I am referring here to Harmony's extreme swings in mood. For example, when Harmony was angry, she was in a rage, but when Harmony was happy, she was the happiest person alive. Her happiness could change to blind rage at the drop of a hat. Worst of all, when Harmony was in a rage, she was not in control of her actions. More than once I have seen Harmony hurl her purse at the floor after storming into class and then, shortly thereafter, actually mourn the breakage of some object contained in the purse. Harmony was in my class for one hour a day, and her extreme shifts in mood did not occur daily. In fact, weeks would go by without incident. However, from day to day it was impossible for me to predict what mood Harmony would be in when she entered the classroom, or to determine why these mood shifts occurred or what triggered them.

Even though I never understood Harmony's behavior, I did develop a close relationship with her outside of class. My class was the last one of the day and Harmony would routinely, along with a couple of other students, "hang out" in my room after school. She didn't open up to me often, but I was able to gather that outside of school, Harmony was allowed to interact socially with church members only. Also, she told me that her father was disabled and that his children from a previous marriage visited periodically. I never met Harmony's father, but I did have the opportunity to meet her mother. Harmony was described by her mother as "having a bad temper just like her father" and advised me not to take Harmony too seriously.

I also knew Harmony's family from the perspective of her half-brother, Joe, who was in another class of mine. Joe and Harmony got along extremely well; however, Joe made no bones about it, he thought his sister was "crazy." Unfortunately, this opinion was also held by most students, and I had even heard Harmony refer to herself this way. Despite the label, Harmony was accepted by the other students. In fact, it may be that she was accepted *because* of the label. It seemed to provide a way for the other students to rationalize her behavior. For example, when a student, for no apparent reason, received the brunt of Harmony's anger, he or she simply took cover and chalked Harmony's behavior up to craziness. Keep in mind, though, that Harmony was a beautiful girl and when she was in one of her good moods, she was considered really fun to be around. So, more often than not, she was sought after, especially if her mood warranted it. The incident I am about to relate involving Harmony took place at a high school located in a large city. The school serves a predominantly Hispanic (60 percent) and low-income population. The area could best be described as "blighted."

Incident

As I was answering a question for Harmony and her partner on some newly introduced science problems, Harmony began to shake and scowl, and finally let go with the foulest language imaginable. Even the night after the incident occurred, I still could not remember exactly what I had said to set Harmony off. Thankfully, these foul mutterings were not aimed at me or anyone else in particular, but mostly directed at the floor. Nonetheless, the room went quiet. At first, I flinched almost simultaneously with the rest of the class. For several seconds, I simply stood in shock. Finally, somehow, I got Harmony out of the room and into the hall. Almost immediately she calmed down and was filled with remorse. She could not tell why she had exploded but said that she was sorry. I explained to her that no matter how sorry she was, I would have to call her parents and tell them what had happened. Although I had threatened to do this several times before, I made it very clear that I intended to follow through this time. Harmony immediately became hysterical. It wasn't until after school, when I had Harmony calmed down again but still in tears, that she told me her father abused her. "How does he abuse you?" I kept asking her, and she kept answering as if it were basically verbal abuse—her father would pin her down and yell at her.

Discussion

Based on my relationship with Harmony, I felt that she was exaggerating to get out of trouble, and I did not believe her story of abuse. Obviously though, she was very much in fear of her parents. For that reason, I gave Harmony another chance. We developed a contract which stated that, if the behavior occurred again, I would call her parents. The contract worked out satisfactorily for the rest of the year. However, this incident still haunts me because I realize that I failed to call in outside help for the alleged abuse. Even though the abuse was verbal rather than physical, the student still referred to it as abuse and I didn't follow up on the accusation.

Questions

1. Should I have called Harmony's parents even though she claimed that her father would abuse her? Was there something else I could have done to find out if her claims were true?
2. I didn't really believe Harmony when she said her father verbally abused her, yet even her mother said that Harmony's father had a "bad temper." Is verbal abuse something that I, as a teacher, should be concerned with? Should a report of verbal abuse be reported to the proper authorities, no matter what the context of the situation?
3. Should I have spoken to Harmony's brother about her claim of abuse to see if he could confirm or deny it? Would this be putting him on the spot? Does a teacher sometimes have to put a student on the spot in order to get at the truth? Was any of this really any of my business?
4. Are there signs of abuse that I should be aware of? Was Harmony's change in moods one of those signs?
5. If I were to encounter a similar situation with another student, what steps might I take to help the student?

Response of
Patti Ritchey, Teacher

Upon reading the case study of Harmony and the incident with her classroom teacher, my immediate reaction is that if this teacher is letting one student's single incident of misbehavior weigh on his or her mind throughout an entire semester, that teacher won't last long in the profession or he or she doesn't really teach in a "blighted" school. Considering that most teachers on the secondary level deal with an average of 25 to 30 students an hour for five class hours a day, the teacher involved in this incident cannot carry the burden of one decision for his or her entire career.

She—and I use the female pronoun because, I suppose, I assume a male teacher wouldn't as easily question his actions—reacted to one very slight discipline problem in a positive and constructive manner, achieving success with the student and maintaining control of the class. Most teachers in "blighted" schools deal with drugs, guns, fights, and obvious abusive language directed at the teacher. Why, then, does this cussing-at-the-floor incident have this teacher concerned even after a viable solution was achieved?

Assuming the teacher is bothered enough to ask me, her supervisor-coach, for an opinion on the incident, I would have to answer her questions in the following manner:

1. It probably wouldn't have achieved much to call Harmony's parents specifically about the alleged abuse. It may have helped to call her parents to inform them that the teacher is working with Harmony to help her maintain more self-control in class. Her parents could be told that this is an area in which Harmony is trying hard and doing well, but that the teacher wanted them to be aware that Harmony is focusing on improving her behavior in this area.

2. Any time a teacher feels—and sometimes it is just a gut feeling— that any type of abuse toward a child is occurring, I would suggest that the teacher notify the student's counselor. Counselors, in our district, are instructed to deal with the issue, and their expertise makes them good at it.

3. Contacting the brother about Harmony's claim is probably not in anyone's best interest. Not only does it put him on the spot, it also puts Harmony and her parents on the spot, especially if the claims are unfounded.

4. District workshops and seminars held regularly during the school year are designed to make teachers aware of signs of abuse. Harmony's mood changes could be one of those signs; they could also be signs of puberty, manic-depression, or a "bad hair" day, depending on her age.

Personally, I believe that the teacher developed an instructive and constructive solution to what is possibly a single incident of misbehavior. The teacher should let go of Harmony and move on to one of the other 150 unique student situations he or she has to deal with in one day.

Response of
Dennis C. Black, Teacher

My first reaction in reading this case report was that there really wasn't much of a problem here. The teacher handled things appropriately.

What do we know about Harmony?

1. Harmony has powerful mood swings.
2. She has a terrible temper that erupts unexpectedly.
3. She can control it if necessary.
4. Her father has a similar temper.
5. She has the potential for other kinds of episodes, evidenced by the use of foul language.
6. Students accept her and excuse her behavior as "crazy."

What are we unsure of?

1. Her temper may be learned or pathological.
2. She may or may not act as she does for effect.
3. She may be the victim of abuse.
4. The foul language could be the early manifestation of anger or a disturbed personality. Harmony may in fact be mentally disturbed.

What do we know about the teacher?

1. The teacher is sensitive to Harmony's problem.
2. The teacher handled an awkward classroom situation efficiently.
3. The teacher developed a solution for a problem that threatened to turn up again but did not.
4. The teacher worries that he or she may have ignored a serious case of abuse.

Based on the facts of the case, the teacher seems to have made all the right decisions. He or she does not have sufficient evidence to pursue a case of abuse, which may be verbal only. It is difficult enough investigating the possibility of physical abuse; proving a case of verbal abuse would be even more difficult. "He pins me down and yells at me" is a charge not likely to convince a district attorney to go to court. In addition, any parent, especially one as volatile as Harmony's, who heard about any investigation might well cause a lot of problems for the teacher and the school. Finally, the teacher was not really convinced that Harmony was telling the truth. There was no definite proof that there was serious abuse. The teacher would need independent corroboration to justify Harmony's vague claims. In the absence of such information, the teacher did the right thing.

The issue I don't understand is why the school didn't insist on some sort of evaluation, and, if warranted, a therapy or behavior-modification program. There are experts who can deal with Harmony's aberrant behavior. Harmony had a history of such behavior, yet there is no mention that anything was ever done. I can only assume that because the school was in a blighted area, the district did not have funds for psychological evaluation or treatment of seriously disturbed students.

I was troubled by the fact that the teacher was disturbed by his or her inaction in pursuing the possibility of abuse. If this teacher continues a pattern of assuming some sort of vague guilt for not pursuing the truth of different situations, he or she will not be able to carry the emotional baggage that goes along with that guilt. Teachers deal with sensitive situations and disturbed children all the time. It is not possible to investigate every conceivable course of action and always choose the right one. A teacher cannot play God, minister, therapist, detective, or parent for every child. For those who try, the complexities will drive them "crazy" or drive them out of the profession. I know plenty of "stressed-out" instructors. This teacher needs to develop some professional distance from the students. He or she should care about them and offer them comfort and sensible advice when qualified, but must be careful about becoming personally involved in their lives. Once teachers make a final decision about a student and a situation, they must go on with their work.

Response of
Nancy Meadows, Director of Guidance

The teacher in this case could have consulted with the school counselor about the many incidents of questionable behavior. Both Harmony and the teacher would have benefited from a team approach to investigating the girl's actions. If the team, including the counselor and all of the girl's teachers, found that the behaviors occurred commonly, a team decision could be made on the matter of when and how to involve the parents. The team may have developed insight into possible abuse by sharing their observations and conversations. The counselor could also interview Harmony. Although physical signs of abuse may not have been seen, school personnel could consult with local Children's Services for advice on whether to pursue the issue.

Verbal abuse can be a form of neglect of the child's emotional needs. In severe cases, Children's Services can intervene. Making the judgment on when to report an incident to Children's Services is best determined by the team. The report would appropriately include remarks made by Harmony and her mother. Her brother may also be interviewed by the school counselor to try to obtain more information.

I believe the teacher could report the brother's comments to the school counselor, who would then follow up by interviewing the boy. The counselor could also check school records for previous reports. Counselors and teachers who knew the children in previous years could be another source of information in trying to piece together a pattern of behavior that may be stemming from abuse. I do believe the teacher is properly, and perhaps legally, committed to making Harmony his or her "business." In all states, the laws require public school personnel to report suspected child abuse cases. Most schools have, or should have, clear guidelines for reporting procedures. I also see that most teachers, as a matter of conscience, wish to do the right thing for their students. Today's teachers are trying to teach the whole child and they realize that a student does not reach his or her full potential if abuse is occurring.

Instances of Harmony's behavior indicate a possibility of abuse. Her mood swings, inability to control her severe reactions, fear of her parents being informed, and seeking the companionship of the caring teacher all may point in the direction of abuse and neglect. These same symptoms are also signs of many illnesses or drug abuse. A thorough physical examination should be helpful in determining the nature of Harmony's problem. Testing by the school psychologist could also be helpful. A neurologist with special interest in children's learning and behavior may also lend insights.

If the teacher were to encounter a similar situation with another student, he or she should meet with the school counselor. The counselor could investigate the student's records as well as call a team meeting to discuss the case. If a counselor is not available, a teacher may try to work with the school psychologist or possibly an administrator. Finally, if no results are obtained within the school, the teacher could directly call Children's Services to report the suspected abuse.

Concluding Questions and Activities

1. The teacher respondent makes the comment: "She—and I use the female teacher form because, I suppose, I assume a male teacher

wouldn't as easily question his actions— . . . ." How do you respond to this? Is this a valid assumption? Do male and female teachers react differently to classroom incidents?

2. When you examine the commentary of the three respondents, you find that Ritchie and Black seem to imply that there really wasn't much of a problem here, the situation was handled properly, and the teacher should quit worrying so much. The director of guidance, however, recommends that the problem be handled through a team approach, including a counselor and all of Harmony's current teachers. Do you think this approach is overkill?

3. When and how do you decide to involve a team of professionals to deal with a student's problem?

4. The author of the case noted that the school Harmony attends serves a "predominantly Hispanic (60 percent) and low-income population." Is this important information to consider? Why do you think the teacher felt it important to include this in the case report?

5. Once again, referring to the responses of Ritchie and Black, both felt that the incident was handled properly. What do you think? Is the handling of Harmony's outburst the real issue here? Has the teacher blown a minor incident all out of proportion?

6. What should you do when children claim that they have been abused? Should your actions and reactions be different for verbal, physical, and/or sexual abuse?

7. Find out from your local school district what the guidelines and procedures are for reporting possible child abuse. Outline the procedures that are followed after a case is reported and describe the kind of feedback a teacher who reports the abuse might expect.

Suggested Readings

Bear, T., Schenk, S., & Buckner, L. (1992/93). Supporting victims of child abuse. *Educational Leadership, 50*(4), 42–47.

Bridgeland, W. M., & Duane, E. A. (1990). Principals as secondary enforcers in child abuse. *Education and Urban Society, 22*(3), 314–324.

Davis, S., & Schwartz, M. D. (1987). *Children's rights and the law.* Lexington, MA: Lexington Books.

DiBrezzo, R., & Hughes, H. M. (1988). The abused and neglected child: Strategies for the teacher. *Journal of Physical Education, Recreation, and Dance, 59*(1), 22–24.

Eckenrode, J. (1993). School performance and disciplinary problems among abused and neglected children. *Developmental Psychology, 29*(1), 53–62.

McFadden, A. C., et al. (1992). A study of race and gender bias in the punishment of school children. *Education and Treatment of Children, 15*(2), 140–146.

McIntyre, T. (1990). The teacher's role in cases of suspected child abuse. *Education and Urban Society, 22*(3), 300–306.

Ney, P. G. (1987). Does verbal abuse leave deeper scars: A study of children and parents. *Canadian Journal of Psychiatry, 32*(5), 371–378.

Ney, P. G. (1988). Transgenerational child abuse. *Child Psychiatry and Human Development, 18*(3), 151–168.

Ney, P. G., et al. (1986). Child abuse: A study of the child's perspective. *Child Abuse and Neglect, 10*(4), 511–518.

Slavenas, R. (1988). The role and responsibility of teachers and child care workers in identifying and reporting child abuse and neglect. *Early Child Development and Care, 31*(1–4), 19–25.

Sternberg, K. J., et al. (1993). Effects of domestic violence on children's behavior problems and depression. *Developmental Psychology, 29*(1), 44–52.

Suspension: Bridge from Misbehavior to Appropriate Behavior?

Background

Mike Canner was the second child in a family of four children. His mother, a grade-school teacher, was divorced from his father. Mike's older brother was attending middle school and his younger brother was in third grade. His little sister lived with their father.

There were a lot of discipline problems in my fourth-grade class and Mike was one of the students who was always "acting up." One Friday, several of the students began to challenge my authority. Every time I began to present a new lesson, they started clowning around, disrupting the entire class. Finally, I told one of the boys, Bruce Barker, that he would have to stay after class. Shortly after this, Mike began acting up and I told him that he would have to stay after class as well.

Incident

After school that day, several of my students were helping me clean erasers and doing some other small tasks around the room. Mike and Bruce had stayed after school to receive their punishment. I decided to have them copy certain sections of the dictionary as a punishment. First, I explained the assignment to Bruce. I asked if he had anything to say about his bad behavior earlier that day. He swore at me, calling me an ———. I told him to get out of the room and wait for me in the principal's office. I also informed him that I would be contacting his mother about this.

The next thing I knew, Mike was calling me a ——— as he went running from the room. The other students didn't know what to say or do, but I could tell that they were really upset by the boys' behavior. I tried to remain calm as I explained to the students that the language that the boys had used was wrong and that using such words always got you into trouble.

The principal waited until I arrived at the office and then he called Mrs. Barker and explained what had happened. Bruce apologized to me but he was still suspended for one day. I do believe, however, that Bruce was sorry for his actions. The principal tried to call Mrs. Canner but was unable to reach her until later that weekend. The principal later told me that Mrs. Canner was very upset, not at Mike, but at the school. She argued that the school had no right to punish her child simply because of the language he used. She went so far as to say that she believed the school was trying to censor her son's speech, which was a violation of his right to free speech. The principal spent a great deal of time convincing Mrs. Canner that Mike's behavior was unacceptable. Finally, she reluctantly agreed that she would go along with whatever the principal thought was appropriate punishment, just so long as Mike was not suspended from school. Since she worked all day and there was no sitter available, suspension was out of the question. If we decided to suspend Mike, she would go to the school board and tell them that we had violated her son's rights.

The principal and I decided that it would be best to remove Mike from the classroom until he apologized to those who were present at the time of his outburst and until he promised that he wouldn't disturb the class again. Before Mike arrived at school on Monday, his desk was moved to the principal's office. The school counselor talked to Mike about his behavior but Mike still refused to apologize and so he was given class assignments to work on in the principal's office. Mike worked alone on his assignments, but the principal monitored his work. Every once in a while, the principal would stop and talk to Mike, always encouraging him to reflect on his behavior of the week before. This went on until the following Friday.

On Friday, the principal made another appeal to Mike. He explained that it took a bigger man to apologize than to commit an unacceptable act. Finally, Mike agreed to apologize. The principal insisted that the apology had to be extended to me personally as well as to the other students who were in the room during the incident. Mike did apologize, but I could tell he really didn't mean it.

Discussion

I was a young teacher who had been popular with the students prior to this year. I was hurt when the students were so disrespectful to me and I was disturbed that such young students were using profanity. I know that students at this age have a tendency to be competitive, especially when it comes to getting attention from the teacher. I guess I just didn't realize that it doesn't always matter to the children whether the attention is positive or negative—just so long as the teacher is paying attention to them.

This incident made me realize that sometimes teachers have to spend as much time helping children develop their social behavior as they do helping them develop their minds. We live in a society where children don't get all the social lessons they need at home.

In my opinion, punishing disruptive students in the classroom will work only for a short while. They must be removed if the seriousness of their infractions is to be made known to them. It is often uncomfortable for teachers when this happens, but we must always act in the best interest of the children in our classroom.

The thing that still bothers me about this incident is the fact that Mike's punishment really wasn't as great as Bruce's, and this seems unfair. It also bothers me that we let Mike get away with an apology that he didn't really mean. It's almost as if he outsmarted us.

Questions

1. Is there some way to avoid the escalation of disruptive behavior in the classroom so that it doesn't get to the point where the child must be removed?
2. Is it the job of the school to discipline the child who is not receiving proper guidance at home?
3. At what point, if any, should a child be suspended from school? Who should make this decision?
4. Does this incident reflect the natural tendencies of children at this age or is it deviant behavior?
5. Were we unfair to Bruce by suspending him while all Mike got was in-school suspension?

Concluding Questions and Activities

1. What were the defining elements of this case report? (What was the problem? What did the teacher do to make the situation better or make it worse?)
2. What do you think of the punishment that was originally administered (having the boys "copy certain sections of the dictionary")?
3. Do you agree with the teacher's statement that "Mike's punishment really wasn't as great as Bruce's"? Remember that Bruce

was the first one to swear at the teacher. Also remember that he did apologize but he was still suspended for a day.

4. How would you respond to Mrs. Canner's accusation that Mike should be allowed to say anything he wants and that the school is violating his right to free speech?
5. What other problem-solving techniques might the teacher have used? What advice would you give the teacher?
6. Interview a principal to find out what the school's policy is regarding in-house suspension. Then interview teachers in that school to find out if they are aware of the policy. Finally, interview parents from the district to see if they think the policy is fair.
7. Get a copy of your local school district's suspension policy. Analyze the policy to see if the teacher in this case would have been in compliance with the guidelines.
8. Critique the Wagner article (listed in the following Suggested Readings) in light of this case report.

Suggested Readings

Calabrese, R. L. (1985). Communication is the key to good discipline. *NASSP Bulletin, 69*(478), 109–110.

Daley, S. (1990, December 12). Pendulum is swinging back to the teaching of values in U.S. schools. *The New York Times*, p. B-14.

Huefner, D. S. (1991). Another view of the suspension and expulsion cases. *Exceptional Children, 57*(4), 360–364.

Kohn, A. (1991). Caring kids: The role of the schools. *Phi Delta Kappan, 72*(7), 496–506.

National Association of Secondary Principals. (1981). *Some alternatives to school discipline: Parental liability and restitution. A legal memorandum.* Reston, VA: Author.

Richards, M., & Biemiller, A. (1986). *Project Thrive. Ways and means: Strategies for solving classroom problems.* Toronto: Ontario Institution for Studies in Education.

Tierno, M. J. (1991). Responding to the socially motivated behaviors of early adolescents: Recommendations for classroom management. *Adolescence, 26*(103), 569–577.

Trice, A. D., & Parker, F. C. (1983). Decreasing adolescent swearing in an instructional setting. *Education and Treatment of Children, 6*(1), 29–35.

Wagner, B. R. (1992/93). No more suspension: Creating a shared ethical culture. *Educational Leadership 50*(4), 34–37.

Yell, M. L. (1990). The use of corporal punishment, suspension, expulsion, and timeout with behaviorally disordered students in public schools: Legal considerations. *Behavioral Disorders, 15*(2), 100–109.

SECTION 1

QUESTIONS, EXERCISES, AND ACTIVITIES

1. In two of the three cases, the students were guilty of using profanity. What was similar about the situations and what was different? How do you explain these differences in terms of teacher attitude?

2. Review the commentaries of the respondents to the Harmony case. What do you think their reactions would be to the case involving Mike?

3. In two of the three cases (Kristine's and Mike's), the principal and the students' mothers played a definite role. How would you evaluate the roles that the mothers played? What do you think might have happened in each of the two cases if the mother hadn't been involved? What would have happened in Kristine's case if her mother had been called?

4. If you were responsible for calling the parents to inform them of each of these situations, what would you say? Would you handle each the same way or would there be some differences?

5. In one case (Kristine's), the principal and teacher were at odds with one another. In another case (Mike's), the principal and teacher worked together to solve the problem. What kind of things can you, as a classroom teacher, do to increase the likelihood that the principal will be supportive if and when you come up against a difficult situation?

6. If you were to develop a behavior-management plan for these three students, what elements would you keep consistent in all three plans? How would the plans differ? For instance, would the age of the student affect the plan? What about the gender of the student? Let's say that you know that one of the students is Hispanic. What if you also knew that one of the students was Asian American and the other was an African American? How might these factors affect your plan?

7. Review the plan that you just developed. Does your plan include both the short-term and long-term solutions? Is it more reactive or proactive? Is it easier to be proactive in the short or long term? Why?

SECTION 1

SUGGESTED READINGS

Canfield, J. (1990). Improving students' self-esteem. *Educational Leadership, 48*(1), 48–50.

Canter, L. (1979). Competency-based approach to discipline—It's assertive. *Thrust for Educational Leadership, 8,* 11–13.

Doyle, W. (1986). Classroom organization and management. In M. Whitrock (Ed.), *Handbook of research on teaching* (3rd ed., pp. 392–431). New York: Macmillan.

Engler, M. (1987). *Strategies for classroom discipline.* New York: Praeger.

Good, T. L., & Brophy, J. E. (1991). Management II: Coping with problems effectively. In T. L. Good & J. E. Brophy (Eds.), *Looking into classrooms* (5th ed., pp. 230–274). New York: HarperCollins.

Jones, V. F., & Jones L. S. (1986). *Comprehensive classroom management: Creating positive learning environments* (2nd ed.). Boston: Allyn and Bacon.

McCormack, S. (1989). Response to Render, Padilla, and Krank: But practitioners say it works! *Educational Leadership, 46*(6), 77–79.

McCormack, S. L. (1981). To make discipline work, turn kids into managers. *Executive Educator, 3*(11), 26–27.

Render, G. F., Padillia, J. N., & Krank, H. M. (1989). What research really shows about assertive discipline. *Educational Leadership, 46*(6), 72–75.

Seeman, H. (1988). *Preventing classroom discipline problems.* Lancaster, PA: Technomic Publishing.

Solomon, D., Watson, M. S., Delucchi, K. L., Schaps, E., & Battistich, V. (1988). Enhancing children's prosocial behavior in the classroom. *American Educational Research Journal, 25*(4), 527–554.

Sparzo, F. J. (1985). *Changing behavior: A practical guide for teachers and parents* (Fastback Monograph No. 221). Bloomington, IN: Phi Delta Kappa Educational Foundation.

Sparzo, F. J., & Poteet, J. A. (1989). *Classroom behavior: Detecting and correcting special problems.* Boston: Allyn and Bacon.

Stevens, G. E. (1984). Ethical inclinations of tomorrow's citizens: Actions speak louder? *Journal of Business Education, 59*(4), 147–152.

Section 2

Dealing with Parents

The case reports in this section focus on problems in which parents serve as catalysts to the incidents. In the first case, "Focusing on the Real Target: Classroom Management or Parent Control?" the teacher is faced with a group of unruly kindergarten students. The students in the class misbehave frequently, and when trouble arises it is often difficult for the teacher to determine which students are involved in the infraction. It is not unusual for her to punish the entire class when such situations arise. The parents of one child become upset because they believe their child is being treated unfairly. The mother volunteers to help in the classroom and the teacher feels this is a good idea because she could use the extra set of hands and it might help ease some of the tension between the parents and her. Everything seems to be going well until the mother reports to the principal that the class is out of control. The teacher now wonders if she handled this parent situation properly.

The second case, "Monster Mom," begins when a third-grade child leaves school during recess. The principal calls the mother and explains to her that the child must return to school. The mother returns to school with the child and is very upset, not with the child, but with the principal for making the child return to school. This incident is followed by a series of incidents in which the mother's behavior becomes more and more disruptive. She threatens both the teacher and the principal and complains about their incompetence to the superintendent. On at least two occasions, the police are called and the situation is finally brought under control. The teacher, however, is concerned because she feels that the situation was mishandled and could easily have turned out less positively than it did.

In the final incident, "Unfair Accusation or Blind Prejudice?" a mother accuses the staff at her son's school of being racist. She airs her complaint at a school board meeting in which the local media are in attendance. The story appeared in the paper the next day and was, in the words of the teacher, "blown all out of proportion."

In the first two incidents, educational respondents provide you with insights into how they view the incidents. The third incident is left open for your own interpretation. As you read the episodes, remember that you are hearing only one side of the story. More than likely, the parent will have a different interpretation of what happened and why. Think about how the case reports might have changed if they had been written from the perspective of the parent.

As you review the cases, you will notice that the incidents deal with elementary students; however, the problems faced by the teachers are not limited to the lower grades. A teacher at any level may find it necessary to deal with parents who complain to the principal about the teacher's ability to control a class. Parents can be just as disruptive at middle school and high school as they are at elementary school, and teachers anywhere may find themselves unfairly accused of inappropriate behavior. As you read the case reports, think about how the consequences might have been different if students at a middle school or high school were involved.

You will also want to examine the case reports to see if you can determine how each of the major participants (e.g., teacher, student, mother, administrator) affected how the incident unfolded. For instance, in the mind of the teacher, did the principal's action help lessen the severity of the incident or help exacerbate it? Was the student really an innocent bystander? Finally, compare and contrast the three incidents to see if anything that was learned from one incident could be applied to the others.

Focusing on the Real Target: Classroom Management or Parent Control?

Background

Last year was probably the most challenging year of my teaching career. I had a group of kindergarten students who just couldn't get along. The class consisted of a mixture of children with Attention Deficit Disorder, children who were emotionally impaired, a child who was autistic, and one with cerebral palsy. Some of the children were very high functioning and others were very low functioning. In addition, there were several "bullies" in the class.

A great deal of class time was spent on talking to the children about getting along and accepting each others' differences. However, the more I talked, the worse things got, and my classroom management skills and discipline methods were challenged to the maximum. It seemed as if I was spending all my time on discipline and no time at all on developing the children's academic skills.

Spending so much time on working out problems and squabbles between the children resulted in a real reduction in my energy supply *and* my enthusiasm for teaching. Prior to last year, I had always been positive and energetic. Last year, I tended to be snappish, even at home. In fact, I was so depressed at one point I thought about leaving teaching. Despite the uphill climb I saw myself facing, I tried desperately to hang on to my sense of humor and enthusiasm.

Winter break helped to relieve some of my tension. When I returned to the classroom in January, I was determined to make the second semester one in which learning (rather than discipline) became central in my classroom. One of the things my children really enjoyed was recess and I decided that I would use this as a reward for the class—when they were good, they would get an extra recess. This worked for a while, but it wasn't long before their behavior began to deteriorate. Because of the students' poor behavior, I eliminated the extra recess, and on days when they really acted badly, I canceled the regular recess as a punishment.

Incident

During parent-teacher conferences in mid-March, the parents of one little girl expressed concern about their daughter's seating arrangement. They said that just because Karen was the "quiet type" she shouldn't be the child who always had to sit next to the problem students. Indeed, Karen was the "quiet type" and was very affectionate and happy, but also very nervous. I explained to the parents that I often changed the seating arrangement in the classroom and that sometimes their daughter might find herself next to a child who had behavior problems. I did, however, say that I would take their concerns into consideration the next time I changed the room around.

In early April, I received a note from Karen's parents indicating that their daughter never told them how school was going except to tell them that "we hardly ever go out for recess because of the 'bad' kids in our room." One afternoon, not too long after I had received the note, Karen's mother appeared after school and started telling me how unhappy her daughter was over having to miss recess. She also added that it wasn't fair that the whole class had to suffer the consequences of some of the children's misbehavior and that I should be able to pick out the trouble-makers and have *only them* sit out. In response, I told her that when a single child was disobeying the rules, that particular child was due to sit out at recess. However, when the *entire* class was being inattentive or excessively loud, it was very difficult to pick out the sole perpetrator(s). It was then that I elaborated on the chemistry of the class, which only made the mother feel more concerned over the unfairness of allowing special education or problem children into the regular classroom.

After this meeting, the little girl got into the habit of asking me how she was doing in class and I always responded positively because that is exactly how she was doing! Her constant questioning bothered me because I had always prided myself on providing feedback to the children on a daily basis and Karen was kept informed of her performance. Also, she seemed very worried now and more nervous than before.

A few days later, Karen's mother sent me another note asking if I could use her help on any projects or activities in the classroom, since she had some time off work from now until the end of the school year. I agreed to have her help out, thinking that it might help to alleviate some of her daughter's worry. As a result, Karen's mother helped out once a week for about three weeks and everything seemed fine. She read to the class and even brought some treats for everyone.

Then one day, my principal came in to talk to me about a note she had received from Karen's mother. The note informed the principal that my class was out of control, that the students were wild, and that I had no control over them! The mother's comments did not surprise me, yet I was hurt because I had tried so hard to maintain a learning environment in the classroom. I felt as if all of my extra energy had been a waste of time and, although my principal was very understanding, I still felt embarrassed.

Discussion

Because it was very close to the end of the year, I was not able to do too much to improve, solve, or alleviate the problem. I merely continued to treat the little girl in the same positive manner, telling her that she was doing a terrific job in class. I also let her work on extra activities when she wanted. All of this was done in the hope that maybe it would help Karen feel more productive or successful. I am pretty stumped on what more I could have done.

Questions

1. Should a teacher let the parents know when the class is composed of an unusual number of disruptive children?
2. Was I wrong in allowing the mother to be involved in the classroom and hence making me vulnerable to parent criticism?
3. Does a teacher have the right "to draw the line" with the parents when they tell him or her where they want their child to sit or not sit?
4. Should I have looked more closely into the reason for the little girl's nervousness and why she worried so much?

Response of Sandra E. Cornwell, Teacher

Last year I also had one of the most challenging years of my teaching career, thanks to a class full of special education students, low achievers, and discipline problems. I like to use cooperative learning groups, do partner work and creative activities, and maintain a flexible schedule.

However, this class could not handle an unstructured classroom or "working together" activities. Also, since several of my students received special education services, my schedule was quite rigid. Although mine was a fourth-grade classroom, I can identify with the problems this teacher encountered.

It is extremely frustrating not to be able to use your preferred teaching style effectively. I felt like a clown punching bag. I began each day standing up with a smile and a positive attitude. By the end of the day, the students had knocked me down. But I popped back up the next morning and went back to try again! I had to change some of my goals to adjust to the makeup of the class. With such a class, one can only keep trying to accomplish what one can, provide some fun learning experiences, and realize that another year is coming!

I believe in being honest with parents concerning problems in the classroom, especially if they ask about the class. Communication with parents is important at any grade level. I have strived to send newsletters at regular intervals (weekly or biweekly), whether teaching kindergarten, second grade, or fourth grade.

I know how an entire class can be so loud or disruptive that a teacher cannot pick out the "few" causing the problem from the "many" joining in. But I've reached the conclusion that if I withhold recess because of behavior, I'm the one being punished because, in the long run, canceling recess does not improve the situation. In fact, a rowdy group probably needs recess to "let off steam!"

I believe the teacher handled the seating arrangement problem very well by telling the parents that she changed seating arrangements often and that next time she would take their concerns into consideration. Teachers do have the right to "draw the line" with parents on the way the classroom is handled, whether it is the seating arrangement or making class rules.

Because of the previous contact and communication this teacher had with Karen's mother, I would have been suspicious when the mother offered to help in the classroom. There are times when extra hands can be helpful when teaching kindergarten. I would have agreed to have her help, but I would have also asked for other parent volunteers. Then I would have asked them to help with specific projects or activities at a specific time. For example, helping students learn to sew on a button when studying the letter *b*; sorting, classifying, and eating different kinds of nuts while studying the letter *n*; or directing small groups in playing learning games. If more than one volunteer is present, students can receive more individual attention and there will be more than one opinion of what is happening in the classroom.

I imagine much of the little girl's nervousness and worry stem as much from her mother's attitude about the classroom situation as from the learning environment itself. By continuing to treat Karen in a positive manner and offering her the opportunity to do extra work, I feel that the teacher did all she could do to help the child have a good year.

Sometimes a teacher has to adapt to the chemistry of the class, to not take all problems too personally, and to listen to parents and take their ideas and concerns into consideration. But it is important to remember that as the teacher, you are in charge of your classroom and it is your responsibility!

Response of
Tracy Robinson, Professor

Parents have the right to ask teachers about classroom process only as it affects their children. This particular teacher was extremely stressed and was in need of support. Going to a counselor or a therapist may have helped her sort out her feelings and perhaps would have assisted her in identifying some unresolved issues that were preventing her from having more pleasure in both her career and personal life.

Karen's parents may have been overwhelmed by the presence of the children with special needs in her daughter's classroom. If I were a parent in this situation, I would have been concerned as well. The following are important questions to consider:

- Are the teachers given instruction and support when their classrooms contain a mixture of children, some with special needs?
- If this parent had known from the beginning about the classroom's composition and had been confident that the teacher was adequately supported and resourceful in addressing the unique issues that would undoubtedly arise in the classroom, would the problems between her and the teacher have occurred?

It is not possible to ascertain whether Karen's nervousness was exacerbated by her classroom surroundings, a function of her home environment, or a product of some other source (e.g., personality). Perhaps the teacher could have engaged Karen's mother in a discussion about the child's anxiety. It might also have been a good idea to consult with the school psychologist.

Given this taxing situation, a preventive approach is needed to combat extreme levels of teacher stress and parent dissatisfaction. Administrative intervention and personal management might have been helpful.

Response of
Judith Spitler-McKee, Professor

The frustrated kindergarten teacher speaks for many colleagues across the nation when she describes her agony in not being able to establish a climate conducive to learning for her young students, whom she describes as being unable to "get along." Additionally, like many conscientious and sensitive teachers of young children, the writer was very aware of the problems that were occurring as she attempted futilely to establish and maintain relationships and assert her authority. The saddest aspects are that she was unable to establish rules and teach Karen how to comply and behave appropriately, both of which are essential for kindergarten children and are common expectations of other teachers, administrators, and parents.

Teachers are faced with situations over which they have no control, some control, or little control. Always, they must do the best they can within those parameters of control. In this incident, some of the factors undergirding the building of relationships, such as the various personalities within the class, were beyond the teacher's control. Every year, caring teachers think about the mix of personalities they will face throughout the school year. Many early childhood teachers are reporting that they have more kindergarten children who seem to have definite special educational characteristics such as Attention Deficit Disorder (ADD), autism or autistic-like behavior, and sensory or motor impairment or developmental delays. When this happens, a reflective teacher will not try to "go it alone" and hope that interpersonal encounters will be more positive than negative, but will seek specialized help from other authorities. These authorities may include experienced colleagues in early childhood who have faced similar classrooms and have been successful in helping children internalize rules and develop autonomy and self-control. Help could be sought in some cases from a hands-on, nonjudgmental administrator who might be able to provide an extra person, such as an experienced aide or a trained volunteer, to lower the adult-child ratio. Two other major sources of support for many teachers are competent social workers and special educators who could observe the classroom and make specific suggestions for modifying disruptive or delayed children's behavior.

The factors over which teachers do have varying control are those of professional organizational skills, curriculum design and implementation, and teaching strategies. Organizational skills involve a teacher's use of classroom space, selection and use of appropriate and interesting materials, recordkeeping, and scheduling of blocks of time. At the same time, it is to be noted that the use of desks and specific seating arrangements is not considered developmentally appropriate for kindergarten children by the National Association of Education of Young Children. Curriculum design and implementation refer to the planned opportunities for active engagements that are provided (or not provided) so children will grow, learn, and develop. More specifically, were there adequate and daily provisions for play and child-initiated learning so that children would learn through several modalities such as visual, auditory, tactile, and kinesthetic? Or were there inappropriate requirements for too much sitting and listening to the adult, which is not the way young children assimilate, consolidate, or apply information, skills, and values? Were interesting, age-appropriate materials provided so that the children's individual developmental and academic needs were met? Did the teacher systematically record the children's behavior in an attempt to see patterns and individual differences, or were the children unfairly lumped into a "whole class is difficult" view?

It may be that the cure is the cause. In this instance, a developmentally appropriate curriculum replete with multiple and varied materials and media (e.g., sand, water, play dough, clay) would have engaged the children's interests and, to a large extent, diverted them from negative interactions. When problems arose over materials and rules, as they invariably do with young children as they are learning the ways of the larger social culture, they could have been discussed and modeled at circle time. Role-playing of rules and rule breaking could have been used to help children grasp the reasons for the rules. The early childhood years are crucial for the development of social and communicative competence. This is mastered through daily interactions with peers and understanding adults, through daily squabbles over materials and media (e.g., "He took my book," "I never get a turn at the water table!"), and through learning how socially to negotiate power and take turns. These are developmental tasks for children this age, and in this classroom they seem not to have been provided.

Too many teachers use recess and playtime deprivation as punishment when children misbehave or fail to follow class rules. Depriving children of the unique benefits of playtime, recess, or physical education time results in deprivation of opportunities for development of the gross motor functions, emotional release, emotional expressiveness, and social

interchanges with other children. All of these deprivations and lost opportunities for growth produce less intellectual attainment and dimin-
ished academic skill development. A more effective prescription would
be to add more playtime, more gross motor exercising, more expressive
arts, and more individual activities if children's learning is to be truly
enhanced.

The child who displayed nervousness was showing clear and dis-
cernible signs of stress resulting from the tense class climate and the lack
of opportunities for individual expression at recess time. Surely there
were other children who were very stressed by the lack of management
and positive relationships with the teacher and peers. The antidotes for
school-related stress are the expressive arts of movement and music, two-
and three-dimensional art (collage, clay), pretend play (house, dress-up),
and three-dimensional model construction (with blocks and put-together
materials). A well-conceived and monitored kindergarten program, built
on the principles of learning and development, would include all of these
antidotes and foster progress in all of the children.

Concluding Questions and Activities

1. What do you believe are the key elements of the problem? Did
   the consultants identify the same key elements that you did?
2. What did the teacher do to make the situation better?
3. What did the teacher do that may have made the situation
   worse?
4. What other problem-solving techniques might the teacher have
   used? What advice would you give the teacher?
5. Did the consultants offer some techniques that you had not
   thought of or that were unfamiliar to you? Did you come up with
   some techniques that the consultants didn't mention? If you did,
   do you still believe that your suggestions are valid?
6. Do you agree with one of the consultants more than the others?
   What, if anything, does this say about your philosophy of education?
7. From the questions and comments of the teacher, do you believe
   that she focused on the central problem or did she focus on the
   quiet child and her parent as a way of avoiding the "real" issue?
8. Do you think that the teacher should have allowed the parent to
   help in the classroom? How do you interpret the teacher's comment, "Then one day, my principal came in to talk to me about a
   note she had received from Karen's mother. The note informed
   the principal that my class was out of control, the students were

wild, and that I had no control over them! The mother's comments did not surprise me, yet I was hurt because I had tried so hard to maintain a learning environment in the classroom. I felt as if all of my extra energy had been a waste of time and, although my principal was very understanding, I still felt embarrassed"?

9. The three consultants appear to be at odds about how well the teacher handled the situation. The teacher consultant makes the statement, "I feel that the teacher did all she could do to help the child have a good year." The first professor sees the teacher as "extremely stressed" and suggests that she needs counseling. The second professor contends that the teacher is "conscientious and sensitive" and "very aware of the problems that were occurring." Take the position of one of the three consultants and support your case with statements from the classroom teacher.

Suggested Readings

Boisen, M. A. (1992). The relationship between the length of play period and the frequency of reported conflicts by preschool children. *Education and Treatment of Children, 15*(4), 310–319.

Christie, J. F., & Wardle, F. (1992). How much time is needed for play? *Young Children, 47*(3), 28–32.

Elkind, D. (1993). Whatever happened to childhood? *Momentum, 24*(2), 18–19.

Graue, M. E. (1993). Expectations and ideas coming to school. *Early Childhood Research Quarterly, 8*(1), 53–75.

Hill, D. (1990). Order in the classroom. *Teacher Magazine, 1*(7), 70–77.

Marshall, H. H. (1989). The development of self-concept. *Young Children, 44*(5), 44–51.

Michels, S., et al. (1993). Parents self-reports of discipline practices and child acting-out behaviors in kindergarten. *Early Education and Development, 4*(2), 139–144.

Neel, R. S., & Cessna, K. K. (1993). Replacement behaviors: A strategy for teaching social skills to children with behavior problems. *Rural Special Education Quarterly, 12*(1), 30–35.

Nummela, R. (1982). The number of teacher adaptations can predict burnout. *Education, 103*(1), 79–81.

Sherburne, S., et al. (1988). Decreasing violent or aggressive theme play among preschool children with behavior disorders. *Exceptional Children, 55*(2), 166–172.

Sobel, M. A. (1982). One point of view: "I love to teach," a formula for coping with burn-out. *Arithmetic Teacher, 29*(5), 2.

Wassermann, S. (1992). Serious play in the classroom. *Childhood Education, 68*(3), 133–139.

Wheldall, K., & Lan, Y. (1987). Rows versus tables. The effects of classroom seating arrangements on classroom disruption rates, on-task behavior, and teacher behavior in three special school classes. *Educational Psychology: An International Journal of Experimental Educational Psychology, 7*(4), 303–312.

Monster Mom

Background

I assumed my teaching responsibilities in September. There were 15 teachers in our building and for 7 of us this was our first year of teaching. It was also our principal's first year. The remaining 8 teachers each had over 15 years of experience. It didn't take long for the staff to divide into a "new" versus "old" mentality. The newer staff would meet in the teachers' lounge after school and at recess, and would go out for an hour or two after school on Friday. Very rarely did the older members of the staff join us.

Incident

About four weeks into the school year, one of my third-grade students did not return to the class after recess. I immediately reported the incident to the principal and we checked the restrooms, the playground, and the halls. The child was nowhere to be found. The principal immediately called the mother and was told that the child had left the playground and gone home. The mother confirmed that the child was not ill. The principal then asked if something had happened at school to make the child want to leave. The mother responded, "No, she just wanted to come home." The principal then informed the mother that the child would have to return to school and would be required to make up the time she had missed. She would do this by staying after school for a few days.

When the child returned to school, her mother accompanied her. The mother let the principal know that she thought it was unreasonable to make the child return to school. When she brought the child to my room, she berated me and threatened that if I laid a hand on her "kid," she would "break my ———— arm." She then implied that it was my fault that her daughter found it necessary to leave school in the middle of the day.

Once the mother left, the girl was very cooperative and almost too docile. We had a talk about staying at school. I told her that if she was not feeling well, she should talk to a teacher and that she should never leave school during the day without first going to the office and telling the principal. The child seemed to understand and she agreed that she wouldn't leave again.

The mother, however, didn't seem to understand. She went to the school superintendent and complained about the "incompetence" of the principal and me. The superintendent's office called the principal to inform her of the incident, but little else was said.

A few days later, the mother stormed into the principal's outer office, screaming for her children. When the principal went to the outer office, she was greeted with, ". . . and if you ever keep any of my kids after school again, I'll hit you between the ———— eyes." The mother also uttered a few choice words about me and my lack of ability. The principal asked her either to leave or to go into the inner office. The mother refused to do either and so the principal walked to the phone and called the superintendent's office. The superintendent was out of the building, but, in a matter of minutes, two assistant superintendents arrived at the school office. The mother calmed down and left the office. However, two days later, she went to the superintendent's office to complain about my performance.

Several days after this, she again came into the school office and said she had come for her "kids." Hearing her voice, the principal went to the outer office. The mother screamed at the principal, "I want my kids now!" The principal explained she would send for them but the mother said, "I'll get them myself!" She went out in the hall and yelled the names of each of her children.

The principal went back into her office to call the police. Just as she picked up the phone, the mother came charging in, screaming, "Go ahead and call your goons. I'm not afraid of any of you!" She then proceeded to every classroom, opened each door, and called the names of her four children. By the time the mother had reached the last door, a policeman had arrived. The principal asked the policeman to remove the mother from the building. However, he insisted that the mother had the right to take her children. The principal explained to him that she was not object-ing to the mother taking the children out of school but to the manner in which she was doing it. The whole building was being disturbed. The policeman just shook his head, but he did remain in the building until the mother left.

After school we had an emergency teachers' meeting and it was quite obvious that the principal was very upset. We could see that the principal was beginning to question the way she had handled the situ-ation and that she was suffering from some self-doubt. She asked us for our suggestions, but the younger members of faculty had few sugges-tions to offer. We tried to be supportive, but we had just had a very traumatic experience and we were wondering ourselves if she had han-dled it properly. After all, that mother could have had a gun rather than just a loud voice. Then what would we have done? At first, the older members of the faculty seemed to enjoy our uneasiness and, through their comments, implied that we would learn how to deal with situations like this once we had more experience. However, after a short time, they began to realize just how nervous we were about the situation. Slowly, they began to work with us and we were able to come up with some good suggestions for what we were to do if anything like that happened again.

In the meantime, the mother went to the superintendent's office again. This parent was always very calm and well controlled when she went to talk to the superintendent. The superintendent arranged a meet-ing with both parents to be held in our school office. The superintendent arrived a few minutes early to meet with the staff. Although he didn't come right out and say it, it appeared as if he thought that part, if not all, of the problem arose because of the staff's lack of experience and from our inability to work together. The principal tried to defend us, but the superintendent silenced her with a rather stern look.

When the conference began, the mother did most of the talking and the father listened, neither agreeing nor disagreeing with what his wife said. Suddenly, the mother jumped up, shook her finger at the superin-tendent, and, in a very loud voice and using a few choice words, berated him and the entire school system. When she finished, the superintendent told the parents that the principal was in charge of the school and that their children would be expected to observe the rules of the school. The mother left very upset.

The superintendent stayed and called the chief of police. He ex-plained the situation and the chief agreed that this was a serious situ-ation. He said that he would inform his department that when the principal called, the officers were to come to the building immediately and do whatever the principal thought was best.

Discussion

Later, the principal told us that she understood the superintendent's hesitation in this situation, especially since we were a young staff and since he was getting two very diverse stories—one from the parents and one from us. As teachers, we weren't really certain that we agreed with her. Couldn't the superintendent have at least apologized when he saw how the mother acted? Would he have supported us if something more drastic had happened? Besides, half of our staff had over 15 years of experience. We didn't have a counterargument for the fact that we had a reputation for not getting along as a faculty because, up until this incident, we didn't get along. This incident helped pull us together as a staff, but there were one or two teachers who felt as if the principal defended the superintendent when perhaps she should have stood up to him.

Questions

1. Did the superintendent owe the faculty an apology for his behavior and lack of support?
2. Is there emotional damage done to children when their parents behave like this?
3. According to news reports, situations such as this one are happening more frequently. What can be done to change the poor relations between the school and parents?
4. What can be done about parents who display erratic and unreasonable behavior?
5. Should counseling be given or required for children in these situations?
6. Is it the responsibility of the experienced teachers to make the new members of the faculty feel welcome? The newer members automatically went to one another for support. Did they have a responsibility to make certain that the older faculty members were invited to their "night out"? Should the principal have done something to help the teachers see themselves as a united faculty rather than as "new teachers" and "experienced teachers"?

Response of Charline Socci, Teacher

This is an unusual situation in that the mother was reasonable at times and then totally irrational. Since the superintendent had dealt with the parent only when she was rational and the faculty had a reputation for not getting along, it is understandable that the superintendent might question how the faculty handled the matter. However, he should have kept an open mind and reserved judgment until after the meeting. I don't think he owed the faculty an apology, but he should have spoken to the faculty after the incident and offered his support. It would have been an excellent opportunity for him to point out the benefits of being a cohesive staff.

Children learn from their parents. Unfortunately, in a situation like this, the children are learning some very negative behavior patterns. Their mother's behavior and attitude toward the school will undoubtedly affect them. This mother probably has some mental difficulties that cause her to react the way she does. The children should be given counseling. There is probably some law or requirement governing how much counseling can be received/given without parental consent. It seems unlikely that this parent would consent to counseling. Perhaps the case could be referred to child protective services for review.

Poor relations between the school and parents (when dealing with rational people) can be improved through sincere communication. The parents need to feel welcome at the school and understand that they are a vital part of their children's education. Parents and teachers need to work together to establish goals for the children. School-based management is a step in the right direction. A management team comprised of faculty, parents, and other community members can make everyone feel that they are a *part* of the school—not that it is the parents *versus* the school. There is little that can be done about parents who display erratic and unreasonable behavior other than to offer support and protection to the staff members who have to deal with these people.

A cohesive faculty is built through the efforts of the principal. It should not be left up to the new teachers or the experienced teachers to see that the faculty works well together. I am assuming that all the faculty members would naturally want a unified faculty that worked together to solve common problems and supported one another when necessary. The principal should arrange committee assignments so that there is a mixture of new and experienced teachers. She could also pair new and experienced teachers at grade level so that they can assist and learn from each other. Although it may help if the new teachers invite the experienced teachers to join their "night out," it isn't necessary. Chances are that the experienced faculty members have family obligations that make a "night out" more difficult. There should be opportunities for the staff to get together socially on occasion. If a faculty does not have a good working relationship, it is unlikely that social occasions would be very enjoyable.

Response of
Pat Olive, Principal

The following are responses to the questions provided by the case report writer:

1. The superintendent could come back to the faculty to let them know that he realizes that this parent is irrational. However, it is still important for a staff to work together and come up with a plan if this kind of situation happens again. This is not a totally unusual situation. There are irrational people in the world who may end up at our school doors. The staff needs to discuss these challenging problems together and use their expertise at solving these problems. The superintendent's message might have hurt, but it sounds as if the staff is having a difficult time working together. I don't think that the superintendent has anything to apologize about. He may have hurt the staff's feelings, but sometimes the truth does hurt.

2. When parents act irrationally, they may be telling their child that it is okay for him or her to act the same way. The modeling of inappropriate behavior can potentially be damaging to a child—especially if the modeling comes from a parent or relative.

3. Relationships between home and school need to be improved. In this situation, I am not sure what can be done. It is interesting to note that we do not know the cause for the mother's unhappiness with this teacher. It might help to listen to the parent and get all the information one can about why the parent is unhappy with the teacher. There is a lot of work to be done with parents and schools. Parents need to be involved in making decisions about policies and curriculum. They should be part of task forces, cooperative decision-making committees, and school councils that involve parents, teachers, and students. This will help parents believe they are partners in this process of educating all children.

4. After an incident such as this has occurred, it is someone's responsibility (the police, the principal) to let the parent know that he or she acted irrationally and that it is not to happen again in the school. This sends a message that this behavior will not be tolerated.

5. Children should be invited to talk about the incident. What happens when people get angry? What can be done so that everyone feels as if they can win (win-win philosophy)? Conflict resolution training may help others feel empowered to state their problems with a disputant and to discuss possible solutions. A schoolwide approach to teaching conflict resolution might be appropriate.

6. Everyone has a responsibility for welcoming new staff members. This should be a norm. The principal is responsible for making sure that staff norms are developed. These norms should be created and revised by the staff at least yearly. It is everyone's responsibility to see that the norms are followed. It is the principal's responsibility to model these norms and remind the staff that the norms exist. The idea of collegiality is important; it must be discussed and practiced. Is there a staff social committee? Could this group schedule some "nights out" for everyone? If there are committees operating in the school or if there are small group discussions at faculty meetings, the principal should mix the old and new teachers together. This sends a message that this type of sharing is important.

Concluding Questions and Activities

1. In this case, the mother was definitely out of control. How did each of the following respond to the mother's actions? (You may have more than one response for each.)
   a. Teacher
   b. Principal
   c. Superintendent
   d. Police department
2. Evaluate each of the preceding responses as either appropriate or inappropriate.
3. For those responses that you rated inappropriate, tell what you think would have been a more suitable response.
4. If you were confronted by a parent who was so completely out of control, what are some strategies that you would use in dealing with the individual?
5. The teacher talks about the tension between the older faculty and the younger faculty and how this incident helped to bring them closer together. What do you think would have happened between the faculty members if this situation had not occurred? If you found yourself in a similar situation where such tension existed, what would you do?
6. Pretend you are scheduled to give a speech on situations that threaten both teachers and students in our schools today. You decide the best place to start is by reviewing the literature on violence in schools. Make a list of the descriptors that you would

use to begin your research. Once your list is complete, check Educational Resources Information Center (ERIC) to see how many sources you would have found. Now develop a list of other sources that you might have used in order to collect relevant data on your topic.

7. Write a 5- to 10-page paper on situations that threaten both teachers and students. Make certain that you include possible sources of danger, statistics on recent occurrences, and ways in which school districts have attempted to address the problems. You should include a list of at least five references.

Suggested Readings

Barron, B. G., & Colvin, J. M. (1984). Teacher-talk to parents. *Education, 105*(1), 76–78.

Black, S. (1993). The parent factor. *Executive Educator, 15*(4), 29–31.

Giordano, A. (1992). Strengthening the home-school connection. *Principal, 71*(3), 38–39.

Glenn, J. (1990, Fall). Training teachers for troubled times. *School Safety,* 20–21.

Goldring, E. B. (1990). Elementary school principals as boundary spanners: Their engagement with parents. *Journal of Educational Administration, 28*(1), 53–62.

Harden, G. D. (1993). Parents say the dardnest things. *Principal, 72*(3), 40–41.

Leitch, M. L., & Tangri, S. S. (1988). Barriers to home-school collaboration. *Educational Horizons, 66*(2), 70–74.

Margolis, H., & Brannigan, G. (1986). Relating to angry parents. *Academic Therapy, 21*(3), 343–346.

Margolis, H., & Brannigan, G. (1990). Calming the storm. *Learning, 8*(5), 40–42.

Morgan, E. L. (1989). Talking with parents when concerns come up. *Young Children, 66*(2), 70–74.

Reis, E. M. (1988). Conferencing skills: Working with parents. *Clearing House, 62*(2), 81–83.

Watkins, P. (1993). Five strategies for managing angry parents. *Principal, 72*(4), 29–30.

Unfair Accusation or Blind Prejudice?

Background

I was about halfway through my first year of teaching and everything seemed to be going fine. I was just starting to know my way around the school and to feel comfortable around my colleagues. This enjoyable ambiance was altered when I received a new student in my classroom.

My classroom consisted of 25 second-graders who were either White, African American, or Middle Eastern. Jermaine Carson, a smart and energetic African American boy, enrolled in our school in the middle of January. Jermaine seemed to possess a great deal of self-confidence. In fact, his attitude might have been perceived as arrogant and presumptuous by the manner in which he socialized with the other children. Jermaine had a difficult time associating with the other children in the classroom. He tended to "turn his nose up" at some children and get into boxing and wrestling fights with others.

Consequently, within several days of Jermaine's arrival, I had to phone his mother to let her know what was going on. I told her that few of the methods that I had been using—name on the board, loss of privileges, removal from the classroom—were working. Most of them didn't work at all and those that did only worked for a short time. I hoped to find out from her what methods she used at home when she had to discipline Jermaine and which of these she felt would be successful with him in the classroom.

Through our phone conversation, I found out that Jermaine's father had been abusive toward both Jermaine and Mrs. Carson up until she divorced him. She added that, as a result, she had spoiled Jermaine and had hoped to boost his confidence by telling him that he was the "greatest." This explained his arrogant behavior and attitudes. His mother and I continued to talk and she finally decided that the best way to deal with Jermaine would be through "plus and minus" points just like she used at home.

I decided to go ahead and try her suggestion the very next day. I gave Jermaine points for "good" behavior and took away points for "bad" behavior. Surprisingly, this system seemed to work very well. I continued to use this method with Jermaine at the appropriate times throughout the rest of the week.

Incident

On Monday of the next week, Mrs. Carson came by to visit us while we were outside for recess. She was very complimentary, saying that she thought I was doing a fine job with Jermaine and that he was quite happy in the classroom. We spoke for a few minutes and she walked with us back to the classroom and then she left.

After school that day, the principal informed me that Mrs. Carson had just stopped by the office and had been very upset with my manner of dealing with Jermaine. Evidently, Mrs. Carson said I had been "demeaning" toward Jermaine because I was using a "plus and minus" points system on him! I just about fell out of my chair when I heard this since I was merely using her suggestion! In response, the principal offered me her support and told me to be careful around Mrs. Carson because she sensed that "something was up."

As if in response to the principal's hunches, Mrs. Carson began making daily appearances in our classroom, delivering her phony compliments and then heading to the office to scream at the principal. Now she was complaining about how easy second grade was for her son and that he should be placed in the third grade. She also made it known that Jermaine had been tested at the local state university and was considered to be a "genius." (We found out later that his score did not classify him as a "genius").

As time went on, Mrs. Carson began approaching me during and after class, and accusing me of not challenging her son and of not paying enough attention to his needs. By now I was really frustrated, and I told her she would have to go talk to the principal if she was unhappy with my performance.

After several meetings between the principal and Mrs. Carson, Jermaine was moved to the third grade. However, this went well for only a few months. Soon, Mrs. Carson began complaining about Jermaine's new teacher, claiming that she also was not challenging Jermaine enough. Mrs. Carson insisted that Jermaine needed to be placed in the fourth grade. Mrs. Kelly, Jermaine's third-grade teacher, reported that he was having a difficult time both socially and academically in the third grade and that there was no way he could handle fourth grade.

Consequently, Mrs. Carson became furious with the entire school. She attended a school board meeting and aired her concerns about the school, the principal, and especially the teachers to the entire board and in front of the local media. In her speech, she commented on how racist the staff and principal were. Of course the entire incident was blown all out of proportion in the paper the next day. The press didn't even mention that I am Mexican American and that Mrs. Kelly, Jermaine's teacher, is African American.

Following this incident, the principal had a meeting with Mrs. Carson, the equal opportunity coordinator, and the superintendent. The final decision was to keep Jermaine in the third grade for the remaining two months of school. This did not keep Mrs. Carson from badgering Mrs. Kelly, however. For example, Mrs. Carson had now begun telling Mrs. Kelly what a good teacher I had been!

A newspaper reporter came to the school the day after the school board meeting to interview the principal, Mrs. Kelly, and me. The principal spoke to the reporter but Mrs. Kelly and I didn't. The reporter wasn't able to get any supporting data for the accusation and so a follow-up story was dropped. However, I am convinced that even the mention of possible racism at our school affected some of the teacher-parent interactions for several months to follow.

Discussion

From that point on, Mrs. Carson basically left me alone, but not before taking a toll on me. It obviously had affected my self-confidence. I was extremely cautious when I dealt with my African American students and I know that, for a while at least, I treated them differently, going out of my way not to offend them. Jermaine must have been undergoing a lot of stress because of his mother's actions and I couldn't help but feel sorry for him.

Questions

1. Should I have refrained from asking Mrs. Carson for some discipline methods to use with Jermaine or was it a good decision to try to use the same methods that she had found to work?
2. Should the principal and staff have given in to Mrs. Carson's request to have Jermaine placed in the third grade? What kind of

problems could this create when dealing with other parents in the future?

3. What other techniques could the principal and I have used in dealing with Mrs. Carson?

4. Should counseling have been suggested to Mrs. Carson? Should this family situation have been further investigated?

5. How can a teacher deal with the accusation of racism?

6. Before this incident, I thought of myself as "color blind." The incident caused me to be "color sensitive." Is there a healthy balance between these two perspectives or is it better to be one way than the other when dealing with the children in the classroom?

Concluding Questions and Activities

1. Why do you think the principal agreed to move Jermaine from the second to third grade?

2. Do you think the teacher was right in asking the mother for ways of dealing with her son's discipline problems?

3. What additional information would you like to have had about this case? What kind of supporting data do you think the newspaper reporter might have been looking for?

4. How do you respond to the teacher's observation that "I was extremely cautious when I dealt with my African American students and I know that, for a while at least, I treated them differently"?

5. The teacher stated, "The press didn't even mention that I am Mexican American and that Mrs. Kelly, Jermaine's teacher, is African American." Do either one of these facts play a role in this case? Is it possible for Mexican American or African American teachers to be racist or to react to their students in a racist manner?

6. Write an analysis of this case. Compare your analysis with those written by two or three other students. As you discuss your responses to the case, also discuss how you went about your analysis. If there is some disagreement about the responses within your group, compare your responses with another group and see if you can reach consensus.

7. Share the case report with a principal and a teacher. After they have had an opportunity to read the case, set up an interview with each of them to discuss their reactions to the case. Prior to the interview, you will need to develop a set of questions that you would like to ask. As you develop your questions, you may find it helpful to review the reactions of the respondents to the

other case reports earlier in this section. Begin your interview with a very general question, such as "How did you react to this situation?" As the interview proceeds, you may ask more specific questions, such as "Do you think the teacher responded appropriately?" and "What about the way the principal reacted?" Toward the end of the interview, ask your respondents how they would handle a similar incident in their school. Don't be surprised if you get a comment like "Such an incident couldn't happen in our school," but if you do get a response like this, probe to find out why they would make such a statement. Make certain throughout the interview that your questions do not "lead" the respondents to answer the way *you* think they should. Once you have completed this exercise, share your findings with your fellow students.

Suggested Readings

Brophy, J., & Good, T. (1970). Teachers' communication of differential expectations for children's classroom performance. Some behavioral data. *Journal of Educational Psychology, 61,* 365–374.

Carew, J., & Lightfoot, S. (1979). *Beyond bias.* Cambridge, MA: Harvard University Press.

Frisby, C. L., & Tucker, C. M. (1993). Black children's perception of self: Implications for educators. *Educational Forum, 57*(2), 146–156.

Hale-Benson, J. (1986). *Black children—Their roots, culture, and learning* (rev. ed.). Baltimore: Johns Hopkins Press.

Harrison, A. O., et al. (1990). Family ecologies of ethnic minority children. *Child Development, 61,* 347–362.

Marcus, G., et al. (1991). Black and white students' perceptions of teacher treatment. *Journal of Educational Research, 84*(6), 363–367.

Murphy, D. (1986). Educational disadvantagement: Associated factors, current interventions, and implications. *Journal of Negro Education, 55*(4), 495–507.

Saunders, S. (1991). Reflections on my educational experiences as an African-American. *Teaching Education, 4*(1), 41–48.

Schultz, R. A. (1983). Sociopsychological climates and teacher-bias expectancy: A possible mediating mechanism. *Journal of Educational Psychology, 75*(1), 167–173.

Slaughter-Defoe, D. T., et al. (1990). Toward cultural/ecological perspectives on schooling and achievement in African- and Asian-American children. *Child Development, 61,* 363–383.

Wilson, M. N. (1989). Child development in the context of the black extended family. *American Psychologist, 44*(2), 380–385.

QUESTIONS, EXERCISES, AND ACTIVITIES

1. Lightfoot (1978) (see the Suggested Readings that follow) stated, "Most parents are viewed as a critical force that, if permitted to interfere, would threaten the teachers' already insecure professional status and self-image." How would you evaluate Lightfoot's statement in light of the three case reports presented in this section?

2. In all three cases, the mothers felt as if their children were being unfairly treated by either the teacher specifically or the school staff in general. Compare and contrast the strategies that the mothers used to try to change the way their children were treated.

3. Do you think the teachers were remiss in not detecting how upset the parents were? If they had become aware of how upset the parents were, what should they have done?

4. Of the three mothers, is there one who you would sympathize with more than the others? Is there one of whom you would be more fearful? Is there one that you feel may have been right in her judgment that her child was being mistreated? Explain your answers.

5. Pretend that you are to give a speech to the local parent-teacher organization on home/school relationships. You know that all three mothers in the case reports are going to be in the audience. All of the teachers will also be in attendance. Prepare an outline of your speech, indicating where and how you are going to address the concerns of both the teachers and the parents.

6. Prepare a flow analysis of both "Monster Mom" and "Unfair Accusation or Blind Prejudice?" The flow analysis on "Focusing on the Real Target: Classroom Management or Parent Control?" is provided in Figure 2–1 as an example. After you have completed your flow diagram, review your answer to question 3 and then, for each incident, indicate on your diagram where you think the teacher should have become concerned with the mother's attitude.

Figure 2–1   Flow Diagram of "Focusing on the Real Target: Classroom Management or Parent Control?"

Parent complains about child's seating arrangement during parent-teacher conferences

Teacher receives note that student is complaining about lack of recess

Mother comes to school to talk to the teacher

Student repeatedly asks teacher how she is doing, although teacher praises her frequently

Mother volunteers to help in classroom

Mother complains to principal that class of out of control

SECTION 2
SUGGESTED READINGS

Carlson, C. G. (1991). *The parent principle: Prerequisite for educational success, 26.* Princeton, NJ: Educational Testing Service.

Davies, D. (1991). Schools reaching out: Family, school, and community partnerships for student success. *Phi Delta Kappan, 72*(5), 376–380, 382.

Epstein, J. (1984). *Effects on parents of teacher practices in parent involvement.* Baltimore: Johns Hopkins University, Center for Social Organization of Schools.

Greenwood, G. E., & Hickman, C. W. (1991). Research and practice in parent involvement: Implications for teacher education. *The Elementary School Journal, 91*(3), 279–288.

Henderson, A. T. (1987). *The evidence continues to grow: Parent involvement improves student achievement.* Columbia, MD: National Committee for Citizens in Education.

Henderson, A. T., Marbuger, C. L., & Ooms, T. (1986). *Beyond the bake sale: An educator's guide to working with parents.* Columbia, MD: National Citizens in Education.

Hoover-Dempsey, K. V., Bassler, O. T., & Brissie, J. S. (1987). Parent involvement: Contributions of teacher-efficacy, school socioeconomic status, and characteristics. *American Educational Research Journal, 24*(3), 417–435.

Lightfoot, S. L. (1978). *Worlds apart: Relationships between families and schools.* New York: Basic Books.

Lindle, J. C. (1989). What do parents want from principals and teachers? *Educational Leadership, 47*(2), 12–14.

Rich, D. (1987). *Teachers and parents: An adult-to-adult approach.* Washington, DC: National Educational Association.

Swap, S. A. (1987). *Enhancing parent involvement: A manual for parents and teachers.* New York: Teachers College Press.

Vernberg, E. M., & Medway, F. J. (1991). Teacher and parent causal perceptions of school problems. *American Educational Research Journal, 18,* 29–37.

Walde, A. C., & Baker, K. (1990). How teachers view the parents' role. *Phi Delta Kappan, 72*(4), 319–320, 322.

SECTION 3

PLACEMENT
OF STUDENTS

All three of the case reports in this section deal with the grade placement of special-needs children. Although the cases involve children at the elementary level, the teacher concerns are prevalent at all grade levels.

In "Social Promotion versus Retention: Is It Really a Question of Self-Esteem versus Achievement?" a teacher is faced with the decision of whether to advance a student whom she feels does not have the necessary skills to perform at the next grade level. The teacher can't decide if the problem is the result of immaturity or inability. She concludes that, if it is inability, retaining the student will do little to alleviate the problem. If, on the other hand, the problem is immaturity, another year at second grade would help. The mother refuses to have the child tested and the principal has made it clear that he does not support retention of students except in very clear-cut cases. The teacher makes a decision that she considers to be a compromise.

The second case, "Special Effort versus Special Placement" is about a student who is autistic. It is very clear that the child needs special help, but he must be tested and the paperwork must be completed before he can be placed in a special program. In the meantime, he is placed in a traditional classroom. The teacher develops a special bond with the student and the student makes great progress over a short period of time. Based on this progress, the decision is made to keep the child in the regular classroom for the remainder of the year, but at the end of the year, the evaluation team must make a decision about where to place the child the following year.

The section concludes with "Bright and Disruptive: Should You Concentrate on the Gift or the Wrapping?" a case about a disruptive third-grade student who happens to be gifted. The child is placed in the regular classroom but the teacher struggles with how best to meet the needs of the child.

Commentaries are provided for the first two cases and the third case is left open-ended for your interpretation. This will allow you to practice and develop your analytical skills.

Social Promotion versus Retention: Is It Really a Question of Self-Esteem versus Achievement?

Background

Last year, Sherri Jackson came to my second-grade classroom possessing very few of the skills necessary to succeed in my room. However, this looked like a challenge, so I decided to keep her in my room, thinking, "All children can learn and I can teach her how to read." This child was not the only low achiever I have had. In the six years I've been teaching in the inner city, virtually all my students have been low achievers or have had behavioral problems.

As the months passed, I noticed that Sherri was persistently tardy— some days she wouldn't get to school until 9:30 or 10:00 o'clock, other days she wouldn't get there until around 11:00, and there were times when she didn't come until the afternoon. There were even a few days when Mrs. Jackson came and took her home right after lunch. Her attendance was not so poor that the truant officer had to check into it, but it was poor enough to have a drastic effect on her time on task. One time when I spoke to Mrs. Jackson about her daughter's poor attendance, I was told, rather defensively, "I'm doing the best I can in getting my daughter to school every day and on time. Whether you believe it or not, other things do come up!" I nodded and replied, "Yes, I understand." However, the times that I had asked Sherri where she was when she was not in school, she told me she went shopping with her mom, or she was at the zoo, or she went with mom to the doctor's, and so on.

I knew this child needed help and I decided that I was going to give her as much help as possible. As the semester advanced, I noticed that

Sherri and another student, Markita, were always together. Wherever Markita went or wanted to go, Sherri went or wanted to go. Markita had also been a nonreader when she entered my room, but through a lot of hard work I was able to help her learn to read. Many of the same techniques that I had tried on Markita I tried on Sherri, and as long as Markita was in class, Sherri did a pretty good job.

Whenever Sherri missed school, Markita would bring her up to date without being asked to do so. However, it wasn't long before Sherri's attendance pattern became contagious. Markita was now following Sherri's attendance pattern. Not only did Markita's attendance change but Sherri's achievement did too. Sherri seemed to be losing all that she had gained. She was confusing some of her concepts, and many of her reading skills, acquired thus far, began to disappear. I could tell that she was trying by the way she gave me her undivided attention, by the way she participated in group activities, and by the amount of time she spent on task. I tried peer tutoring, counseling, the after-school tutorial program, and giving her extra instructional time, yet nothing seemed to help.

Incident

I spoke with Mrs. Jackson about Sherri's yo-yoing academic performance. Mrs. Jackson was not surprised by my statements because she also had noticed Sherri's inconsistent performance when she was helping Sherri with her homework. I suggested that we have Sherri evaluated by the school psychologist. Immediately, with tears in her eyes, Mrs. Jackson screamed, "Definitely not! My little girl is not crazy." Once I calmed her down, she explained that she had allowed her older son to be tested and the test results did disclose a learning disability. He was placed in a special education class and many of his friends made fun of him. He was labeled as "learning disabled" and he continued to wear this label even after he dropped out of school. I asked if his academic performance improved when he was in the special classroom and her response was, "Yes, it helped him a great deal, but he was depressed all of the time because all of the kids thought that he was retarded and called him a moron." She was determined that this was not going to happen to her daughter.

I tried to be understanding while reassuring her that we both wanted what was best for her daughter. I agreed not to have her daughter tested, but told her that we needed to look at other ways of helping Sherri. I explained that, in spite all of Sherri's hard work, she had not developed the skills that she would need to be successful in the third grade. Therefore, I was going to recommend that she repeat the second grade.

I thought this parent was upset when I mentioned the possibility of psychological testing, but it was nothing compared to the way she reacted when I suggested that her daughter repeat a grade. She began to shake and then she yelled, "No! You can't fail her; I won't let you! Because if she doesn't pass, it will bother her so much that she just won't try at all. I know my child." I tried to calm the mother down by telling her that I would try to come up with some other solution. She left my room in tears, convinced that I was out to get her child.

I spent a long time trying to decide whether to retain Sherri. Then I remembered something that I had heard at a staff meeting. The principal had stated that too many students in our school had had to repeat a grade last year and that unless we decreased the number of retentions this year we would lose some of our allocated funds. I couldn't remember the statement exactly, but it boiled down to this: If the school reported too many failures, it would make the administration look bad. If the principal was made to look bad, he was going to make it bad for those teachers who were flunking their students. Of course he didn't come right out and say this, but his message was clear and there could be no doubt about what he meant.

Discussion

Having listened to all of the arguments against retaining Sherri, it was now time to focus on the student. I talked to Sherri and explained the situation. I told her that her choices were either to stay in the second grade where the work would be easier or to go on to the third grade where the work would be harder. I also explained that if she went to third grade but couldn't do the work, the teacher would send her back to second grade. She thought about it for about two seconds and then said, "I want to go to third grade. I'll work really hard so that the teacher will want to keep me." It was obvious that Sherri did not want to stay in the second grade.

I called the parents and informed them that I was going to assign Sherri to the third grade next year, but if the work proved to be too difficult for her, she would be sent back to the second grade. I really wasn't certain that this was the best solution, but there was a possibility that Sherri would mature over the summer and she might be able to handle the third-grade work. By assigning Sherri to the third grade, I was giving her a chance to prove herself. Besides, the administration had made it clear that "put backs" wouldn't count against the teacher. In addition, the parents were pleased with the decision. I just hoped it was the right one.

Questions

1. Was listening to what the child wanted before I made my decision a wise thing to do?
2. Was there something else I could have done to convince the mother to have her daughter tested?
3. As a teacher, how should I have reacted to the principal's threat?
4. What are some of the positive and negative effects of retaining a student at this young age?
5. What are some of the positive and negative effects of sending a child back a grade after the child has been assigned to the higher grade?

Response of
Sandra E. Cornwell, Teacher

My first concern would have been Sherri's tardiness and poor attendance. A child needs to be present to learn. At second-grade level, students who miss out on class discussions and hands-on activities are at a disadvantage. I wonder how poor the attendance must be before it would be investigated by a truant officer. Since the teacher had discussed the problem with the mother without success, I believe the teacher should have discussed the attendance problem with the administration.

I feel that the teacher tried several avenues to help Sherri, including peer tutoring, counseling, extra instructional time, and the after-school tutorial program. Since Sherri seemed to be trying her best but did not experience success, I believe the teacher should have pursued psychological testing even though the mother objected. When I had this same type of problem, my principal said that there is a law concerning children's rights that allows a child to be tested even if a parent does not approve.

I would have explained to the mother that the testing did not necessarily mean that Sherri would be put into a special education program. The testing would simply determine if the child had a learning disability and would help detect those areas in which she had specific weaknesses. It would also assist the teacher and/or Sherri's next teacher in deciding which instructional approach would be most effective for her.

If the testing revealed a learning disability or a below-average intelligence, I do not feel retention would be beneficial.

The adage about retention—the earlier, the better—is certainly true. Early prevention through early childhood programs, prekindergarten programs, and, in some cases, keeping a child home for a year can better prepare a child for the school situation. If retention is needed, I feel it is better to retain children at an earlier age. Children who are younger seem to be more accepting of the decision and also tend to accept peers who have been retained.

I have retained students in kindergarten, second grade, and fourth grade. I believe the students repeating kindergarten benefited most by the retention. If parents are supportive, retention in lower grades can have a positive effect on the student. The child experiences success rather than another year of failing. Some students improve in gross and fine motor skills by having another year to develop, and as they go on through school, this gives them more self-confidence in physical education classes and in playing recess games with peers.

Children often say and do cruel things to the child who is repeating a grade, especially an older child. This can affect the repeater in a negative way. However, one must keep in mind that these same children often say cruel things to the child who is not repeating but who is not working up to grade level. In larger school districts, other children may not realize the student is repeating a grade. Self-esteem is important, but it seems to me that trying to do work at which one cannot succeed is just as devastating to a child's self-esteem as repeating a grade.

I feel a second-grader is not mature enough to make a decision about his or her educational future. Almost all students want to go on to the next grade. At this age level, the decision needs to be made jointly by teachers and parents. Experience has shown me that if parents are not behind a retention, the retention is usually not a positive step.

As a classroom teacher, I feel I must hold a child's best interest in mind when making decisions. It helps to discuss a child's problems with the parents, other teachers who have had the student, and the school counselor or psychologist in order to gain help in deciding what is the best course to follow. When considering a recommendation for retention, I have had a joint conference with parents, the principal, and the next year's teacher. Sometimes when parents see the texts and objectives for the next grade, they realize their child is not ready to handle the required work. I have also asked parents of students who have repeated successfully if they would be willing to talk with parents who are making a decision about retention. A teacher needs to weigh all possibilities before making a decision to recommend retention. But if a teacher feels that it is best for the child, he or she should go on record by making that recommendation.

I strongly feel that sending a child back a grade after being assigned to a higher grade is, for the most part, a negative decision. It almost seems like a threat—"You must help this child all summer and if she isn't doing better, she might have to go back to second grade." I believe it would be better for the student, parent, classmates, and teachers if a child begins at the correct grade level at the beginning of the year. I have *never* experienced a child getting enough help over the summer to be ahead of where he or she was at the end of the year.

In summary, I believe this teacher should have been more aggressive in correcting Sherri's irregular attendance problem, had psychological testing performed, and thought more about retention in second grade rather than sending her back after being assigned to third grade. As the saying goes, "Hindsight is often better than foresight." All we teachers can do is try our best, with the resources available to us, to help each child to succeed.

Response of Sarah Huyvaert, Professor

In my judgment, the teacher in this case was a good-hearted individual who found it difficult to confront others, even when she believed that the decisions made by the others would have negative effects on students. For instance, the teacher knew that Sherri's poor attendance was affecting her academic performance and so she spoke to Sherri's mother about the problem. However, when the mother became defensive, the teacher backed down. As a result, Sherri's poor attendance continued. In another example, the teacher believed that Sherri needed special help and asked that she be tested. When the mother became upset, the teacher made little effort to persuade the mother but rather agreed not to have the child tested. Finally, when the teacher had to make the decision of whether to retain Sherri, she made the decision, not on what she believed was best for the child but rather on what would be the least upsetting to everyone, including the mother, principal, and child. She justified this with the statement, "I really wasn't certain that this was the best solution, but there was a possibility that Sherri would mature over the summer and she might be able to handle the third grade. . . . Besides, the administration had made it clear that 'put backs' wouldn't count against the teacher. In addition, the parents were pleased with the decision."

This teacher has a great deal of potential. She is caring, hard working, willing to go out of her way to help a child, and eager to try different instructional approaches. She listens to the input of others and she appears capable of making sound professional judgments. Her fear of upsetting other people, however, makes it difficult for her to live up to her potential.

If I were to serve as a consultant to this teacher, I would begin by showing her that her basic understandings of Sherri's needs were accurate and that she had the data she needed to support her conclusions. She knew the child lacked skills coming into second grade, but as a teacher she had worked with other children with the same basic deficiencies and she had been able to help them, so there was reason to believe that she could help Sherri. She knew that Sherri's attendance pattern was unacceptable and the mother's explanation was inadequate. What's more, she had data to support her conclusions. I would try to show that by appearing to agree with the mother's conclusion that "things come up," the teacher was inadvertently saying that Sherri's attendance pattern was understandable and acceptable. I would follow through the rest of the case in the same fashion, examining the testing and retention issues from the data she had available and analyzing the manner in which she handled the issues. Only then would I begin to answer her specific questions. The first three questions I would answer as openly and honestly as I could. My answers would go something like this:

1. *Was listening to what the child wanted before I made my decision a wise thing to do?* It's never wrong to get the child's input *but* its very wrong to have a child make a decision just because you can't decide what to do.
2. *Was there something else I could have done to convince the mother to have her daughter tested?* You could have asked the counselor to be present in the meeting. This is not an unusual response to the suggestion that a child be tested. Most counselors have tips and techniques on how to help parents understand that the purpose of testing is not to label a child but to find specific ways to help the child learn.
3. *As a teacher, how should I have reacted to the principal's threat?* First of all, I am concerned that you used the word *threat*. Are you really certain he was making a threat or was it frustration on his part? You should have made an appointment with the principal

and shared your observations and the data that you had collected. Find out what his real position is on retention and how you can work together to help not only Sherri but also other children who are in the same position.

For the last two questions, "What are some of the positive and negative effects of retaining a student at this young age?" and "What are some of the positive and negative effects of sending a child back a grade after the child has been assigned to the higher grade?" I would work with the teacher to find the answers. I would do this through a review of the literature and interviews with parents, students, and teachers in her building.

My consultation with this teacher would not be complete until we had an open and honest discussion about what I consider to be the fatal flaw in this case. I think this good-hearted, caring teacher set the child up for failure, not once but twice. She did it first when, at the beginning of the school year, she decided to keep the child in second grade even though the child had "very few of the skills necessary to succeed." The teacher set the child up a second time when she sent her to third grade. She told Sherri that the work is harder in third grade, and Sherri responded, "I'll work really hard so that the teacher will want to keep me." What will happen to this child's sense of self-worth and self-esteem when she tries *very hard* and still fails?

If this case does nothing else, it should serve to remind us how much damage we, as caring adults, can do to a child when we are unwilling or unable to accept our professional responsibilities, no matter how unpleasant they may be.

Concluding Questions and Activities

1. The teacher knew right away that Sherri possessed "very few of the skills necessary to succeed" in the second grade. Should she have requested a change in Sherri's placement as soon as she realized this?

2. Sherri is absent a great deal of the time and the mother seems to think this is okay. Is there anything the teacher could have done to help the mother see why it is important for Sherri to be in school as much as possible? What are some strategies that the teacher could have used?

3. Sherri and Markita started spending a great deal of time together and the togetherness seemed to have had a negative effect on Markita's attendance and Sherri's achievement. What, if any-

thing, should the teacher have done about this? Should she have tried to separate the girls? Do teachers have a right to intervene in a friendship among their students when they know the friendship is having a negative effect on both students?

4. The mother doesn't want the child tested, she insists that the child be promoted, and she isn't concerned about Sherri's absences. The teacher doesn't indicate that she makes any real attempt to change the mother's attitude, but makes the comment that "I knew this child needed help and I decided that I was going to give her as much help as possible." Wouldn't changing the mother's attitude go a long way toward helping this child? Is there anything a teacher should or could do about a parent's attitude when the attitude is negatively affecting the child?

5. How would you have resolved the issue of where to place the student the following year, knowing that the principal, parent, and student were all against retaining the student? How, if at all, would Sherri's third-grade teacher come into play?

6. Read Jim Grant's book, *Worth Repeating: Giving Children a Second Chance at School Success* (see the Suggested Readings that follow). After you have read the book, critique this case report once again and compare your new critique with your original one. What insights did you gain from Grant's book?

7. Find out what your school district's policy is for retaining students. Who is involved in the decision-making process? Can children "try out a grade" and, if it doesn't work, go back a grade? How many children are retained in each school in your district? Who (parents? teachers? students? administrators?) served on the committee that wrote the policy?

8. As a student, were you aware of anyone in your high school class who was retained in elementary school? If so, how successful were they in high school? Is this consistent with the literature on retention?

Suggested Readings

Byrnes, D., & Yamamoto, K. (1986). Views on grade repetition. *Journal of Research and Development in Education, 20*(1), 14–20.

Carstens, A. A. (1985). Retention and social promotion for the exceptional child. *School Psychology Review, 14*(1), 48–63.

Grant, J. (1989). *Worth repeating: Giving children a second chance at school success.* Rosemont, NJ: Modern Learning Press/Programs for Education.

Hoffman, S. G. (1989). What the books don't tell you about grade skipping. *Gifted Child Today, 12*(1), 37–39.

Jennings, J. M. (1992) Parent involvement strategies of inner-city schools. *NASSP Bulletin, 76*(548), 63–68.

Karweit, N. L. (1991). *Repeating a grade: Time to grow or denial of opportunity?* Report No. 16. Baltimore, MD: Center for Research on Effective Schooling for Disadvantaged Students.

Mantzicopoulos, P., & Morrison, D. (1992). Kindergarten retention: Academic and behavioral outcomes through the end of second grade. *American Educational Research Journal, 29*(1), 182–198.

Miller, S. A., et al. (1991). Parental beliefs, parental accuracy, and children's cognitive performance: A search for causal relations. *Developmental Psychology, 27*(2), 267–276.

Robinson, T. (1992). Transforming at-risk educational practices by understanding and appreciating differences. *Elementary School Guidance & Counseling, 27*(2), 84–95.

Schuyler, N. B. (1985). A matter of time: retention and promotion. *Spectrum, 33*(4), 40–44.

Shepard, L. A., & Smith, M. L. (Eds.). (1989). *Flunking grades: Research and policies on retention. Education policy perspectives.* Bristol, PA: Falmer Press, Taylor & Frances, Inc.

Smith, M. L., & Shepard, L. A. (1987). What doesn't work: Explaining policies of retention in the early grades. *Phi Delta Kappan, 69*(2), 29–34.

Thomas, A. H. (1992). Alternatives to retention: If flunking doesn't work, what does? *OSSC Bulletin, 35*(6).

Tomchin, E. M., & Impara, J. C. (1992). Unraveling teachers' beliefs about grade retention. *American Educational Research Journal, 29*(1), 199–223.

Special Effort versus Special Placement

Background

A new school year was beginning. I took my file box of students' cumulative folders to my classroom to read and gather information about this year's first- and second-graders. When I opened the box, my heart sank. I had the 25 folders that I was supposed to have, but it didn't take me long to realize that one huge folder was as fat as all the rest put together. That was my introduction to Scott, a first-grader who had just transferred from another school in the district.

After reading the other folders, I turned to Scott's. It was a litany of intervention and problems—early childhood programs since he was age 3, speech and language classes for two years, test scores that indicated a two-year developmental lag, numerous observations, diagnosis of Attention Deficit Hyperactivity Disorder (ADHD), aggressiveness, and a call for "HELP!" from his kindergarten teacher (who eventually just let him wander around and do his own thing). There was also a recommendation for a full-time aide for Scott this year. His family background was dysfunctional: a father in prison, some suspicion of child abuse, a younger sibling with special needs, and a stepfather who was unemployed.

My first step was to enlist help from resources in my building. I set up meetings with the speech therapist, the school psychologist, the Chapter 1 reading teacher, and the social worker. Our building consultation team convened to discuss Scott and to see what help I could expect. It was noted that I couldn't get any help until a formal placement had been made. We agreed to speed up all the paperwork, do evaluations, and then make the decision about Scott's long-term placement in a program for children with autism. Until then, however, he was mine to teach as best I could.

I had never taught a child with autism before. How was I going to teach him? How could I reach him in his narrow world? How could I assess if he was learning? What help would come from home? Most importantly, was Scott's assignment to my room the right placement for him or should he be sent across town to the school with the program for children with autism?

To get more information, I called on colleagues who had experience teaching children with autism. I turned to college texts to find additional information on autism. I got information from a local group of parents who have children with autism. I began reading what information I could find at the library. Even armed with this knowledge, the central question remained: Which would be better for Scott—the autism program or staying with me? This question became even more central during the next month as school got underway.

Scott was immediately recognizable the first day. He was smaller than almost all of the other children, wiry, and fidgety. I showed Scott his desk, greeted the other students, and the new school year began.

I decided right away to keep my own file on Scott to document what I was observing. That first day, Scott displayed these behaviors: rocking while standing and seated, fixating on objects (30 minutes with a pair of scissors), unusual noises (moaning, occasional howling), wandering off from class, inability to follow one-step directions, poor coordination, no eye contact, no verbal interaction with other students, and no interaction during free play. In the course of the day, I "lost" him twice (he wandered off to watch gym classes), he sharpened all his pencils down to tiny nubs, and he cut his clothes with his new scissors.

In trying to assess Scott's academic skills, I quickly discovered that he could write his name (with reversals), knew left to right orientation of print, and could distinguish the different primary colors. He would talk in single words to me but not to anyone else. At the end of the day, I was sure that, without substantial help, Scott would not be able to function in my room.

Incident

Over the next two months, I continued to teach Scott while waiting for all the paperwork to flow through the system. I actively pursued avenues to get Scott engaged in class. I placed him in a reading group, individualized his instruction, attempted to involve him in all class activities, engineered ways to get him to interact with other children (when he wished to), kept close track of him, tried to treat him just like all the other students whenever possible, and all the while added to my file about him. I met daily with his mother after school to share what he had done that day.

Ever so slowly, he began talking more with me and making occasional eye contact, and he even learned some of the daily routines. He was no longer getting lost in the school, he told a story once to the class (without looking at them), and he wrote in his journal. Scott seemed to be growing intellectually and changing right before my eyes. And I grew more fond of him every day.

My dilemma came with the meeting of the official team in early November. We met to discuss and decide if Scott should be placed in the program for children with autism. I knew the other members of the team would be leaning toward placement in the special program, yet I had seen such growth and change that I felt continuing with me might actually be better for Scott. I wondered, though, if I was being objective. Was keeping Scott the right decision for him? Would he benefit more from the daily one-on-one instruction (which he clearly needed) that he would get in the autism program than he would from working with me?

At the team meeting, we listened to the reports of the speech therapist, the school psychologist, the social worker, and the teacher from the autism program. It was clear from our conversations that they all felt placement in the autism program was the best thing for Scott. Then I spoke up and said I disagreed. I told them that I realized the testing and other observations indicated placement but that I had seen Scott reach out of his world to me. I saw him begin to reach out to others. I was learning to read his writing (talk about invented spelling!); we were communicating. He was trusting me more and more each day. I even said, "I am being selfish about this, I realize, but I am seeing such growth and I enjoy Scott so much. In my opinion, leaving him with me would be the best decision for Scott."

His mother sided with me immediately because she too had seen the positive change in Scott at home. She could tell that Scott was indeed learning—he demonstrated a willingness to read with her each night, he talked with her about school, he played school with his sister, and he even had a friend he called every once in a while. All of these were things Scott had never done before—things that his Mom attributed to Scott being in my class.

The discussion continued for another 30 minutes. The decision was made to keep Scott in my class, to get as much one-to-one intervention as possible with the Chapter 1 teacher and speech therapist, and to have the autism program teacher available to me for consultation and help.

Discussion

At this point, I believe that keeping Scott was the right decision. He has continued his growth, he reads out loud in group (better than two other students), he interacts with two children (although he still never calls his classmates by their names), he does regular first-grade work consistently (I can even read every word now, although no one else can), and he can go anywhere in the building and return (within a reasonable amount of time).

In looking at the evaluation and testing, we had a limited picture of the "testable" Scott. Those tests clearly said to place him in the appropriate program for children with autism, not in the regular classroom. Yet those tests did not reveal the little boy who loves to laugh, who gets thrilled at new discoveries, and who tries to catch sunbeams in his hands.

Questions

1. Was I being professional in wanting to keep teaching Scott or is it possible that my personal, positive feelings for Scott were interfering with my making a better decision?
2. What other avenues could have been pursued prior to making the placement decision?
3. What would be the best way to evaluate our final placement decision?
4. Although we have seen a great deal of short-term growth, would placement in the program have benefited Scott more in the long term?
5. What kind of transition problems are we likely to encounter next year when Scott is moved out of my classroom?

Response of Nicholas Byrne, Teacher

Looking at the case report as a whole, not in separate parts, I wonder how correct the original diagnosis was, as well as the opinion that the family was dysfunctional. There was no indication that the mother was not supportive. I'm not sure if she was or not. She met every day with the teacher. This is not the characteristic description of a dysfunctional family.

I feel that teachers often welcome challenges (such as Scott). By the way this teacher handled the situation from its inception, he demonstrated himself to be highly professional and a competent teacher. He created excellent programs for Scott and was involved with both the study team and parent. Having positive feelings for Scott only aided in Scott's growth. Having a good year in first grade with a caring and interested teacher, in the mainstream, is the best of all possible worlds.

The final placement for Scott is a tough one because of his positive experience with this capable teacher. The questions that have to be asked are:

1. Will the second-grade teacher be able to continue the program effectively?
2. Will Scott continue to progress, regress, or remain at this level?
3. Will Scott resume aggressive behavior if his peers notice regression or "different" behavior?

I believe Scott could benefit if he was moved to a supportive second grade with a willing teacher. If there was no willing teacher, and I emphasize *willing*, then I would definitely send him to the class for autistic children. The second-grade teacher, with the help of the team and the previous teacher, could continue to press forward with Scott's program, making adjustments as deemed necessary. I feel this could continue indefinitely throughout Scott's schooling as long as the interest, attitude, and professionalism demonstrated by the first-grade teacher is maintained throughout Scott's school years.

Finally, practically, if Scott cannot continue to progress, then his placement should be reconsidered. Forcing a square peg into a round hole will just cause frustration and failure for all concerned.

Response of
Barbara Lowenthal, Professor

When I first read the information about Scott, I questioned the composition of the team that evaluated the child for placement in a program for children with autism. Professionals such as the teachers, speech therapist, psychologist, Chapter 1 reading teacher, and social worker were mentioned as team members. However, there was no mention about the role of the family except to characterize it as dysfunctional. Public Law 99–457 and the Individual with Disabilities Act (IDEA) stress that the family be part of the evaluation team. Not only must the family consent to the evaluation but they also are empowered to assist, as much as they wish, in planning and evaluating the placement for their child if he is eligible for special education (Dunst, Trivette, & Deal, 1988; Lerner, 1993; Cook,

Tessier, & Klein, 1992) (see the Suggested Readings that follow). In order to work with any family, whether it is considered "dysfunctional" or not, it is necessary to be nonjudgmental and to find family strengths as well as needs. The strengths of the family can be used to aid the education and development of a child such as Scott, and family involvement should be encouraged. One of the strengths demonstrated by the mother was her interest in the child's continuing placement in the mainstream class because of her observation of his progress there.

Continuing placement of Scott in the regular class agrees with current thinking about inclusion and the requirements of the Individual with Disabilities Act (Public Law 99-142), which guarantees that all children have an inherent right to be educated to the maximum extent appropriate with children who are not disabled. The law further specifies that special classes, separate schooling, or other removal of children with disabilities from the regular educational environment should occur only when the nature of the disability is such that education in regular classes, with the use of supplementary aids and services, cannot be achieved satisfactorily. Scott appears to be making appropriate progress in both academic and social areas according to the observations of both his teacher and his mother.

Standardized testing may not, and should not, be the only way to evaluate Scott's growth and development. Ecological assessment can include such things as informal testing, criterion- and curriculum-based evaluation, observations, interviews, and the use of portfolios. From the observations and interviews with Scott's teacher and mother, from anecdotal records, and from informal testing, we obtain a holistic view of a child with autistic behaviors who has developed cognitively, linguistically, creatively, and, most significantly, in view of his disability, socially. Scott belongs in the regular class in which he can remain with typically developing children and have further opportunities to grow, to model appropriate behaviors, to further his language and communication, and to form friendships with his peers.

Transition problems that can occur when Scott is ready to move on to second grade should be anticipated and planned for before the change in placement. There needs to be good communication between the family and the school team, which includes not only related service personnel and administrators but also his sending and receiving teachers. Scott and his mother should be encouraged to visit the prospective new class, and the parent needs to be informed about other placement options. The receiving teacher can tell Scott's present teacher what she or he feels are "survival" skills for the children in the new class so that Scott's present teacher can start preparing him for the new placement. The receiving teacher needs to know Scott's present levels of achievement and the extent of his participation in classroom activities. With careful planning and teamwork involving the family and school personnel, Scott should continue to make progress and, as his teacher so aptly states, to keep on trying to catch sunbeams in his hands!

Concluding Questions and Activities

1. List the techniques the teacher used to make this situation work. Are there additional techniques that you might have used? Would these same techniques work with most mainstreamed students, regardless of age? Identify any techniques you would modify, add, or delete if you were working with older students and provide a rationale for your changes.

2. If a special-needs student were assigned to you next year, what are some of the questions that you would like to have answered about the student? Of whom would you ask these questions and in what format (e.g., conference, written documentation, etc.)? Assuming you are a member of a team of professionals working with the student, how would you prepare for an initial team conference?

3. What are the challenges faced by a teacher who has mainstreamed students in the classroom?

4. Most teachers will tell you that they have little time left over during the school day and/or year for extra planning. Yet we see that this teacher spent a lot of time working with Scott individually and communicating with Scott's mother after school. How do you think this teacher managed to find the time? What might be the trade-offs involved when a teacher works so closely with just one student? Is this always positive or are there some negatives involved?

5. The teacher made the comment, "I knew the other members of the team would be leaning toward placement in the special program, yet I had seen such growth and change that I felt continuing with me might actually be better for Scott." Do you think this teacher was objective in his judgment? Is it important for a teacher always to be objective or should a teacher occasionally make decisions that are based on professional intuitions and subjectivity?

6. Develop a written argument either for or against the mainstreaming of special-needs students into the regular classroom. In your argument you should address the impact on both the special-needs student and the other students in the classroom.

7. Read the articles by Campbell and colleagues ("Peer Tutors Help Autistic Students Enter the Mainstream"), Handleman ("Mainstreaming the Autistic Type Child"), and Raab and colleagues ("Promoting Peer Regard of an Autistic Child in a Mainstreamed Preschool Using Pre-Enrollment Activities"), which are listed in the following Suggested Readings. Develop a plan that you might use to integrate a student with autism into your classroom.

Suggested Readings

Brinker, R. P., & Thorpe, M. E. (1984). Integration of severely handicapped students and the proportion of IEP objectives achieved. *Exceptional Children, 51*(2), 168–175.

Campbell, A., et al. (1983). Peer tutors help autistic students enter the mainstream. *Teaching Exceptional Children, 15*(2), 64–69.

Cook, R. E., Tessier, A., & Klein, M. D. (1992). *Adapting early childhood curricula for children with special needs.* New York: Merrill.

Dunst, C., Trivette, C., & Deal, A. (1988). *Enabling and empowering families.* Cambridge, MA: Brookline.

Handleman, J. S., (1984). Mainstreaming the autistic type child. *Exceptional Child, 31*(1), 33–38.

Handleman, J. S., et al. (1991). A specialized program for preschool children with autism. *Language, Speech, and Hearing Services in Schools, 22*(3), 107–110.

Jenkins, J. R., Speltz, M. L., & Odom, S. L. (1985). Integrating normal and handicapped preschoolers: Effects on child development. *Exceptional Children, 52*, 7–17.

Lerner, J. (1993). *Learning disabilities: Theories, diagnosis, and teaching strategies.* Boston: Houghton Mifflin.

Lovaas, O. I. (1987). Behavioral treatment and normal educational and intellectual functioning in young autistic children. *Journal of Consulting and Clinical Psychology, 55*(1), 3–9.

Lowenthal, B. (1987). Mainstreaming—Ready or not. *Academic Therapy, 22*(4), 393–397.

Lowenthal, B. (1991). Ecological assessment: Adding a new dimension for preschool children. *Intervention, 26*, 148–152.

Machado, G. (1983). A center for "special students" can teach kids and save money. *Executive Educator, 5*(12), 29–30.

Raab, M. M., et al. (1986). Promoting peer regard of an autistic child in a mainstreamed preschool using pre-enrollment activities. *Child Study Journal, 16*(4), 265–284.

Snow, R. E. (1984). Placing children in special education: Some comments. *Educational Researcher, 13*(3), 12–14.

Strain, P. S., et al. (1985). Normally developing preschoolers as intervention agents for autistic-like children: Effects on class deportment and social interaction. *Journal of the Division for Early Childhood, 9*(2), 105–115.

Bright and Disruptive: Should You Concentrate on the Gift or the Wrapping?

Background

John Amos is an only child. His parents divorced when John was about a year old. Since that time, John has had no contact with his father. When he was a student in my third-grade class, John lived with his mother and her boyfriend, Ray. From the first day of the school year, I could tell that John was a bright boy. His vocabulary was excellent, he paid attention in class, and he often contributed orally to class discussions. At the beginning of the year, John was completing about two-thirds of the assigned written work.

Incident

I talked to John's mother during parent-teacher conferences about John's work and his complaints to me that he could never do things well enough to please Ray. I shared two of John's examples with his mother: Ray said that John couldn't play Nintendo right and couldn't shovel snow right. John's mother indicated to me that her son had been a perfectionist since he was just two years old. She stated that she had told Ray to stop expecting perfection from her son. She also told me that she was going to move out of Ray's house and try to make it on her own.

As the year progressed, John was doing less and less written work in the classroom and little or none of his homework. I talked to his second-grade teacher about his work habits. She indicated that during the second grade he did most of his class work, but not much of his homework. I told John what his second-grade teacher had said about his work habits and questioned him as to why he wasn't performing in third grade. He said that I was giving him a lot more work to do than he had in second grade and that the work wasn't fun. He also stated that he hadn't wanted to work since kindergarten.

During the course of the year, I found that John wanted to do only what came easily for him. He did not want to practice. He did less and less written work. He finally refused to take a spelling test and wouldn't take a timed fact test in math. I cut back some on written work for him, had him dictate his answers orally to another student for timed fact tests, and offered rewards for work completed. Nothing seemed to satisfy him.

Thinking that the work might be too easy for John and that he might be bored, I provided an opportunity for him to advance to fourth-grade math with two other boys from my room. He tried for one day and then gave up, saying he couldn't do the work. He compared himself to the two boys, saying he wasn't as smart as they were and that he was stupid. I tried to provide some independent study for John, but he made a point of telling me that I should make him do only the work the other students were doing.

John then started being mean to fellow students, kicking and tripping them. Anytime I asked him to do something, he refused to do it. He always wanted to do the opposite. At one point, he had to be carried out of the room, kicking and screaming.

I had not requested in-school counseling for John because I knew he needed more help than our counselor could give, especially since the counselor was in the school only one day a week. Early on I talked to John's mother about getting professional help for him. She made an appointment for him with a counselor, but did not follow through because of the cost. At a later time during the school year, she took him to another counseling agency, but did not continue these sessions, again because of the costs.

Right after Christmas, the principal tried to get John's mother to sign a form that would allow the school system to have John tested. The mother was reluctant and kept putting off giving her permission. The school contacted the counseling agency and they agreed that they would test him and share the results with us if his mother agreed. John's mother finally agreed and John was tested. However, when a conference was set up to discuss the results, the mother did not keep her appointment.

By the end of the school year, John was spending much of his time in the principal's office. He did a minimum amount of written work, but enjoyed reading books beyond his grade level.

When test results came back from the state test for educational process, it was confirmed that John indeed had a high IQ of 141. Thinking that perhaps he might benefit from placement in a gifted and talented program, my principal recommended that we try placement in our school system's program. I filled out a recommendation form and waited for a decision. The head of the program telephoned the principal and me to inform us that she couldn't place John in the program because of his behavior problems.

The next school year, John started out in the same pattern of refusing to do work and hurting other students. The principal finally got the mother's signature for psychological testing within our school system. John did qualify for placement in a class for emotionally handicapped children.

Discussion

Looking back on the situation, I wonder if a behavior modification program would have worked early in the year. Also, perhaps suspension early in the year would have helped the mother realize the severity of John's emotional problems.

I wish I had recommended John for in-school counseling. I think his mother would have given her permission for that. Even a little help would have been better than nothing. Perhaps I should have tried more one-on-one work between him and the aide. Maybe doing more work on the computer to substitute for some written work and practice would have been more successful.

My class was so good about accepting John with his problems, but I feel guilty for having taken so much class time in dealing with John. I feel that the other children were somewhat shortchanged in their instructional time.

Questions

1. When reasoning didn't work, should I have asked the principal to suspend John?
2. Should I have been more forceful in trying to convince John's mother of the seriousness of her son's problems?
3. Should I try to individualize my instruction more in the future to meet the special needs of my students?
4. Should I require less practice and more creative work from the more talented students?
5. According to John's mother, John was a perfectionist. Is it possible that he was avoiding the work so that he could avoid failure? If so, what should I have done to help him?

Concluding Questions and Activities

1. What were the defining elements of this case report? (e.g., What was the problem? What did the teacher do to make the situation better or make it worse?)
2. What other problem-solving techniques might the teacher have used when dealing with John? What advice would you give the teacher?
3. Was the teacher wrong in not requesting in-school counseling even though she was certain that it wouldn't help John and it would take time away from other students who might be helped? Explain your answer.
4. The results of John's IQ test confirmed that he was very bright. His behavior problems, however, prevented him from being accepted in the gifted and talented program. Is this fair to John? Is it fair for the classroom teacher to have to "put up" with his problems when the special teacher does not?
5. Should the fact that John is a bright student influence the way the teacher responds to his behavior problems? If so, how? If not, why not?
6. Interview a classroom teacher to find out how the teacher would deal with a similar problem. Then interview a school counselor or a teacher from the gifted and talented program to see how that person would respond to a case such as this. Do the teachers agree? What additional information would they want before they would be willing to make a decision? What kind of advice would they give this teacher?

Suggested Readings

Adderholdt, E. M. (1989). Perfectionism and underachievement. *Gifted Child Today, 12*(1), 19–21.

Adderholdt, E. M. (1990). A comparison of the "stress seeker" and the "perfectionist." *Gifted Child Today, 13*(3), 50–51.

Dubelle, S. T., & Hoffman, C. M. (1987). When an attention seeker gets under your skin. *Principal, 66*(4), 28–30.

Janos, P. M., et al. (1985a). Self-concept, self-esteem, and peer relations among gifted children who feel "different." *Gifted Child Quarterly, 29*(2), 78–82.

Janos, P. M., et al. (1985b). Friendship patterns in highly intelligent children. *Roeper Review, 8*(1), 46–49.

Peretti, P. O., et al. (1984). Effect of parental rejection on negative attention-seeking classroom behaviors. *Education, 104*(3), 313–317.

Petty, R. (1989). Managing disruptive students. *Educational Leadership, 46*(6), 26–28.

Roeper, A. (1982). How the gifted cope with their emotions. *Roeper Review, 5*(2), 21–24.

Tuttle, F. B., Jr. (1979). *Providing for the intellectually gifted.* Urbana, IL: National Council of Teachers of English.

Yewchuk, C., & Jobagy, S. (1991). The neglected minority: The emotional needs of gifted children. *Education Canada, 31*(4), 8–13.

QUESTIONS, EXERCISES, AND ACTIVITIES

1. Each of the students in this section had special needs, and their teachers were concerned about the best ways to meet these needs. Do you think the same amount of deliberation is given to placing the "regular" student? Should placement of all students be given equal consideration regardless of their status as "regular" students or special-needs students? Defend your answer.

2. Compare and contrast the roles the adults played in these cases. What did the teachers do to get the parents involved? How did the professionals interact with one another? At what point were team meetings called? What were the reasons for the team meetings? What effect did the school climates have on the placement of the students? How do the reflections of the three teachers compare?

3. Prepare an annotated bibliography on one of the following topics:

   The Disruptive Student
   The Gifted Student in the "Regular" Classroom
   The Child with Emotional Disorders
   Mainstreaming the Student with Special Needs
   Retention versus Social Promotion

   Your bibliography should follow the accepted format of your university. (*The Publication Manual of the American Psychological Association* and *The Chicago Manual of Style* are two of the more frequently used style manuals.) Your bibliography must include a brief summary of the document and you may also want to include quotes that you feel are noteworthy.

4. Interview several teachers about the procedures that their school uses to place students. What role, if any, do parents play in the process? Are there different procedures for different types of students (e.g., students who are gifted, students who are emotionally impaired, "regular" students)? If there is a conflict between two or more parties concerning the placement, who resolves the conflict? What course of action is taken if it appears that a student has been placed incorrectly? See if you can find out (a) what the teachers' responsibilities are (e.g., do they make recommendations or do they actually assign students to groups?); (b) what tasks must they perform (e.g., fill out forms,

attendance at meetings, etc.); and (c) when most of these activities occur.

5. Compare your findings from question 4 with the findings of other members of your class. As a group, see if you can determine how practice differs from theory. (In order to do this, you will need to rely on the readings that you did for your annotated bibliography.)

SECTION 3
SUGGESTED READINGS

Chandler, H. N. (1986). Mainstreaming: A formative consideration. *Journal of Learning Disabilities, 19*(2), 125–126.

The Chicago Manual of Style (13th ed.). (1982). Chicago: The University of Chicago Press.

Downing, J. A., et al. (1990). Regular and special educator perceptions of nonacademic skills needed by mainstreamed students with behavioral disorders and learning disabilities. *Behavioral Disorders, 15*(4), 217–226.

Forman, E. A. (1988). The effects of social support school placement on the self-concept of LD students. *Learning Disability Quarterly, 11*(2), 115–124.

Fuchs, D., et al. (1990). Mainstream assistance teams: A scientific basis for the art of consultation. *Exceptional Children, 57*(2), 128–139.

Gearheart, B. R., Weishahn, M. W., & Gearheart, C. J. (1992). *The exceptional student in the regular classroom* (5th ed.). New York: Macmillan.

Gillet, P. (1986). Mainstreaming techniques for LD students. *Academic Therapy, 21*(4), 389–399.

Humphrey, M. J., et al. (1984). Mainstreaming LD students. *Academic Therapy, 19*(3), 321–327.

Publication Manual of the American Psychological Association (3rd ed.). (1984). Washington, DC: American Psychological Association.

Snow, R. E. (1984). Placing children in special education: Some comments. *Educational Researcher, 13*(3), 12–14.

SECTION 4

CURRICULAR AND
INSTRUCTIONAL DECISIONS

The three case reports in this section deal with some aspect of instructional decision making. In the first case, "Time Is of the Essence," the teacher shares an incident in which her students were unable to finish a test during the assigned class period. Most of the students stay after class to complete the test, but one student protests because he is unable to stay after school and he believes it is unfair that the other students have been given an opportunity that is unavailable to him. The teacher discusses how she handled the incident, but questions the events that led up to the situation and wonders if her decisions were appropriate.

The author of the second case in this section, "Student Needs versus School Logistics," develops a plan for meeting the needs of high school students who take longer than "normal" to meet course objectives. He discusses problems associated with tracking students, "dumbing down" textbooks, and trying to change the system to meet the needs of the students.

"Cooperation through No Fault of My Own—Or How to Succeed without Really Trying" involves gifted students in the ninth grade. The students have been grouped together throughout most of their school years and they are very competitive. In the words of the teacher, "Up until the incident I am about to describe, which occurred near the end of the second six weeks, I had tried just about everything, including cooperative learning, to get these students to work together, but I had only limited success." She goes on to describe an incident that caused the students to change from competitive to cooperative. Although the teacher is pleased with the outcome, she is disturbed by the triggering event that caused the change to take place and wonders what else she could have done.

All of the cases in this section deal with high school students. But the concerns—improper time allotted to instructional activities, balancing student needs with school requirements, and helping students become less competitive and more cooperative—are applicable at all grade levels. This section differs from the previous sections in that none of the case reports have individual commentary. Instead, at the end of the section, you will find one commentary on all of the cases. This commentary was written by Billie Hughes, a faculty member at Phoenix College. Hughes is involved in outcomes assessment and evaluation and is noted for her work on classroom research.

As you review the cases in this section, think about your role as a classroom teacher and/or a former student. Have you ever encountered similar problems within your environment? If so, how did you address them? See if you can identify other problems that might possibly have been addressed in this section. Finally, try to write your own commentary in response to the teachers. As you do so, remember that these reports are written only from the perspective of the teacher and, although data and information may be incomplete, the perspective is valid, at least in the eyes of the teacher.

Time Is of the Essence

Background

On March 5th, my general chemistry students—84 students in four classes—took a test covering material from Chapter Eight in their text-book. When I was writing the test, I had the feeling the test might be too long. The students would have to know the material well and recognize patterns as they moved from one problem to the next in order to complete the test within the time given.

As I had expected, I had not allotted enough time for the test. In third- through fifth-period classes, students who needed extra time stayed in the classroom and finished their tests. They were sent to their next classes with a pass that explained why they were late. The students were stressed by the end of the test but there were no complaints. The sixth-hour class proved to be a different story.

One student, Jeff, said he was unable to stay after school and com-plained that it was not fair that other students were given the chance to spend more time on their tests while he was unable to. Jeff added that he knew the material, but didn't have time to answer all the problems. He didn't explain why he couldn't stay after school.

I graded the tests and passed them back the next day. The average grade was 63 percent, much lower than the 77 to 82 percent range in which the students normally performed. Many of the students were disappointed in the scores. Although I agreed that the test was too long, I attributed at least part of their failure to a lack of effort. Those students who really knew the material were able to complete the test within the allotted amount of time. Some students were aware they had difficulties with the material before taking the test, but they hadn't asked questions in class or attended tutoring sessions. This resulted in those students not knowing the material well enough to complete the test in the allotted time. Even when given more time, they were still unable to complete the test satisfactorily. I did attribute part of their failure to task difficulty. I believe that the questions on the test were too difficult for them to answer at the time they were asked to perform.

Whatever the reason for the poor student performance—lack of time, not enough effort on the part of the students, or a test that was too demanding—the situation had to be corrected. I spent the next week going over the test with the students and reteaching the material. I hoped this would take care of the problem if it was related to task difficulty. I wrote and gave a new test that was much shorter than the first. This would take care of the problem if it was caused by lack of time. If the problem was a result of the students not putting in enough effort, then their poor scores would have to remain.

The average on the second test was 81 percent. Jeff's test score improved from 39 percent on the first test to 75 percent on the second test. I still believed that Jeff didn't know the material on the first test. If he had, I think his second test score would have been even higher. At least now he wasn't going to be able to blame the lack of time for his performance. Both test grades were counted. The test scores accounted for one-third of the marking period grades. When the marking period ended on April 3rd, Jeff received a D– (62 percent).

Incident

Jeff had a "fit" when he was told his final grade. He argued that the first Chapter Eight test score should be dropped. I tried to be rational and discuss the problem from my perspective. I admitted that I had made a mistake in gauging the time needed to complete the test. I explained that I did not make the test too long on purpose, that I tried to create a situation in which everyone could succeed, and that I viewed the extra time on the test as a privilege—not as a right. I pointed out that I had tried to correct for my mistake by curving the first test score, by spending time reteaching the material, and by offering a second test. The majority of the students in the class accepted my viewpoint and understood that I had been accommodating, but Jeff persisted with his argument. I then attempted to show Jeff that if he had been fulfilling his responsibilities in the class, his grade could have been higher. I pointed out to him that he had neglected to turn in three assignments and had turned in two assignments late. If his missing assignments hadn't counted as zeroes, his marking period grade would have been a D (66.3 percent). If the first test score was dropped from his grade, his marking period grade would be only 0.5 percent higher (66.8 percent). This fact finally convinced Jeff that he was just as responsible for, and in control of, his grade as I was.

Discussion

I think it was possible to resolve this conflict for a couple of reasons. First, Jeff felt he was able to question what occurred in class. If he had never raised the issue with me, he could have continued to blame one test score for his failure. Second, I was receptive to discussing the issues with Jeff and the rest of the class. Seeing that I was trying to correct for my mistake was important. Third, I had documentation of Jeff's performance to support the grade I had given. Finally, I had demonstrated that I was trying to be fair by weighing both scores equally.

One issue that was not resolved was what action should be taken when a student does not complete a test in the given amount of time. I accepted suggestions from the class but none of the suggestions were as fair and as practical as the method I was currently using. The following shows the suggestions and my rebuttals:

Suggestion: Let students finish the test the next day in class.

Rebuttal: Would it be fair to the students who finished the test on time to give the students who didn't finish, and who have viewed the test, another night to study?

Suggestion: Pass out the pages of the test separately. When a student finishes a page, he or she picks up the next one. Therefore, the students don't see the material ahead of time.

Rebuttal: When a student picks up a new page, how will I know if he or she will have enough time in class to finish it? It is obvious that students finish tests in different lengths of time. If I could predetermine how long it would take to finish the test, we wouldn't have this problem.

Suggestion: If the students in third hour take a long time to finish the test, the method of giving the test could be adapted for the next three classes.

Rebuttal: Would this be fair to the third-hour class? Again, just because someone in third hour has difficulty finishing the test doesn't necessarily mean the rest of the students will have trouble.

Suggestion: Grade only the work that is finished.

Rebuttal: How do I then distinguish between a question left unanswered because a student didn't have time to finish it and a question left unanswered because the student didn't know the answer? Students could answer only the questions they knew they were going to get right.

Needless to say, I'm open for more suggestions. I see the best solution as being to not let it happen again, but, try as I might, this is probably unlikely.

Questions

1. I assumed the students were ready for the test because they had not communicated otherwise to me. Who is responsible for determining if students are ready to take a test?
2. What should be done if a student does not have enough time to complete a test or an assignment?
3. Would it be acceptable to allow different methods or different times for test taking for different students? How could this be fairly justified?
4. Should I have spent so much time explaining to Jeff why I had counted the tests the way I did?

Concluding Questions and Activities

1. Do you think the teacher's response to Jeff was an appropriate one?
2. If you were in Jeff's place, how would you have reacted? How would you have reacted if you had been one of the other students?
3. Do you think the teacher spent too much time justifying his actions?
4. What do you think about the teacher's rebuttals to the class? Are they logical? Do they make sense?
5. One thing a teacher must always try to avoid is getting into a "power struggle" with the students. When you attempt to justify your actions to a student, you may very quickly find yourself in just such a struggle. At the same time, when students are upset by your actions, you need to help them understand why you did what you did. How might you avoid turning a discussion of your actions into a "power struggle"? How close do you think this teacher came to a power struggle?
6. The teacher gives you a long list of alternative strategies that could have been used to remedy the problem and then explains why he chose none of them. Identify some other alternatives that

might have been used and discuss the possible consequences of their use.

7. Read a journal article on authentic assessment and then evaluate this case in light of the information provided.

8. Develop a notebook of alternative testing ideas that could be used with students. Include samples of different types of evaluation approaches. Also include samples of the different types of questions that could be included on a paper/pencil test.

9. Interview classroom teachers to find out how they plan a class period so that the time available is wisely used. Discuss what they do if they inadvertently plan too much or too little for the time allotted.

Suggested Readings

Bacon, R. K., & Beyrouty, C. A. (1988). Test retakes by groups of students as a technique to enhance learning. *Journal of Agronomic Education, 17*(2), 99–101.

Evans, C. S. (1993). When teachers look at student work. *Educational Leadership, 50*(5), 71–72.

Fleener, M. J., & Marek, E. A. (1992). Testing in the learning cycle. *Science Scope, 15*(6), 48–49.

Hambleton, R. K. (1987). Determining optimal test lengths with a fixed total testing time. *Educational and Psychological Measurement, 47*(2), 339–347.

Nimmer, D. N. (1984). Measure of validity, reliability, and item analysis for classroom tests. *The Clearing House, 58*(3), 138–140.

Shepard, L. (1979). Norm-referenced vs. criterion-referenced tests. *Educational Horizons, 58*(1), 26–35.

Stiggins, R. (1987). Design and development of performance assessments. *Educational Measurement: Issues and Practices, 6*(3), 33–42.

Stiggins, R. (1988). Revitalizing classroom assessment. *Phi Delta Kappan, 69*, 5.

Wiggins, G. (1988). Rational numbers: Scoring and grading that helps rather than hurts learning. *American Educator, 12*, 4.

Wiggins, G. (1992). Creating tests worth taking. *Educational Leadership, 49*(8), 26–33.

Student Needs versus School Logistics

Background

As do most high schools our size, we offer courses for different ability levels. In algebra, we offer Honors Algebra, Algebra, and Technical Algebra I as well as Technical Algebra II. The last two courses were created to help students obtain algebra skills and to give them two years to obtain these skills. From discussions that have occurred in department meetings, it has become evident that there is great dissatisfaction with these two courses. Many students who sign up for the courses have motivational and/or disciplinary problems. A lot of the problems stem from the students' previous math history. They have had trouble with math throughout the grades and are convinced that math is not for them or—even worse—that they can't do math. Another part of the dissatisfaction with these classes is the textbooks that are being used. The book for Technical Algebra I is "too easy" according to several of the teachers. Typical comments revolve around the fact that it is a general math book that doesn't really teach algebra. I cringe inside when I hear comments like this. I want to say, "Books don't teach students—teachers have been hired to do this. If you're not happy with the book, find or create other material."

Finally, many of the teachers in our department have low expectations for the students who take these courses. Some evaluate the students, in part, on the number of discipline problems the students create and on how much effort the students show. There is little regard for whether the students demonstrate any of the algebra skills. I believe some of the teachers in our department feel that many of the students taking these classes are not capable of learning algebra. There is a strong feeling that these classes should be eliminated altogether.

About five years ago, our high school got a new principal. Never before have I worked with a principal who has taken such a leadership role in curriculum. He recognized that many of our high school students go on to college and that algebra is a "gatekeeper" course to success in math, science, and business courses. He instituted three changes in the math department. First, any student who gets a D or F for the first semester must go back and successfully repeat the first semester before going on to second semester Algebra. Second, he created an "algebra block" class. In this class, the students take a regular Algebra class for two hours of their school day, not just one. This course was created with the same rationale as the Technical Algebra I and II courses, but uses two hours out of the school day instead of two years out of a total high school stay. The third change was the creation of an Applied Algebra class. This class is intended to be more of a hands-on course, integrating other areas of curriculum, especially science. All of these changes are recent and have not been adequately evaluated to assess their success.

Incident

This past school year, I was assigned to teach two Technical Algebra II classes. This turned out to be a very frustrating experience. The classes were larger than normal (they started out with 29 and 26 students, respectively) and were scheduled for the last two hours of the school day. There were many juniors and seniors taking what is considered to be a sophomore class. As I checked student records, I found that many of them had had two teachers in the department who were known for being "easy graders." This meant to me that some of these students did not learn very much in Technical Algebra I. Also, there were students in the class who were taking my Technical Algebra II course without the recommendation of their Technical Algebra I teacher.

It is the practice at my school that the math teachers recommend a math course for their students for their next year and that the counselors meet with the students and advise them on which course to take. However, the ultimate decision rests with the student and his or her parents. If the parents disagree with the course a teacher has recommended and insist that the student be placed in a different course, the parents are required to sign a waiver that states that the student may not withdraw from the course for any reason.

During the semester, there was a major crisis in each class that had to be resolved. One class felt that they had a "right" to talk to each other any time they wanted. Many of them had experienced this "right" during their previous year. I don't allow unnecessary talking in my classroom and so there was a lot of conflict between the students and me at the beginning of the year. It took a long time to reduce the tension in the room. The other class had two students who couldn't and wouldn't get along. This culminated in a physical confrontation where neither student would back down. I sought to have one of these students reassigned to my other class. He ended up in one of the Technical Algebra II classes taught by another teacher.

Toward the end of the first semester, it became clear that many of the students in my two classes, especially the last-hour class, did not have the algebra skills necessary to be successful in the second semester of the course. I struggled with the question: Should I continue with my responsibility to teach the objectives in the course outline or should I try to meet the needs of each individual student? I decided to approach the assistant principal in charge of schedule changes to see if I could create one class that would continue on with the course content and one class that would go back and try to master the first semester content. He thought this was a great idea and wanted to expand it to involve the other teacher who was teaching Technical Algebra II. Also, he wanted to check with the principal and counselors to resolve some issues, such as how to assign a student a grade for first semester and how to award credit for the second semester of the course.

A meeting was scheduled with the assistant principal, the other teacher, and me. I considered the other teacher to be a very bright person and a good teacher. Therefore, I was surprised to hear what he had to say. I was advised to lower my expectations for these students because if I thought about it, I would realize that the students in Technical Algebra were in the lower part of the bell curve of human intelligence, and because of this, many of them would never be able to learn algebra. When I protested that the department's course outline and description of the course states that this was an algebra course, he stated that the course is not really teaching algebra and that what was really needed was a change in the course outline and description. It was obvious that this teacher did not want to involve his classes in any of the changes I was interested in making.

Shortly after this meeting, I was informed that the counselors had grave concerns about making any changes. They did not know how to assign credit for those students who would repeat or how to apply the credit for meeting graduation requirements. (At our high school, at least two math credits are required in order to graduate.) Also, they did not want a "can of worms" opened. They feared other teachers might want to try something similar. I was basically told, both within and outside of the department, to continue with the course content. I went to the person in the department that I respected most (he retired this year) and told him of this experience. I asked for ideas about evaluating student performance. He gave me a few, all of which I had already tried and none of which worked with my students.

Discussion

I continued with the course content. I tried to reinforce first semester skills whenever possible, tried to show students the big picture of what algebra is and how it can be used, and attempted to convince students that, even though they might not be successful now, that did not mean they would never be able to do algebra. I did the best I could for these students, but I am still thinking that my original solution would have been a better one for these students.

Questions

1. The history of our math department has been to create new courses to better meet student needs whenever students appear to be doing poorly. Is this the best way to solve this problem?
2. Is the creation of courses by ability level educationally sound or should concepts and content be the organizing principles?
3. Should I have "stuck to my guns" and individualized within my classes? How could I have explained the second semester grade for those students who hadn't covered the course content in one semester?
4. It is quite obvious to me that low teacher expectations for these courses contribute to the lack of student learning. What are the responsibilities of the principal and me (the math department chairperson) when it comes to affecting change, especially in regard to teacher expectations and resulting behaviors?
5. Is it the responsibility of the teacher to teach the objectives of the course or to meet the needs of the individual students within the class?

Concluding Questions and Activities

1. Do all students need algebra in high school? Are the teachers right when they imply that "not all students can learn algebra"?
2. How do you react to the teacher's statement, "Books don't teach students—teachers have been hired to do this. If you're not happy with the book, find or create other material"?

3. The teacher notes that two of the teachers in the department are "easy graders," and that when students have an "easy grader" it indicates to him that the students have not learned very much. Do you think this means that the student who has a "hard grader" has learned a lot? What does this mean? What is a "hard grader"?

4. What consequences, both pro and con, result from a teacher being an "easy grader"? What are the consequences of a teacher being a "hard grader"? Which would you rather be and why?

5. The Technical Algebra II classes were scheduled for the last two periods of the day. Teachers often consider these to be the worst periods of the day because everyone is tired and the students are suffering from "information overload." If you buy this argument, what would you schedule for the last two periods of the day? As you think about your answer, remember that you don't want to waste any of the instructional day and not all teachers can have study hall the last period!

6. When the teacher was told to continue teaching the course outline, he went to another teacher to get ideas for evaluating the students' performance. Do you think this means he accepted the other teacher's suggestion that he lower his expectations? What should be the relationship between course objectives, students' needs, and student evaluation?

7. Which is more important—the curriculum or individual student needs? In other words, do you think it is more important to teach content or to teach students? Would your answer be different for the elementary grades than for high school? How would your approach to grading change as you moved from one focus to the other? Think about your answer in terms of the purpose of grades, remembering that one of the functions of grades is to communicate to other educators the competence of students in relationship to the curriculum.

8. Working with a partner, see if you can devise a way to address the counselors' concerns (how to assign the credits for those students who would repeat the course, how to assign the credits in terms of graduation requirements, how to address their fear of "opening a can of worms").

9. Pair up with a partner and prepare a simulation of a follow-up meeting between the teacher and the counselor. One of you take the position of the teacher and the other take the position of the counselor. From these positions, you are to debate the question: Should the teacher continue with his responsibility to teach the objectives in the course outline or should he try to meet the needs

of the individual student? Support your argument with data from outside sources (e.g., selected articles, interviews with educators, previous class discussions, etc.).

Suggested Readings

Black, S. (1992). On the wrong track. *The Executive Educator, 14*(12), 46–49.

Black, S. (1993). Derailing tracking. *Phi Delta Kappan, 74*(5), 27–30.

Braddock, J. H., II, & McPartland, J. M. (1990). Alternatives to tracking. *Educational Leadership, 47*(7), 76–79.

Canady, R. L., & Reina, J. M. (1993). Parallel block scheduling: An alternative structure. *Principal, 72*(3), 26–29.

Carbo, M. (1992). Eliminating the need for dumbed-down textbooks. *Educational Horizons, 70*(4), 189–193.

Gamoran, A. (1992). Is ability grouping equitable? *Educational Leadership, 50*(2), 11–17.

Ornstein, A. C. (1992). The textbook curriculum. *Educational Horizons, 70*(4), 167–169.

Sharma, M. C., & Travaglini, L. E. (Eds.). (1988). *Math notebook (from theory to practice). Information for teachers/parents of children with learning problems in mathematics. Vol 5 and 6.* Framingham, MA: Center for Teaching/Learning of Mathematics.

Useem, E. L. (1992). Middle schools and math groups: Parents' involvement in children's placement. *Sociology of Education, 65*(4), 263–279.

Cooperation through No Fault of My Own— Or How to Succeed without Really Trying

Background

During my second year of teaching, I was assigned the responsibility of teaching the gifted students at a high school in a large metropolitan area. In total, there were 11 students in my ninth-grade science class and I had them for 90 minutes a day. Out of the 11, one was White, 4 were African American, and the rest were Hispanic American. Only 4 of the 11 were female and all came from low-income families.

The academic achievements of these students were inspiring. They exceeded all my expectations for gifted students and provided a challenge for me as a supposed expert. In fact, our most rewarding learning experiences were usually the result of my not knowing the answer. Needless to say, these students were highly motivated, but not due to any strategies that I had supplied. Winning was the name of the game and the emphasis was not on *what* was won, but on *who* had won. Consequently, the atmosphere in the class was charged and nonsupportive, with students constantly trying to outdo one another. To make matters worse, there were several different pairs and groups of students who were outwardly hostile to one another. The pairs and groups were formed based on race and the hostilities had developed over a long period of time. In addition, the hostilities were reflective of the community in which the school was located. Most of the 11 students had been in the same classes since elementary school and they spent the majority of their day together at high school as well. Up until the incident I am about to describe, which occurred near the end of the second six weeks, I had tried just about everything, including cooperative learning, to get these students to work together, but I had only limited success.

Incident

The day before science fair projects were due, two of the students' projects, Amy's and Angela's, were nowhere near completion. During study hall, Amy started crying in frustration. I didn't have much sympathy for either Amy or Angela because neither had been willing to give up even one band practice to attend a science fair class. Both science fair class and science tutoring were offered every Wednesday after school; transportation home was provided via an activity bus. I also sponsored a science club that met on Wednesdays and, even though I was compensated for the time I spent on the science class, I hated not being able to attend the club meetings when my name came up on the rotation schedule. I considered this a sacrifice and I expected no less of a sacrifice from my students. I had made this quite clear more than once.

I was really disgusted with the girls and their lack of preparation, and I let them know it in front of the entire class. I reminded them that if they didn't pass this class, they could be dropped from the gifted program. This stunned all of the students and Amy began to cry even harder. I don't know if it was Amy's tears, my refusal to help them, or the fact that the girls could be kicked out of the gifted program, but one by one, the rest of the class started helping Amy and Angela. Sidney showed Amy how to organize her data for statistical analysis, Jesus punched in numbers, and Brittney covered the backboard for the display.

At one point, I almost relented and was about to help the students when I realized that something wonderful was happening. All 11 were pulling together to achieve a common goal for the first time ever. Angela and Amy were actually allowing themselves to be tutored. All past wrongs had been forgotten. And best of all, by helping Angela and Amy, the rest were sacrificing their chances of winning the science fair competition—a fact of which they were very much aware.

Recognizing this as the behavior I'd been trying to achieve since the beginning of the school year, I praised the students generously. That evening, I spent a lot of time reflecting on what had happened that day.

Discussion

For the rest of the year, without knowing it until just recently, I employed peer tutoring strategies on a regular basis. I was even considered one of the "peers" and the class tutored me in Spanish. The students taught me a new Spanish word every day, then required me to use it somehow twice during the hour. They occasionally gave me a written quiz and they especially delighted in making and grading the quizzes. Whether or not academic achievement was improved more than it would have been otherwise, I do not know. I do know, however, that all 11 students made tremendous gains in socialization skills. It was almost as if peer tutoring unlocked the door and a whole new world was opened to them. I know it sounds corny, but the unofficial class motto became "Be Kind." In fact, every once in a while the students would whisper to one another, "Be kind."

Questions

1. I believe that it was the peer tutoring strategy that turned this class around. However, I know that the turning point was when Amy and Angela almost failed, and I am not certain that the peer tutoring strategy would have worked without this turning point. At the same time, I don't think I should purposely create such an intense situation in my class. If I ever encounter a group like this again, what are some strategies that I might use to make students receptive to peer tutoring?

2. These students were very competitive prior to the incident. Is there ever a place in the classroom for competition, and, if so, how do you control it so that it doesn't get out of hand? Can you control it with a group like this one? Should you try?

3. Is it the responsibility of schools to teach socialization skills, values, morals, and so on? If so, where is that responsibility on the teaching priority list?

4. I plan on using peer tutoring in all my classes. But how do I let students know it is okay to work together on some things but there are other times when it will be considered cheating if they work together?

5. Are there other strategies that can be used to break down some of the hostilities among different racial groups, especially when they reflect the mood of the community?

Concluding Questions and Activities

1. The teacher's questions are very thought provoking. Are there, however, other questions that you think she should have been asking?

2. The teacher notes that she had to give up attending the science club meeting and she states, "I expected no less of a sacrifice from my students." When teachers must make sacrifices for their

students, is it fair for them to expect their students to make sacrifices also? Explain your answer.

3. The incident begins with Amy and Angela about to fail the science class. In front of the entire class, the teacher reminds them that if they fail the class, they will be dropped from the gifted program. This served as the trigger event for the cooperative learning. This is just one of many possible outcomes of the teacher's actions. Describe some other possible outcomes of the trigger event.

4. It appears that cooperative learning broke down many of the barriers that were present in the classroom at the beginning of the year—not the least of which were the racial barriers and the need to be competitive. How can this be explained in light of the literature on cooperative learning?

5. Is competitiveness a characteristic of high-achieving students? Justify your answer and support it with findings from outside readings.

6. Develop a lesson plan that utilizes cooperative learning strategies. In the lesson plan, tell how you would go about organizing the groups, what kinds of activities you would have the group members do, and how you would evaluate the product (the results of the learning activity) and the process. Explain how your lesson plan would be different, depending on the attitudes of the students for whom you were designing it.

Suggested Readings

Ballard, L. (1993). Finding the right button. *Gifted Child Today, 16*(1), 26–29.

Cohen, E. (1986). *Designing groupwork.* New York: Teachers College Press.

Davidson, N., & Worsham, T. (1992). *Enhancing thinking through cooperative grouping.* New York: Teachers College Press.

Ellis, S. S., & Whalen, S. F. (1992). Keys to cooperative learning: 35 ways to keep kids responsible, challenged, and most of all, cooperative. *Instructor, 101*(6), 34–37.

Humphreys, B., et al. (1982). Effects of cooperative, competitive, and individualistic learning on students' achievement in science class. *Journal of Research in Science Teaching, 19*(5), 182–200.

Jacobs, G. (1988). Co-operative goal structure: A way to improve group activities. *ELT Journal, 42*(2), 97–101.

Johnson, D. W., & Johnson, R. T. (1987). *Learning together and alone: Cooperative, competitive, and individualistic learning.* Englewood Cliffs, NJ: Prentice Hall.

Johnson, D. W., & Johnson, R. T. (1989). Toward a cooperative effort: A response to Slavin. *Educational Leadership, 46*(7), 80–81.

Martin, J. E. (1992). Gifted behaviors—Excellence for all. *The Clearing House, 61,* 37–40.

Martino, L. R. (1993). When students help students. *Phi Delta Kappan, 74*(5), 31–32.

Owens, L., & Barnes, J. (1982). The relationships between cooperative, competitive, and individualized learning preferences and students' perceptions of classroom learning atmosphere. *American Educational Research Journal, 19*(2), 182–200.

Slavin, R. E. (1983). *Cooperative learning.* New York: Longman.

Slavin, R. E. (1988). Cooperative learning and student achievement. In R. E. Slavin (Ed.), *School and classroom organization.* Hillsdale, NJ: Erlbaum.

Stavro, S. (1992). Bringing it all together. *Middle School Journal, 24*(2), 67–69.

Thorndike, T. A. (1988). Theories of education among academically able adolescents. *Contemporary Educational Psychology, 13*(4), 323–330.

Response of Billie Hughes, Professor

These three cases left me thinking about the underlying assumptions associated with the purpose of schools: grading, testing, and passing to the next level. As I read and thought about what these teachers were saying, I sifted through ideas in current writing about restructuring and I pondered how much I have learned from using cooperative learning and shifting from a focus on teaching to a focus on learning.

As we move from talk of reform to talk of restructuring or systemic change, we move from making *adjustments* in the way we currently teach to making *philosophical shifts* in the way we think about teaching and learning. The restructuring movement calls to question many of our basic assumptions and long-held beliefs about schools.

These three cases raise issues related to several broad education restructuring issues: (1) What are the appropriate outcomes of education? (2) How do cooperative versus competitive structures fit into education? and (3) What signals do we send to students on what matters in school?

The Outcomes of Schooling

Ultimately, one of the most important issues all teachers face is: What is the purpose of schooling? The teacher who wrote the case report about the gifted students directly raised this when posing the question, "Is it the responsibility of the schools to teach socialization skills, values, morals, and so on?" The Secretary's Commission on Achieving Necessary Skills (SCANS) calls for schools to prepare students in a number of areas that cross disciplines. Even though this report was originated to define workplace skills, its recommendations consist of critical skills for citizenship as well as employment. As you read the list of skills (see Figure 4–1), you will see that many of the difficulties that arose in the preceding case reports occurred because students did not possess some of these skills.

Recurring themes in the SCANS report are personal responsibility, decision making, independent learning, teaching others, and self-assessment. Repeatedly, in the cases presented, teachers were making most of the decisions. Students were not involved in planning their learning, developing self-assessment, monitoring their own progress, or working together to attain a common learning goal. The chemistry teacher set the standards, determined when the test would be given, and decided that including both scores in the final grade was fair. Clearly, Jeff's goal was not to learn certain skills. He was not self-assessing his skills. Jeff was focusing on the percentage of correct answers he received on his test—so was his teacher. No shared vision of what success in

---

Figure 4–1 Workplace Skills from the SCANS Report

Workplace Know-How

The know-how identified by SCANS is made up of five competencies and a three-part foundation of skills and personal qualities that are needed for solid job performance. These are the following:

WORKPLACE COMPETENCIES: Effective workers can productively use:
Resources—They know how to allocate time, money, materials, space, and staff.
Interpersonal Skills—They can work on teams, teach others, serve customers, lead, negotiate and communicate, and work well with people from culturally diverse backgrounds.
Information—They can acquire and evaluate data, organize and maintain files, interpret and communicate, and use computers to process information.
Systems—They understand social, organizational, and technological systems, they can monitor and correct performance, and they can design or improve systems.
Technology—They can select equipment and tools, apply technology to specific tasks, and maintain and troubleshoot equipment.

FOUNDATION SKILLS: Competent workers in the high-performance workplace need:
Basic Skills—Reading, writing, arithmetic and mathematics, speaking, and listening.
Thinking Skills—The ability to learn, to reason, to think creatively, to make decisions, and to solve problems.
Personal Qualities—Individual responsibility, self-esteem and self-management, sociability, and integrity.

Source: Secretary's Commission on Achieving Necessary Skills, *Learning a Living: A Blueprint for High Performance.* Washington, DC: U.S. Department of Labor, 1992.

---

chemistry "looked like" existed. Jeff had no plan for attaining skills in chemistry and no means of monitoring how he was doing on his learning goals.

The math teacher had a class that wanted the right to talk. The teacher believed in setting rules and expected the students to follow them. Obviously, other teachers have different rules, so the students believed the rules to be arbitrary. What is missing from this picture is an understanding that rights are linked with responsibilities—that talking in class needs to be associated with attaining important learning goals. The students lack learning goals that they care to achieve and the teacher is in a position of "forcing" the students to learn. One way to "force" learning is to prohibit talking. But, by prohibiting talking, we can also stifle learning. When we focus exclusively on teaching content, students graduate from high school without skills in setting goals, assessing quality, and managing their lives. We want lambs in the classroom and responsible citizens once they graduate.

I contend that this lack of involvement in developing the goals, in setting standards, and in monitoring their own progress is a major reason for a lack of motivation and a lack of commitment to learning. The students in the algebra class had no control over what they learned nor how they learned it. Students need to be involved in making decisions about their own learning and to feel the sense of accomplishment associated with attaining goals they set for themselves. I am not suggesting that external standards do not exist. But I think we need to look for alternative models of assessment that include the students in the goal-setting process. Students should organize themselves to work toward goals, much the way Eagle Scouts or Black Belts in karate strive for excellence.

Not involving the students indicates that we do not believe they want to learn and are not capable of setting high standards for themselves. As a result, teachers are in the position of "forcing" students to learn by threats of poor grades, fear of retention, or "being dropped from the gifted program." The underlying measures of success are external and consist of external rewards rather than the intrinsically good feeling that comes from accomplishing a goal and developing competency.

Competition versus Cooperation

The SCANS report is clear on the need for skills in working with others. In my classes, I clearly state that I *do not* define cheating as helping someone who needs help. I tell the students that one day they will be in a classroom of 25 to 30 students and that one teacher cannot ensure the success of all of these students. However, if they can develop a supportive community in their classrooms, with all students committed to the success of the entire group, then all can learn. The day of the rugged individualist is gone. Many of us are still holding onto individual performance and questioning whether or not it is "fair" to penalize the high performers who are stuck in groups with low performers.

But overall, my experience with emphasizing sharing and caring is overwhelmingly positive. The teacher of the gifted saw this when she unknowingly united her students around a common goal. These students do care about each other. Clearly, these students have never been given a reason to work together; they have not experienced a shared vision, participated in working toward a common goal, nor had the opportunity to experience the pleasure of being a part of an effective team effort. Brandt (1987) acknowledged the argument when he asked:

But are these trends [cooperative versus competitive] contrary to basic American values? Is it fair that students should benefit from each other's efforts and share responsibility for what others do or don't do? Ask doctors, who more and more engage in group practice, consulting with one another on difficult cases. Ask ministers, who depend on volunteer committees for much of the work of their churches. Ask military officers who train young men and women in intricate maneuvers. Ask members of work teams in automated factories. Ask executives involved in team management. (p. 3)

I find that removing competition from my classroom leads to more learning than would ever occur if I pitted students against each other. I focus on learning and quality. Students understand quality and they understand caring.

Outcomes versus Credits

Another recurring theme in these cases is the message we send about what is important in school. We have evolved a system of education based not on competency, but rather on passing to the next grade or acquiring enough credits to graduate. As Wiggins (1989) stated:

An "A" in "English" means only that some adult thought the students' work was excellent. Compared to whom or what? As determined by what criteria? In reference to what specific subject matter? The high school diploma, by remaining tied to no standard other than credit accrual and set time, provides no useful information about what students have studied or what they can actually do with what was studied. (p. 42)

Earning credits, rather than becoming competent, becomes a game students play to move through the system. Moving to the next grade level, regardless of the competence level, becomes the measure of success. Thus, not only have we developed a content-driven system that does not provide students with goal setting, interpersonal relations, and self-assessment, but we have arbitrary standards applied by teachers. This was clear when the math teacher referred to students having "easy" teachers. Students have no reason to strive for quality. All they have to do is get through the classes and earn credits.

Final Comments

The changes needed to resolve the issues in these three cases cannot be found in "quick fixes." As Michaels (1988) said, "We need to examine our basic philosophical beliefs about teaching, learning, the nature of human beings, and the kinds of environments that maximize growth for teachers and students alike" (p. 3). We need to consider whether we truly believe students have rights as well as responsibilities, whether we believe students *want* to learn, and whether we believe students are capable of self-assessment and self-imposition of standards of excellence. We also have to decide whether we think schools are about learning or teaching, outcomes or credits, communities or individuals. These seemingly little shifts have great impact on what we do in school because we shift our entire emphasis from focusing on what we teach to what students learn. We shift from creating teaching units to creating learning environments. We shift from teachers who police and threaten to teachers who help students set goals, work together, and celebrate competence.

In closing, I believe that we need to share a vision. We need to pull from each others' strengths, to share leadership, and to support each other. All of us—students, teachers, and parents—need to be heading in the same direction. If we are not, teachers will become merely enforcers and our jobs will lose their joy. We are capable of far more than this!

References

Brandt, R. (1987). Is cooperation un-American? *Educational Leadership, 45*(3), 3.

Michaels, K. (1988). Caution: Second-wave reform taking place. *Educational Leadership, 45*(5), 3.

Secretary's Commission on Achieving Necessary Skills. (1992). *Learning a living: A blueprint for high performance.* Washington, DC: U.S. Department of Labor.

Wiggins, G. (1989). Teaching to the (authentic) test. *Educational Leadership, 46*(7), 41–47.

Questions, Exercises, and Activities

1. The cases presented in this section are very different from one another. Develop a rationale for grouping these three cases together. As you do this, try to identify the unifying theme.

2. The chemistry teacher was pleased with the way the testing issue was resolved. The teacher of the gifted was pleased with the way the students finally cooperated, but was not certain, given the same situation, she could obtain the same results. The algebra teacher was unhappy when he couldn't change the schedule for the Technical Algebra class, but accepted it (You could almost see him shrugging his shoulders and saying, "I did all I could do.") Do you agree with each of their evaluations of the outcomes? Justify your answers.

3. The respondent to these three case reports made the statement, "As we move from talk of reform to talk of restructuring or systemic change, we move from making *adjustments* in the way we currently teach to making *philosophical shifts* in the way we think about teaching and learning." What is meant by "philosophical shifts"? Give a specific example of such a shift and compare it to an adjustment in teaching methods.

4. By their actions and comments, the authors of the case reports in this section have provided you with some insight into their beliefs about teaching and learning. Team up with two other students in your class and assign a different case report to each member. As a team member, you are to analyze your assigned case to see if you can determine which model of teaching was most closely adhered to by the teacher. Share your analysis with other members of the class. How much agreement is there among those who analyzed the same case? How do you account for any disagreement among the analyses? Did the class find that one model was most prevalent in these cases or are there a variety of models being used? (*Models of Teaching*, by Joyce, Weil, and Showers, provides a description of a variety of teaching models and should serve as a useful aid in this exercise.)

5. In two of the three cases, "Time Is of the Essence" and "Students Needs versus School Logistics," time played a role. In the first case, there wasn't enough time for the students to complete a test in the given time period. In the second case, students were unable to meet the course objectives in the semester framework.

The National Educational Commission on Time and Learning, whose report, *Prisoners of Time* (1994), studied the issue of the relationship between time use and student achievement. Write a brief paper that examines the issues in these two cases in light of the Commission's recommendations.

SECTION 4

SUGGESTED READINGS

Baker, G. P., & Desrochers, C. G. (1992). A head start for student teachers. *Executive Educator, 14*(5), 23–24.

Borko, H., et al. (1990). Teachers' thinking about instruction. *Remedial and Special Education (RASE), 11*(8), 40–48, 53.

Glidden, P. L. (1991). Teachers' reasons for instructional decisions. *Mathematics Teacher, 84*(8), 610–614.

Johnston, S. (1990). Understanding curriculum decision-making through teacher images. *Journal of Curriculum Studies, 22*(5), 463–471.

Joyce, B., Weil, M., & Showers, B. (1992). *Models of teaching* (4th ed.). Boston: Allyn and Bacon.

Katz, L. G. (1990, February). On teaching. *Child Care Information Exchange, 71*, 3–4.

Klevin, T. A. (1991). Interactive teacher decision-making. Still a basic skill? *Scandinavian Journal of Educational Research, 35*(4), 287–294.

National Educational Commission on Time and Learning. (1994). *Prisoners of time.* Washington, DC: Office of Educational Research and Improvement.

Orstein, A. C. (1990). The evolving accountability movement. *Peabody Journal of Education, 65*(3), 12–20.

Pine, P. (1985). *Raising standards in schools: Problems and solutions. AASA critical issues report.* Arlington, VA: American Association of School Administrators.

Scaps, E., & Solomon, D. (1990). Schools and classrooms as caring communities. *Educational Leadership 48*(3), 38–42.

Schmuck, R. A., & Schmuck, P. A. (1988). *Group processes in the classroom* (5th ed.). Dubuque, IA: Wm. C. Brown.

Webb, N. M. (1985). Student interaction and learning in small groups: A research summary. In R. E. Slavin, S. Sharan, S. Kagan, R. Hertz-Lazarowitz, C. Webb, & R. Schmuck (Eds.), *Learning to cooperate, cooperating to learn.* New York: Plenum.

Welch, M., & Link, D. P. (1991). The instructional priority system: A method for assessing the educational environment. *Intervention in School and Clinic, 27*(2), 91–96.

Westerman, D. A. (1991). Expert and novice teacher decision making. *Journal of Teacher Education, 42*(4), 292–305.

SECTION 5

PROFESSIONAL INTERACTIONS: TEACHER TO TEACHER

The case reports in this section deal with teachers interacting with other teachers. The first case, "Interaction and Reactions," involves a third-grade teacher and the special education teacher. The two teachers were close friends until the classroom teacher began having trouble with one of her special education students. An incident in the teachers' lounge between the teachers leaves the classroom teacher feeling as if she has been treated unprofessionally by the special education teacher.

In the second case, "Caught in the Middle," an assistant principal attempts to help Jane, a high school math teacher, who is exhibiting signs of teacher burnout. The more he tries to help, the more frustrated he becomes with Jane. He shares his frustrations with another teacher, who happens to be a friend of Jane's. He asks the teacher to work with Jane to help her improve her teaching, indicating that, "without a drastic change, Jane will be gone soon." The teacher agrees to help, but in the end, nothing changes except that the *second teacher* becomes frustrated and wonders why she was involved in the first place.

The last case in this section, "When a Sub Isn't a Substitute," focuses on a teacher who was on maternity leave at the end of the school year. This makes it necessary for the substitute to administer the final exam. For whatever reason, the substitute leaves the room during the exam. During this time, a student goes to the teacher's desk and takes the answer key for the second half of the exam that is to be given the next day. That night, several of the students call their regular teacher to tell her what happened. It is obvious that they are very upset and they expect the teacher to do something about the test to be given the next day. The classroom teacher returns to school and gives the students an entirely different test. This seems to resolve the issue of the test, and the students accept the solution as a good one. The teacher, however, is angry and frustrated with the substitute and wonders what she could have done to avoid the situation and what kind of recourse she has if this were to happen again.

The cases involve elementary teachers ("Interaction and Reactions"), teachers in a junior high/high school combination ("Caught in the Middle"), and a high school teacher ("When a Sub Isn't a Substitute"). The issues involved, however, cross all grade levels.

Commentary on the three cases, as a group, is provided by Sarah Huyvaert, associate professor of teacher education at Eastern Michigan University. Prior to reading Huyvaert's comments, you will want to form your own opinions about what went right and what went wrong in each of the cases. The type of teacher interactions presented in the case are not unusual. If you haven't already found yourself involved in a similar incident, you may. As you read the reports, remember that you are hearing only one side of the story—the teacher's. Try to think how the other participants might have felt about the situation and what each of the participants did to make the situation worse and what each could have done to make it better.

Interaction
and Reactions

Background

As a beginning third-grade teacher, I knew very few of the staff, parents, or students in the small elementary school. However, one of my closest friends, Jill, was the part-time special education teacher at the school. Before the school year started, Jill gave me a list of the children who would be in my class who had special needs. These children would be receiving assistance from Jill throughout the year.

Jill told me about one child, Joe, who had some behavior problems in last year's classroom but who had made remarkable progress during the last months of the school year and probably would not need much, if any, special education monitoring. The only suggestion that Jill gave me was that I should set up a behavior modification program similar to the one used by last year's teacher, since it had been so successful. I agreed to post a sheet of paper on Joe's desk and mark it each time he disrupted the class. There were to be specific consequences for each mark and his parents were to be notified if he received more than two marks during one day. If he went one week without a certain number of marks, he was to receive a reward. I began the program the first day of school, and at the end of the second week I called Joe's parents to discuss my expectations for classroom behavior. I encouraged them to support the program at home, and they agreed.

Throughout the first month of school, Joe often called out during lessons, interrupted other students during independent work, was physically very active, and generally appeared distracted and disinterested in school. By the end of the month, I could see that this program was not working, even though I was following it diligently. Joe was getting at least two marks every day and not a week went by without a conversation with his parents. The parents seemed supportive at the beginning of the program, but I found out, through my conversations with Joe, that his parents were not keeping their promise to reinforce consequences of poor behavior in school.

This struggle went on for several months, and during this time I kept Jill informed about the lack of progress, letting her know that things were not working out. She kept telling me that Joe needed time to adjust to a new teacher and "get back into the swing of things" at school.

As I got to know Joe and his family, and became more familiar with his background, I discovered that he was one of the oldest students in my class, because he had repeated his kindergarten year. His grades indicated that he was an average student. He had never been formally tested for any disability, such as Attention Deficit Disorder (ADD). His family had recently encountered several crises, including the onset and treatment of his mother's breast cancer and the pregnancy of his unmarried teenage sister. I also learned from the teacher who had Joe's brother in class that she was battling with Joe's parents over a curriculum issue.

As the months went on, I tried using some other management techniques with Joe. These techniques had worked when I was a substitute teacher, but nothing seemed to work with Joe. His grades worsened and his parents became disillusioned with the apparent lack of progress. Not only did they voice their concerns to me but also to Jill. As the year wore on, I was becoming more and more discouraged.

Incident

In the beginning of November, I walked into the teachers' lounge one afternoon on a break period. Jill, the principal, and the music teacher were all seated at the same table. I stopped to ask Jill if we could meet to discuss Joe's situation. Instead of setting up a time when we could meet, Jill began to ask questions about Joe's behavior problems right then and there. I told her that I had been trying some different techniques, such as withholding recess time, because I wasn't seeing any progress in using the program she had suggested. She informed me, very bluntly, that Joe had done very well last year under the program and she couldn't understand why the program that was used by last year's teacher wasn't working with him now. She also told me, in a very loud voice, that the punishment system I was using right now would not work with Joe because he was a very sensitive child. She finally agreed to observe Joe in the classroom. However, even though she had her appointment book with her, she left to go to her next obligation without setting up a definite time to observe Joe.

I was deeply hurt by Jill's actions in the teachers' lounge. First, I was embarrassed because I felt she criticized my teaching in front of the principal and a colleague. I was offended because she had shown what I felt was a lack of professionalism in choosing to discuss this in front of other parties. I also was more discouraged than before because she did not offer me any alternatives to the discipline procedures that I had already tried, and I felt that she had implied that I was part of Joe's problem. Finally, I was hurt because I expected more empathy from her as a friend.

Discussion

At wit's end with this situation, one day I decided to read through Joe's complete school records. I was amazed to find that the remarks of the kindergarten and first-grade teachers about Joe's behavior—including his inability to attend and his consistent interruption of classroom activities—matched my observations exactly. I also observed Joe in music and art classes, and found that the other teachers had similar problems with Joe's lack of attention in the classroom. As a result of these discoveries, I began to realize that it was not my classroom management strategies that were inadequate, but rather the problem stemmed from the fact that Joe had some kind of attention problem and I simply did not have the skills or knowledge that were necessary to help him.

After a confrontation with Joe's parents, the situation came to a head. I knew I had to do something. Because Jill never did come in to observe me, I chose to go to the principal for advice. He was very supportive. He observed Joe during class, and afterwards offered the simple suggestion that I change his seat placement to the front of the room. I did so. This, combined with the modified version of the original program for behavior management and an increased confidence on my part, led to Joe making remarkable strides in his ability to stay on task during the last three or four months of school.

The principal had Jill read Joe's school records and Jill agreed that his past history was significant enough to indicate that he had a problem with attention in the classroom. She then arranged for him to be tested and it was determined that Joe did indeed have Attention Deficit Disorder. She also agreed that his problems were not a result of my lack of classroom management skills. However, Jill and I remained fairly distant as colleagues for the remainder of the school year.

Questions

1. Should a regular classroom teacher always review the permanent records of children with special needs prior to the beginning of a school year?
2. Should a teacher begin the year by following the exact programs and systems used successfully by a child's previous teacher or special education teacher?
3. Was I wrong to take so much personal offense at the incident with Jill in the teachers' lounge?
4. When I observed Joe in music class, I noticed the same behaviors that he exhibited in my classroom. The music teacher was in the lounge when the incident with Jill occurred and yet she said nothing when Jill implied that Joe's poor behavior was all my fault. Should the music teacher have said something, especially since the principal was there, or was she right to stay out of it?
5. What should I do to improve my working relationship with Jill? I don't want to confront her, but I also don't want to apologize. I don't think I did anything wrong, but I think Jill did do something wrong, and I think it's important that she knows how I feel.

Concluding Questions and Activities

1. The teacher says that she was hurt and embarrassed by Jill's actions in the teachers' lounge. Do you think this is a normal reaction or do you think the teacher was overreacting?
2. With fellow students, role-play the incident in the teachers' lounge. Afterwards, each player should describe how he or she (or his or her character) felt toward each of the other players as a result of the incident.
3. The teacher waited until after she was "at wit's end" to read Joe's school records. Why do you think she waited so long? If she had read the records earlier, do you think her reactions to either Joe or Jill would have changed? Defend your response.
4. How do you think Jill felt when she found out that the teacher had gone to the principal for advice? Do you think the teacher was justified in her actions?
5. More and more emphasis is being placed on teachers working as teams. Why wasn't the team approach more successful in meeting Joe's needs? Pretend that you are the teacher in this case and the principal tells both you and Jill to come up with a plan for working together. The plan must include the purpose for your teaming, a description of the roles each of you will play, and a

way that he (the principal) can monitor your success. What sources (people) and resources (including books and articles) would you use when developing your plan? Explain what you would expect to gain from each source. Also, provide an annotation for each resource that is included. (The key here is not to develop the plan, but rather to develop a list of sources and resources.)

Suggested Readings

Allan, J., & Barber, J. (1986). Teacher needs and counselor response: One example. *Elementary School Guidance & Counseling, 20*(4), 277–282.

Bredeson, P. V. (1991). Teachers and their workplace: Commitment, performance, and productivity. *Educational Administration Quarterly, 27*(4), 558–562.

Burnley, G. D. (1993). A team approach for identification of an Attention Deficit Hyperactivity Disorder child. *The School Counselor, 40*(3), 228–230.

Downing, J. A., et al. (1990). Regular and special educator perceptions of nonacademic skills needed by mainstreamed students with behavioral disorders and learning disabilities. *Behavioral Disorders, 15*(4), 217–226.

Fuchs, D., et al. (1990). Mainstream assistance teams: A scientific basis for the art of consultation. *Exceptional Children, 57*(2), 128–139.

Gearheart, B. R., Weishahn, M. W., & Gearheart, C. J. (1992). *The exceptional student in the regular classroom* (5th ed.). New York: Macmillan.

Glatthorn, A. A. (1987). Cooperative professional development: Peer-centered options for teacher growth. *Educational Leadership, 45*(3), 31–35.

Leggett, D., & Hoyle, S. (1987). Preparing teachers for collaboration. *Educational Leadership, 45*(3), 58–63.

Meadows, N. (1993). The teacher's guidance handbook: An enhancement to consultation. *The School Counselor 40*(3), 231–233.

Mitchell, J., & Marland, P. (1989). Research on teacher thinking: The next phase. *Teaching and Teacher Education, 5*(2), 115–128.

Patriarca, L. A., & Lamb, M. A. (1990). Makers and reflective practitioners: A promising practicum model. *Teacher Education and Special Education, 13*(3–4), 228–232.

Caught in the Middle

Background

When I first met Jane, she had been teaching in our small, rural district for several years. At that time, our school contained grades 7 through 12. My contact with Jane during my first year was limited. She taught Algebra I and Geometry to the upper-level students while I taught seventh-, eighth-, and ninth-grade General Math. Jane and I did interact at department meetings and occasionally we would have lunch together. Over the next year, our friendship grew. We would stop in each other's rooms at the end of the day for some light conversation. Jane and I discovered we shared the enjoyment of several activities. When my husband and I went out West for a summer, Jane even housesat for us.

It was shortly after this time that Jane began to demonstrate some of the symptoms of teacher burnout. She began to question if she wanted to stay in the teaching field. She decided to take a year off to get her master's degree in mathematics and to get a part-time job outside of education to see if see liked working in business better than she did teaching.

Unknown to me at the time, the administration was glad Jane was taking a leave of absence. They had been receiving complaints about her from several of her students' parents. The parents felt that Jane knew her material, but that she wasn't able to bring it down to their children's level. Since the students felt that they didn't understand the material, they weren't taking the next math course, Algebra II.

Upon Jane's return the next year, however, she was warmly accepted back by the administration. The temporary replacement who had been hired for Jane had been a total disaster. Jane was assigned the Geometry classes and also received a Trigonometry class. At the start of the year, Jane was recharged, enthusiastic, and filled with the belief that she could, and would, make a difference in her students' lives.

Unfortunately, things did not seem to change much for Jane in the classroom. This became evident to me since I was now teaching Algebra I and II. Listening to the students' conversations made it apparent that there were problems. The students who had Jane for Geometry and who were in my Algebra II class were reluctant to take Trigonometry because Jane taught the class. My Algebra I students didn't want to take Geometry because of all the rumors that they had heard about Jane's classes. The administration let the schedules remain the way they were for a year, but the problem only became worse. The number of students who were avoiding Jane's classes could no longer be ignored. Jane was then given Elementary Algebra, Consumers' Math, and an Algebra I class. She was heartbroken. She had crying outbursts in class and could not manage the discipline problems. When she found out she was pregnant, she immediately requested a maternity leave for the following year.

At the end of her leave, Jane asked to return to a half-day position. The administration honored her request. However, when Jane learned of the classes that she would be teaching, she indicated that she wanted a full-time position. Again, the administration honored her request, but informed her that her full-time status would not bring about any change in the classes that she would receive for the following year. When the teaching schedules were released, Jane was given Elementary Algebra, Consumers' Math, and General Math.

Incident

When Jane returned to teaching, she was not assigned a room. She had to teach in a number of different classrooms throughout the day. For a couple of class periods, Jane was assigned a classroom down a short hall from mine. It was evident that the atmosphere in her class did not lead to a learning environment, due to all of the shouting that was going on by both Jane and her students.

This was the year Jane was to be evaluated by the relatively new assistant principal, Mr. Hines. Mr. Hines was a former math teacher and for the past year we had worked together on changing the math curriculum. During this time, we became very good friends. When it became evident to Mr. Hines that Jane, a veteran teacher, was having major problems, he checked her file for explanations. Upon seeing a clean record, he spoke to several administrators and found that Jane's problems had been overlooked, but not forgotten, by the administration. Mr. Hines began immediately to work with Jane on trying to improve various aspects of her teaching.

Throughout the year, Mr. Hines would stop by my classroom and express his frustration at being placed in the situation of trying to do something with a teacher who had shown problems for years. He indicated that he tried to work with her, but she was not open to his suggestions. According to Mr. Hines, their relationship deteriorated to the point of Jane crying as soon as he would open his mouth. He finally decided to put Jane on an extended evaluation plan. This meant that Jane had to work with others to show some improvement within a set time frame or be dismissed within the year.

It was at this point that Mr. Hines asked me to go into Jane's classroom and give her some helpful teaching hints. He indicated that, without a drastic change, Jane would be gone soon. He also shared with me some of his frustration at not being able to make a difference in her teaching, and told me that he was upset with the other administrators because they had not taken care of the problem earlier. He begged me, as a friend, to help him out in this difficult situation. This put me in an awkward position. I told Mr. Hines that I would not go into Jane's classroom unless she asked for help. It was important to me that she knew that I was not trying to tell her how to run her classroom. The other thing that bothered me was that we had less than nine weeks left in the school year. I didn't know what I could tell Jane to do differently in her classes when the patterns had already been well established and there was such a short time left in the school year.

It was few days after my discussion with Mr. Hines that Jane came to me and asked if I would sit in on several of her classes and give her some suggestions to improve her teaching. She let me know that this was not her idea but was the only way that she would be able to keep her teaching job. She also implied that the reason she was having difficulty was because I had "stolen" the good classes and she was left with the ones that nobody wanted to teach.

Discussion

I observed Jane's classes for several weeks and made some suggestions about classroom management that she used, but the situation didn't really improve. The students would behave themselves when I was there, but as soon as I left the room, the shouting would start again. I really didn't know what kind of suggestions to make about her teaching methods. It was obvious that she was talking over the heads of the students, that her examples weren't relevant, and that the students really didn't care. I pointed these things out to her and she agreed, but I didn't know how to help her change the situation. Things that worked well for me only seemed to backfire when Jane used them. I became really frustrated because it seemed as if all of my comments were negative, that my evaluation was affecting my friendship with Jane, and, if possible, that I was making a bad situation even worse.

Questions

1. Was I overstepping the bounds of friendship and being unprofessional when I let the assistant principal tell me about the problems with another teacher?
2. Could I have helped Jane and her students if I had stepped into the situation earlier? Do I have the right to tell another teacher what to do before I am asked for help?
3. Should Mr. Hines have asked for my help without giving me some guidance on how to handle the situation, even though he didn't seem to know what to do?

Concluding Questions and Activities

1. The teacher in this case felt as if she were "caught in the middle" between the assistant principal and the other math teacher. Is there anything that she could have done to get herself out of this position? Do you think she handled the situation appropriately?
2. Rewrite this case report from Jane's perspective. Try to remain as true to the facts (as they are presented in this report) as possible while at the same time presenting the other point of view.
3. Teachers are often criticized because they do not monitor one another's professional activities. At the same time, teachers need to be respectful of professional differences, in both style and approach to teaching. What are some indicators that a teacher may need to intervene in the activities of another teacher? Are student complaints, in and of themselves, enough? What about parent complaints? If a teacher sees another teacher "behaving inappropriately," should he or she intervene immediately or should the activity be documented and the teacher given the benefit of the doubt? If you were working with a good friend and you heard rumors about how bad his or her teaching was, what would you do?

4. Many of the Suggested Readings in this section address peer coaching as a strategy for helping teachers to assist other teachers. However, one of the key elements in peer coaching is that both teachers must be open and willing. Do you think Jane would have been receptive to peer coaching at the beginning of the case report? How about midway through? At the end? Were there defining elements that might make her more willing at some points than at others?

5. The assistant principal asked one teacher to help another teacher who was in need. Much of the literature on teacher evaluation and growth supports this type of approach. However, what started out as a positive approach seems to have deteriorated into gossiping and griping sessions. Was it the teacher's responsibility to bring these sessions back to "the higher plane" or, because of lines of authority, did she act appropriately?

6. With your classmates, develop a survey to assess the degree to which peer coaching is being used in your area. Is it used more at the high school, the middle school, or the elementary school? Where it is being used, who initiated the process—teachers or administrators? If it is not being used in a school or school district, why not? What techniques are being used to help the teacher in trouble? Where peer coaching is being used, how is it implemented, who is involved, and how do the teachers feel about the process? Once you have the results of your survey, compare the findings to the recommendations and conclusions presented in the literature on peer coaching.

Suggested Readings

Barnes, R. E., & Murphy, J. (1987). Help teachers help themselves. *Executive Educator, 9*(9), 23, 29.

Batesky, J. (1991). Peer coaching. *Strategies, 4*(6), 15–19.

Blank, M. A., & Sindelar, N. (1992). Mentoring as professional development: From theory to practice. *The Clearing House, 66*(1), 22–26.

Bridges, E. M. (1992). *The incompetent teacher: Managerial responses.* Bristol, PA: Falmer Press.

Chrisco, I. M. (1989). Peer assistance works. *Educational Leadership, 46*(8), 31–32.

Cox, C. L. (1991). Peer coaching: A process for developing professionalism, achieving instructional excellence, and improving student learning. *Thresholds in Education, 17*(4), 23–26.

Evans, R. (1989). The faculty in midcareer: Implications for school improvement. *Educational Leadership, 46*(8), 10–15.

Glatthorn, A. A. (1987). Cooperative professional development: Peer-centered options for teacher growth. *Educational Leadership, 45*(3), 31–35.

Greene, B. Z. (1985). Improve the quality of teaching in your schools. *Updating School Board Policies, 16*(3), 1–3.

Grimmett, P. P. (1987). The role of the district supervisors in the implementation of peer coaching. *Journal of Curriculum and Supervision, 3*(1), 3–28.

Joyce, B., & Showers, B. (1987). Low-cost arrangements for peer coaching. *Journal of Staff Development, 8*(1), 22–24.

McNeil, J. (1971). *Toward accountable teachers: Their appraisal and improvement.* New York: Holt, Rinehart and Winston.

O'Neil, I. R., & Adamson, D. R. (1993). When teachers falter. *The Executive Educator, 15*(1), 25–27.

Phillips, M. D., & Glickman, C. D. (1991). Peer coaching: Developmental approach to enhancing teacher thinking. *Journal of Staff Development, 12*(2), 20–25.

Raney, P., & Robbins, P. (1989). Professional growth and support through peer coaching. *Educational Leadership, 46*(8), 35–38.

Showers, B. (1985). Teachers coaching teachers. *Educational Leadership, 42*(7), 43–48.

Shulman, J. H., & Colbert, J. A. (Eds.). (1987). *The mentor teacher casebook.* San Francisco: Far West Laboratory for Educational Research and Development.

Witmer, J. T. (1993). Mentoring: One district's success story. *NASSP Bulletin, 77*(550), 71–78.

When a Sub Isn't a Substitute

Background

I was a high school science teacher in my fifth year of teaching at a large suburban high school. Near the end of the school year, I gave birth to my first child. I taught until the day the baby was born, and a substitute teacher finished out the last two weeks of the school year. I had prepared all the final review materials and prearranged for the substitute to administer the final exams.

Incident

While I was at home enjoying my new bundle of joy, I began to receive calls from upset students—one was even in tears. All the students who were calling were from one of my chemistry classes. Their comprehensive semester final was a two-day test. During the first day of testing, the students alleged that the substitute teacher had left the room during the exam. While he was absent from the room, students started talking and sharing answers. The upset students told me that one student had gone up to the teacher's desk and stolen a copy of the second day's exam, which the substitute had left on top of my desk. The teacher's answer key for the entire exam was also in that pile. Although the key was not stolen, it could easily have been read and copied. The second part of the test was scheduled for the following day. This final exam was worth a significant number of points and would have a definite impact on the final grades. The test was an open-notes test so that the students would have formulas available to them. It was the chemical concepts and problem-solving skills that were being tested.

After three or four students had called with complaints, I was very upset. With my maternal hormones swinging into full force, I decided to call the substitute. I told him that I was getting calls from students, who were saying that he had left the room during the chemistry final. I asked him if this was true and he said, "Yes, that's true. I went down to the lounge for some coffee and was back shortly." I asked him if copies of the exam and answer key had been left out and he replied, "Yes." I told him about the students' phone calls and allegations I had been receiving. He thought the students were overreacting. He said, "I could not have been gone more than 5 to 10 minutes. What harm did it do?"

I told him I would not be needing his services anymore and I would be coming back to finish up the final exam myself. We went around and around—he wanted me to stay home because substitutes make more pay from a maternity leave than they do from just a temporary five-day assignment. He promised that he would not leave the room again when the students were there. Although he persisted, I told him, "No, I'm definitely coming back." I then called the principal in charge of substitutes and told him about the situation and he agreed to release the substitute.

That night I was very distraught. Between breast feeding and diapering, both of which I had not yet mastered, I found myself writing a new comprehensive chemistry exam. I returned to school on the last day of finals to find many surprised expressions, especially on the faces of the students in my chemistry class. I administered the new final, which was a combination of the day 1 and day 2 exams. I explained to the students that the new final would be their only exam grade and that this was being done because of reported cheating. This new exam tested the exact same concepts as the first two exams, so if the students had studied and understood their notes, there was no cause for concern. The students would still be allowed to use their notes, since that was what they were expecting.

Discussion

There were definitely some bewildered-looking students, some sweaty palms, and lots of smiles. The boy who had allegedly stolen the test failed the final exam and ultimately the semester. Individual student grades were similar on this test to what they had been on previous exams. It was a very unfortunate situation and it was the last thing I wanted to deal with at this time in my life, but I felt I had no alternative but to offer a new test to which the students had not had previous access. I felt it would be a grave mistake for any educator to be aware that cheating had occurred and not act on it. By not taking action, students would receive the message that it is okay to cheat and that if they are clever enough, they can get away with it.

There were no parental complaints following the cheating ordeal, and although it would have been much easier to have looked the other way and let the substitute finish out the school year, I felt I had an obligation to stand up against cheating. I did request that this particular substitute never be assigned to my room again.

Questions

1. How else might I have handled this situation? Was it really necessary for me to rewrite the test and then administer it personally?
2. Should I have called the substitute and talked directly to him or should I have left it to the principal in charge of substitutes?
3. Should the substitute teacher have been reprimanded in any way for leaving the classroom during a final exam?
4. Was I, in some way, responsible for this incident? Is it okay to leave a final exam to be administered by a substitute? If not, how should a final be administered when a teacher can't do it? If it is okay, then how can a situation like this one be avoided?
5. If the substitute had denied leaving the room, what should I have done?
6. Should the boy who allegedly stole the exam have been confronted or was the fact that he failed the course enough of a consequence?

Concluding Questions and Activities

1. The teacher makes the comment, "I had no alternative but to offer a new test." Do you agree? Is it the teacher's responsibility to repair the damage done by the substitute? If the teacher had been too ill to come to school to give the final, what should have been done?
2. The teacher also makes that the comment, "I did request this particular substitute never be assigned to my room again." Should a formal complaint have been filed against the substitute? Why or why not?
3. If you were the substitute, and a teacher became upset with the way you handled his or her classroom, what would you do? What if the complaint was accurate but was a result of your lack

of knowledge regarding school policy? What if the complaint was inaccurate and based on student comments?

4. How should a teacher prepare for a substitute? How should a substitute prepare for a substitute teaching assignment? Prepare a "substitute teaching kit" that contains materials that would make a substituting job easier. You may prepare the kit as if you were the classroom teacher or as if you were the substitute. Among the things that you will want to include in the kit will be tips and techniques for making the day go smoother, a checklist of things that should be done at the beginning of the "subbing" day, and a checklist of things that should be done at the end of the "subbing" day. You will also want to add additional materials that you think would be helpful. Talking to a teacher or a substitute teacher may give you additional information on what to include in your kit.

5. Often, a substitute feels like a stranger in a strange land. What, if anything, should the other teachers do to ease this uncomfortable feeling? What should the principal do?

6. Share with your classmates some of your "subbing" experiences. These may be experiences that you have had as a classroom teacher, a substitute teacher, and/or as a student. Share both good experiences and poor experiences. From these experiences, see if you, as a group, can develop some general hints and guidelines for both the classroom teacher and the substitute.

Suggested Readings

Clifton, R. A., & Rambaran, R. (1987). Substitute teaching: Survival in a marginal situation. *Urban Education, 22*(3), 310–327.

Collins, S. H. (1982). Substitute teaching: A clearer view and definition. *The Clearing House, 55*(5), 231–232.

Fox, B. A. (1988). Where you're absent: Preparing for the substitute. *OAH Magazine of History, 3*(3/4), 7–9.

Keane, B. M. (1984). Are you modeling honesty in your high school classroom? A checklist for teachers. *Momentum, 15*(2), 36–38.

Moses, J. C. (1989). Adventures in subland. *Teacher Educator, 24*(4), 2–7.

Nelson, M. (1983). A few steps by regular teachers can help substitutes with class instruction. *NASSP Bulletin, 67*(466), 98–100.

Pronin, B. (1983). Guerilla guide to effective substitute teaching. *Instructor, 92*(6), 64–66, 68.

Rundall, R. A. (1986). Continuity in subbing: Problems and solutions. *Clearing House, 59*(5), 240.

Seldner, J. K. (1983). Substitute teaching: Is there a better way? *Teacher Education Quarterly, 10*(4), 61–70.

Tracy, S. J. (1988). Improve substitute teaching with staff development. *NASSP Bulletin, 72*(508), 85–88.

Warren, R. (1988). Substitute teachers—Education's relief pitchers. *NASSP Bulletin, 72*(512), 96–99.

Response of
Sarah Huyvaert, Professor

The teacher, as the lone adult in the classroom, is responsible for maintaining classroom control, developing and organizing the instructional day, providing emotional support to the students, and furnishing the minute-to-minute instruction that occurs within the framework of that day. Classrooms are often seen as the sovereign kingdom of the teacher who spends the majority of the professional day sequestered with students and segregated from other adults. Because of this, the classroom can become an isolated environment—one in which the teacher is isolated from other adults. Shedd (1985) has noted, "The relative isolation of teachers—from administrators and, more especially from each other—is one job feature that complicates and impedes the teachers in their performance of their responsibilities" (as quoted in Smith & Scott, 1990, p. 10). Each of the three case reports in this section serves to validate the accuracy of this statement and to demonstrate how this isolation can have a negative effect on students.

In the first case, the teacher needed assistance in deciding how to help a student who was having behavioral problems in the classroom. The special education teacher (Jill) provides the teacher with some suggestions but they don't work. The teacher then tries other approaches of her own, which work a little better, but the results still aren't satisfactory. We can see that the teacher is frustrated and that she feels isolated and abandoned. What we can't see is what effect the "experimentation" had on Joe and the other students in the room. We can assume, however, that if the teacher had been a little less isolated—if Jill and the teacher had had more interactions—the level of frustration would have been lower for everyone involved.

In the second case, Jane's students have had to suffer through the experience of having a very poor teacher, and we can imagine what effect this has had upon them as students. The other educators (teachers and administrators) seem to become aware of the problems in Jane's classroom as a result of gossip and rumor. The assistant principal is frustrated because he doesn't know how to help, and so he asks another teacher to step in. The teacher is uncomfortable about becoming involved and feels that she is "caught in the middle." She does, however, agree to intervene on the condition that Jane first ask for assistance. Once again, we can only imagine how Jane must have felt when she had to go to her one-time friend and admit that she was having trouble and needed help. How much easier it would have been for everyone involved if Jane hadn't been so isolated to begin with—and just think how much better off the students would have been!

In the third case, the substitute teacher left the classroom to "get a cup of coffee." Although most educators would agree that this is unacceptable behavior on the part of the substitute, the really troublesome aspect of this case is what we don't know. We must ask ourselves, When a teacher is this irresponsible, what else may be going on in the room? Unfortunately, we will never know because the substitute teacher is also isolated from the other professionals in the building.

The problems caused by the isolated nature of the classroom have been recognized by the professional community, and many school districts are making conscientious efforts to reduce the isolation of classroom teachers. These efforts take many forms, including the development of teaching teams, the inception of teacher consultants, the introduction of peer coaching, and the initiation of mentoring programs. To some degree, each of these programs involves one or more professionals consulting with the classroom teacher. *Consulting* has been defined as "any form of *providing help* on the content, process or structure of a task or a series of tasks, where the consultant *is not actually responsible for doing the task itself* but is helping those who are" (Steele, 1975, p. 2). However, as demonstrated by two of these cases, "Interaction and Reactions" and "Caught in the Middle," simply understanding that a consulting or team approach is needed will not guarantee that the attempt to improve collegiality will be effective.

There are several factors that can help to assure the success of collegial interactions. First, the classroom teacher and the other professionals must respect one another's professional knowledge, and everything possible should be done to maintain this respect throughout the consulting process. Nothing destroys a collegial relationship faster than when one of the colleagues develops an attitude of superiority or inferiority. This is true whether the relationship is being established through peer tutoring, mentoring, consulting, or teaching teams. This element of professional respect was missing in both "Caught in the Middle" and "When a Sub Isn't a Substitute." In the third case, "Interaction and Reactions," it appears that there was some level of mutual respect at the beginning, but it had dwindled by the time the principal finally made his visit to the classroom. If lack of respect is interfering with a collegial relationship, it may be necessary for a third party to intervene.

In many cases, the first factor—collegial respect—fails because the second factor—direct and open lines of communication—is missing. Often, lines of communication break down simply because good communication takes time and no provision is made for the additional time required. An example of this is seen in "Interaction and Reactions" where the teacher is forced to bring up her concerns in the teachers' lounge during Jill's break. Poor communication is also evident in "When a Sub

Isn't a Substitute." In this case, the teacher fails to communicate to the substitute that he is expected to be in the room whenever the children are there and that he is to proctor the exam. This may appear to be common sense, but the substitute appeared to be unaware that this was the expected behavior. By the time he was told that leaving the room was unacceptable behavior, it was too late—the teacher had already decided to release the substitute and return to the classroom.

Good communication takes time and effort and is affected by the time and place of the interaction. It takes time and effort to meet with colleagues, to write quality reports so that others understand the history of the students, and to read and analyze the reports that others have written. Meaningful communication also requires special attention be given to the time and place of the communication so that other variables will not unduly affect the communication process. These variables may include such things as the mood of the communicators or an intervention by someone who accidently overhears a conversation. In the case of "Interaction and Reactions," it is apparent that the teachers didn't invest enough time or effort into communicating with one another. It is also obvious that the classroom teacher was not prudent in picking the place for this discourse. Approaching Jill in the teachers' lounge, on her break and in front of the principal was *not* a good communication strategy. In order for communication between colleagues to be effective, it should not be haphazard, as it appears to have been in this case, but rather deliberate and purposeful. Remember that, even though time and effort are two resources that are often overtaxed in the educational system, the chances of improved communication, and hence an improved collaborative relationship, is greatly influenced by the investment of these two resources.

Collaboration is also affected by the assumptions team members bring with them. It is normal for all parties involved in the collaborative process to have their own assumptions about what should and should not happen during, and as a result of, the collaboration, and it is important for everyone involved in the process to be aware of these assumptions. If the assumptions are not addressed at the onset and subsequently clarified throughout the process, it is fairly certain that conflicting assumptions will create problems at some point.

A fourth factor that will affect the collegial relationship is the amount of stress involved. Understanding that a certain amount of stress is normal in a collegial relationship goes a long way toward helping to keep stress under control. Some of the most common sources of stress include the following:

1. One colleague may be suspicious of the other colleague's motives or competence.

2. Teachers may feel that the collaborative process creates a threat to existing traditions, ways of working, relationships, and/or professional rewards and acknowledgment.
3. There may be pressure for early results.
4. There may be some confusion about the amount of perceived power that other team members should have.
5. Stress may arise from competition among team members or from feelings of inferiority, superiority, or insecurity by one or more team members.

The author of "Caught in the Middle" demonstrated that she was sensitive to the first source of stress—suspicion of a colleague's motive—when she stated, "It was important to me that she [Jane] knew that I was not trying to tell her how to run her classroom." Examples of the second source of stress—a fear that the collaborative process will interfere with, and serve as a threat to, existing conditions—are present in all three case reports. This is especially true in the case of Jane because the purpose of the intervention is, in fact, to disrupt the status quo. The case involving Jane also provides a good example of the third source of stress—pressure for early results. The author of the report states, "He [the assistant principal] indicated that, without a drastic change, Jane would be gone soon. . . . I didn't know what I could tell Jane to do differently in her classes when the patterns had already been well established and there was such a short time left in the school year."

Confusion about the amount of perceived power—the fourth source of stress—is evident to a slight degree in "When a Sub Isn't a Substitute." The teacher asks, "Should I have called the substitute and talked directly to him or should I have left it to the principal in charge of substitutes?" This question indicates that the teacher was uncertain whether she should have accepted the responsibility for reprimanding the substitute teacher. Examples of stress arising from the feelings of individuals—the final source of stress that was included on the list—can be found in at least two of the case reports. For instance, we get the impression that the classroom teacher in the case "Interaction and Reactions" is hurt by what she perceives as Jill's attitude of superiority. In the case with Jane, we see a hint of competition among the teachers when the author notes, "She also implied that the reason she was having difficulty was because I had 'stolen' the good classes and she was left with the ones that nobody wanted to teach."

Although the five sources of stress listed are among the most common sources, the list is by no means exhaustive. Time pressures, conflicting sets of priorities, and uncertainty about roles and responsibilities are also sources of stress. Once it is understood that feeling a certain amount of stress is normal, teachers will be more willing to admit that they are feeling stress. This is important because, if the team is aware that a member is feeling stress, the team may be able to help reduce the stress. At the same time, the team and individual team members should not dwell on the issue of stress, because stress tends to grow the more it is discussed. What should be concentrated on is not the feeling of stress, but rather the source of the stress and how to lessen or alleviate its effect. Remember that, even though teamwork is a source of stress, teamwork is also one of the best ways to deal with stress. As team members work together in a spirit of cooperation, the stress on the group and the individual members will be greatly reduced. It is hoped that through these programs, professional educators will begin to work together as a team to address the diverse needs of the students.

The need for increased interaction between teachers is becoming more and more evident, as witnessed specifically by the three case reports in this section and more generally by all of the case reports in this book. To say that the world of the classroom is a complex world is surely an understatement. As an increasing number of students with special needs enter the classroom, as curricula explode, and as we strive to meet ever higher demands for excellence, the complexity will only continue to increase at a very rapid rate. In order to deal with the complexity and to meet the many goals that are being thrust upon our educational institutions, it is imperative that professional educators work together as a team to address the diverse needs of our students.

References

Smith, S. C., & Scott, J. J. (1990). *The collaborative school: A work environment for effective instruction* (p. 10). Eugene, OR: ERIC Clearinghouse on Educational Management.

Steele, F. (1975). *Consulting for organizational change.* Amherst, MA: University of Massachusetts Press.

Questions, Exercises, and Activities

1. Compare and contrast the role of the administrators in "Interaction and Reactions" and "Caught in the Middle." Which of the two administrators would you say was most supportive? What did they do to make the situation better? What did they do that may have made the situation worse? What, if anything, should they have done differently?

2. In two of the three cases, "Interaction and Reactions" and "When a Sub Isn't a Substitute," the teachers were forced to interact with one another simply because they "shared students." In the third case, "Caught in the Middle," the teachers didn't share students but did share content. Should this make a difference in the level of collaboration that goes on between the teachers involved in each case?

3. Imagine that you teach with one of the case report authors, who shares with you his or her frustrations. As the conversation develops, it becomes evident to you that the teacher is under stress due to ____ (fill in the blank with any factor that you wish, including, but not limited to, those outlined in the Huyvaert response). Like most teachers, you are very busy, have been isolated from the actual events, and have heard additional rumors about the situation that the teacher has not shared with you. What would you do? What are your responsibilities as a professional? Who would you turn to for help? How would you decide whether to get involved?

4. Prepare a review of literature on one of the four approaches to collaboration—team teaching, teacher consultants, mentoring, or peer tutoring.

5. Pretend that all three of these cases happened in your school within the course of one school year. Your building has a work improvement team of which you are a member. Your team decides that something has to be done to improve the interactions between teachers within the building. Your subcommittee is given the task of researching different methods that might be used. Working with two of your peers, develop a report that could be delivered to the committee as a whole. Your report should include an executive summary of not more than two pages and should be accompanied with several key journal articles that explain the different approaches that could be taken. Your committee will be given just 10 minutes to present its find-

ings to the committee as a whole (your class). The committee (class) is given one week to study your proposal and then vote on the approach it wishes to take. Therefore, you must make certain that the report is clear and to the point and that you are able to summarize your findings, direct the attention of the committee to key points, and answer any questions that might be asked based on your report.

6. Once the committee as a whole (the class) has voted on the approach they wish to take, have your subcommittee come up with a plan for implementation of the approach.

Section 5
Suggested Readings

Bacharach, S. B., et al. (1990). Work design, role conflict, and role ambiguity: The case of elementary and secondary schools. *Educational Evaluation and Policy Analysis, 12*(4), 415–432.

Berkey, R., et al. (1990). Collaborating for reflective practice: Voices of teachers, administrators, and researchers. *Education and Urban Society, 22*, 204–232.

Flinders, D. J. (1988, Fall). Teacher isolation and the new reform. *Journal of Curriculum and Supervision.*

Fuhr, D. L. (1993). Managing mediocrity in the classroom. *School Administrator, 50*(4), 30–33.

Glatthorn, A. A. (1987). Cooperative professional development: Peer-centered options for teacher growth. *Educational Leadership, 45*(3), 31–35.

Kirst, M. W. (1991). Improving children's services. *Phi Delta Kappan, 72*(8), 615–618.

Leggett, D., & Hoyle, S. (1987). Preparing teachers for collaboration. *Educational Leadership, 45*(3), 58–63.

Lieberman, A. (Ed.). (1988). *Building a professional culture in schools.* New York: Teachers College Press.

McGrath, M. J. (1993). When it's time to dismiss an incompetent teacher. *School Administrator, 50*(4), 30–33.

Munro, P., & Elliott, J. (1987). Instructional growth through peer coaching. *Journal of Staff Development, 8*(1), 25–28.

Phillips, M. D., & Glickman, C. D. (1991). Peer coaching: Developmental approach to enhancing teacher thinking. *Journal of Staff Development, 12*(2), 20–25.

Prager, K. (1992). *Collaborative planning time for teachers.* Madison, WI: Center for Organization and Restructuring of Schools.

Reep, B. B., & Grier, T. B. (1992). Teacher empowerment: Strategies for success. *NASSP Bulletin, 76*(546), 90–96.

Rosen, M. (1993). Sharing power: A blueprint for collaboration. *Principal, 72*(3), 37–38.

Shulman, L. S. (1989). Teaching alone, teaching together: Needed agendas for new reforms. In T. J. Sergiovannie & J. H. Moore (Eds.), *Schooling for tomorrow: Directing reforms to issues that count.* Boston: Allyn and Bacon.

Smith, S. C., & Scott, J. J. (1990). *The collaborative school: A work environment for effective instruction.* Eugene, OR: ERIC Clearinghouse on Educational Management.

Sparks, G. M., & Bruder, S. (1987). Before and after peer coaching. *Educational Leadership, 45*(3), 54–57.

Tater, C. J., et al. (1989). School characteristics and faculty trust in secondary schools. *Educational Administration Quarterly, 25*(3), 294–308.

Welch, M., & Link, D. P. (1991). The instructional priority system: A method for assessing the educational environment. *Intervention in School and Clinic, 27*(2), 91–96.

SECTION 6

CHILDREN IN CRISIS

Each of the teachers who wrote a case report in this section was faced with the grave task of helping students who were in troubling situations. In the first case, "I'll Think of Jerry Until the Day I Die," a tutor shares an experience that involved working with a junior high student who had a learning disability. The student, Jerry, is unable to master the traditional curriculum but is gifted when it comes to working with his hands. Jerry is frustrated by his inabilities and the tutor senses that Jerry's frustration is extreme and that this is a very troubled student. The tutor tries to reassure Jerry, telling him that even if he can't master the skills required in school, he can lead a productive life. In the end, however, the case takes a tragic turn.

In the second case in this section, "How Could I Have Helped?" Wally, a seventh-grader, is faced with the imminent death of his mother. The teacher describes Wally's behavior during this difficult time and then questions her own behavior and how she might have responded differently.

In the third case, "Score One for the System," Steven, a fourth-grade student with Attention Deficit Disorder, is taken off his medication because his mother is afraid that he will become a drug addict. Later, Steven informs the teacher that his mother and her boyfriend are on drugs. Steven also shares several incidents with the teacher that leads her to believe that Steven's mother is being physically abused by the boy-friend. The teacher tries several strategies that she thinks might help. At the end of the report, however, the teacher is frustrated and somewhat bitter. Try to determine if there was something else the teacher should or could have done and if her bitterness is appropriate.

Each of these cases deals with extremely emotional issues that are far from everyday occurrences in the classroom—but neither are they atypical. More and more teachers are facing these types of situations each year. Professional educators must become more astute at handling the needs of children in crisis. After reading this section, it would not be unusual for you to feel limited in your own abilities to handle such tragic situations. It is hoped that through the examination and discussion of cases such as the three presented in this section, you will develop some strategies and techniques that will help you to deal with extreme situations if and when they should occur in your own classroom.

Like the previous two sections, this section does not include commentary for each of the cases, but rather provides commentary that covers all of the cases. The commentary is provided by Jan Collins-Eaglin, who has a doctorate and experience in both clinical psychology and educational psychology.

As you read the cases, think what the author might have done differently, what the warning signs were that indicated the student was having difficulty handling the situation, and what kind of follow-up the school might have conducted. Also, examine the emotional responses of the teachers and see if you can develop a set of strategies that will help you deal with not only your own emotions but also those of fellow teachers who may be suffering because of a tragedy.

I'll Think of Jerry Until the Day I Die

Background

Jerry was a quiet, handsome 13-year-old when he was screened at an agency for learning disabilities. It was determined that his disabilities were severe enough to warrant private instruction, paid for by special "scholarship" funds. His mother, a single parent, never completed high school and struggled to get off welfare by attempting employment at low-paying jobs with very irregular hours—jobs such as being a waitress at fast-food restaurants. Jerry had a 4-year-old sister who he had to watch when his mother was working. When I was assigned to tutor Jerry, I was given very little background information because "it would be an invasion of the child's privacy," and basically I was told it was none of my business. Everything I eventually learned of Jerry's life were things that he chose to share with me.

Incident

Although Jerry fully cooperated with me and attempted to do the best that he could at our lessons, he repeatedly told me, "It's no use. There's no reason for me to learn to read and write. I'll never be able to do anything. This is stupid and boring. School is stupid and boring. All I do is bad work in school and then watch my sister at home. Nobody cares; I don't care. This is a waste of time." For a child his age, this overall despair regarding his life and future concerned me. I spoke with his mother several times about Jerry's attitude, but she seemed more concerned about getting her own life in order than in helping Jerry. She really didn't know how he was actually doing in school, who his friends were, or what he was doing after school. A note that I wrote to one of his teachers concerning his schoolwork went unanswered. The agency that assigned Jerry to me had no support staff, such as a psychologist, that I could speak to about Jerry's problems.

Like most of my students who had learning disabilities, Jerry was very bright in specific areas and loved to work with his hands. A local lumber store occasionally hired him to help clean up and they paid him with supplies. He spoke very excitedly about a great fort he had built in the woods with these materials and how much fun it had been to build things. I tried to encourage him by emphasizing that building homes and other kinds of buildings might be a job he would want to consider as an adult. I noted that he already had many of the skills that he would need and that it wouldn't be necessary for him to go to college in order to get a job in this trade. All we had to do was get him through high school. He refused to believe this. He could not accept the fact that, even with special programs for struggling students, he could graduate from high school. Even if he did graduate, Jerry felt that college was mandatory to get any sort of worthwhile job. He was adamant that college was absolutely out of the question and finishing high school at this point was a big "maybe."

Academically, Jerry did very well with me. I congratulated him on his improvement since our first lessons—he had jumped at least one grade level in the language arts. But still, his terrible undercurrent of despair remained. After approximately nine months of lessons, his mother informed me that Jerry had told her that he was going to quit our lessons and she felt that she couldn't do anything about it. Our sessions were terminated.

About a year and a half later, I read an article in the local newspaper stating that a 15-year-old boy had fallen asleep between the rails of the train tracks near his home. He never moved as the train approached and he was killed instantly. The boy was Jerry. His mother suspected foul play, but the police suspected that drugs or alcohol were involved. Because of the depressed state that Jerry was always in, I believe it was suicide. However, no suicide note was ever found.

Discussion

Naturally, I will think of Jerry until the day I die and of what I didn't do to prevent this senseless, horrible death. More and more of my students are coming to me to share their feelings of worthlessness and stupidity, and I believe now that this is due to the nature of the educational system.

The needs of children who are gifted in any nonacademic area are basically ignored within the school. Jerry's ability to think three dimensionally and his ability to apply that thinking to build structures was not valued or viewed as a viable skill within the school. Studies have indicated that children learn best when utilizing all of their senses, but this multisensory method appears to be used only during the elementary years. When a student reaches the later grades—middle school and particularly high school—reading, writing, lectures, and note taking are preferred over a hands-on technique. The impression is also given that college is required for financial and personal success. Emphasis is placed strictly on test scores, and all tests are demanding higher levels of reading/writing skills. Even math questions have taken on the story format.

If children do not have the support system at home to nurture any alternative special skills and/or do not have an advocate to speak for them within the school system, those children are simply set adrift, left to sway with any tide that may come their way. Today, whether we like it or not, we must be more than just teachers to some of these children. Sometimes we are all they have.

Questions

1. How can the curriculum be revised to accommodate students with skills in areas other than reading and writing?
2. Everyone possesses at least one special skill, but is it the teacher's responsibility to notice this skill, whatever it may be, and then nurture it?
3. How does a teacher prevent the nondisruptive, struggling children such as Jerry from getting lost and forgotten in the shuffle of an everyday classroom?
4. When I met with the intake interviewer upon receiving Jerry's test scores, shouldn't I have been given all the pertinent information regarding his past?
5. How far should a teacher go in "playing" psychologist? Should I have made an effort to contact the principal and/or a counselor at Jerry's school to inform them of his attitude?
6. If there are special programs available at a school that may help a student in trouble, should the student be forced to take part in the programs?
7. Would it have been okay for me to contact the lumber store where Jerry sometimes worked, explain the situation, and inquire if they might let him help out on more difficult tasks? I think this would have helped to build Jerry's sense of self-worth.

8. How far should a teacher push? Is it my responsibility to meet with a struggling single parent and inform her that it appears that her child needs much more help than I, or perhaps even an entire school, can offer?
9. How much resistance from the child, and all parties involved, should teachers subject themselves to before giving up?
10. When a teacher has 35 children in the classroom, should the teacher attempt to meet the needs of all 35 individually or teach the group as a whole and hope to catch those students that seem lost?

Concluding Questions and Activities

1. The tutor states that a note was sent to the teacher but that the teacher failed to respond. Think of at least three reasons why the teacher might not have responded. One of the reasons should be one that you could defend; one should be one that might be understandable but not acceptable; and the third one should be plausible but totally unacceptable. Make certain you are able to defend your answers.
2. The statement was made that "children who are gifted in any nonacademic area have their needs basically ignored within the school." Do you agree? Why or why not?
3. The tutor appears to be very conscientious. He tries to encourage Jerry by concentrating on his strengths, he talks to the mother, and he sends a note to the teacher. None of this helps. In your role as a teacher, what might you be able to do that the tutor was unable to do? (Hint: What support systems are in place that might help you deal with a child such as Jerry?)
4. The question "How does a teacher prevent the nondisruptive, struggling children such as Jerry from getting lost and forgotten in the shuffle of an everyday classroom?" implies that this is a common occurrence. Do you agree or disagree? Give specific examples (from both your readings and your personal experiences) to support your conclusion.
5. The tutor didn't receive certain information about Jerry because the agency said it would be an "invasion of the child's privacy." Find out what the rules and regulations governing invasion of privacy are and if and when exceptions are ever made to such rules and regulations. How might this information affect the classroom teacher? Based on your findings, defend or refute the

statement: Personal information should be revealed to a teacher as a matter of course.

6. The author of this case observes that more and more students are sharing their feelings of "worthlessness and stupidity." Unfortunately, this is a growing trend in schools. Develop a list of strategies that you might use with students who display such feelings. Your strategies should be developed for one grade level and should include instructional and motivational strategies along with techniques for developing the students' self-concept.

7. Develop two different lesson plans to teach the same content. One of the lesson plans should employ the "typical" approach to the lesson and the other should be designed to teach a student whose reading and writing skills are weak.

Suggested Readings

Beane, J. A. (1991). Sorting out the self-esteem controversy. *Educational Leadership, 49*(1), 25–30.

Europa, E. (1982). Alternative education: An educational support program — Union City's innovative prototype for alternative education. *NJEA Review, 55*(9), 16–17.

Ford Foundation. (1987). *The forgotten half: Non-college youth in America.* New York: Author.

Hayes, M. L., & Sloat, R. S. (1988). Preventing suicide in learning-disabled children and adolescents. *Academic Therapy, 24*(2), 221–230.

Mamchur, C. (1990). But . . . the curriculum. *Phi Delta Kappan, 71*(8), 634–637.

McCarty, R. J. (1993). Adolescent suicide: A ministerial response. *Momentum, 24*(2), 61–65.

Mitchell, M. G., & Rosenthal, D. M. (1992). Suicidal adolescents: Family dynamics and the effects of lethality and hopelessness. *Journal of Youth and Adolescence, 21*(1), 23–33.

Orbach, I. (1986). The "insolvable problems" as a determinant in the dynamics of suicidal behavior in children. *American Journal of Psychotherapy, 40*(4), 511–520.

Salimena, R. A., & Brooks, T. P. (1990). It can happen here. *School Leader, 19*(5), 36–37, 44.

Taylor, D. (1990). *Learning denied.* Portsmouth, NH: Heinemann.

Van Dyke, P. (1989). The car chase. *Teaching Exceptional Children, 22*(1), 56–57.

How Could I Have Helped?

Background

My first-hour, seventh-grade class consisted of mostly well-behaved students but a few of them acted very immaturely. These students knew better but "acted out" just for attention.

One student, Wally, especially liked to do things to get my attention. He never did anything really bad, but sticking stuffed animals in girls' faces seemed to be just the thing to get him some of the attention he needed. In addition to this, he would always seem to forget his folder, book, and pencil. If he brought them to class, he would not do his work unless I sat down and worked on it with him. I knew that he was intelligent, but it was out of character for him to do well. When it came time for a test, he would either refuse to take it or he would just fill in the answers without reading the questions.

I had also noticed that Wally was absent a lot but he had never seemed to be sick. Wally had a "bad" reputation with the other kids and was expected to live up to it. He had one brother who was in the sixth grade and they lived with their mother and her boyfriend. Wally would come to school with dirty clothes on a dirty body. He was very embarrassed about this, but didn't seem to do anything to change his appearance. One day he had on a pair of pants with a tear in the leg. When he came up to talk to me, he held his hand over the tear so that I would not be able to see it. The other students would make comments about Wally not doing his homework, saying that it was okay because that was "just the way Wally is." They told me that Wally and his brother smoked cigarettes and that they lived in a cardboard box. He did not live in a cardboard box, but his house was not very nice.

In their own way, the students respected Wally. He was small for his age but the other students never picked on him. He had a tough-guy reputation, but in reality he was a very kind and caring boy who just wanted someone to give him attention.

Incident

During the first week in December, I was called to a meeting in the principal's office. The school counselor, a social worker, and all the teachers in my unit were there, along with the principal. The principal informed us that Wally's mother was dying of cancer and she had only six weeks to live. We were told that, after the death of their mother, Wally and his brother would be living with an aunt and uncle. The aunt and uncle lived in a nearby city and the boys didn't really know them. The boys' father had deserted them when they were young and there were no other relatives to take care of them. We were also told that the mother's boyfriend was going to live with them until her death but that he planned on leaving right after that and did not want the boys.

Discussion

After receiving this information, I began to understand why Wally craved so much of my attention. In an effort to help him, I gave him a special drawer where he was to keep his book. I also gave him a folder and a pencil with his name on them so that he would have his materials for class. I had students work with him on assignments and gave him special things to do to help make him feel important. Each day in class, I went up to him, asked how he was doing and made sure everything was going okay. I tried to make him feel that I was concerned about him. I sat down and read test questions to him and I went out of my way to make sure that he was doing his work. His attendance was becoming a problem, so I did everything I could think of to make school a place where he wanted to be.

In spite of all of my efforts, Wally would come up to me and ask me to send him down to the office because he didn't feel well. The counselor was convinced that Wally wasn't really sick but that he wanted to be sent home. He didn't want to be in school; he wanted to be home with his dying mother. The boy never knew from one day to the next if his mother would be there when he arrived home from school.

Within a short period of time, some of the other students in class began to complain that when they did a class activity on the computer, Wally always got to work on the computer. Some of the more astute students realized that if Wally was not actively involved, he would somehow find a way to interrupt the class. These students let the other students know that it was okay for Wally to use the computer. During this time, I tried to do as much as possible to make Wally feel like he was important to our class and that people did care about him. One thing that really seemed to help was our pet rabbit. The rabbit really liked Wally. In fact, it got to the point that the rabbit would want to play with Wally and Wally would climb up on a table to get away from the rabbit. This was the only way Wally could get his work done.

Near the end of the school year, Wally and his brother moved in with their aunt and uncle. The uncle drove the boys to school every day so that they wouldn't have to change schools at the end of the year. Their mother was still alive and living at home, but someone from the hospice was always there with her. Sometimes Wally would go home after school to visit with her, but this didn't seem to be enough. Wally's behavior became almost intolerable and he would plead with me to send him to the office. All of the professional staff agreed that Wally was acting up because he was hoping that he would get kicked out of school so that he could spend the remainder of the year at home with his mother. During the last few weeks of school, Wally got away with an awful lot. If other students had tried some of the things he did, they would have been strongly reprimanded. The other students in the room seemed to sense something was wrong, but they were never told exactly *what* was wrong. Wally's behavior made it difficult for all of us, but, under the circumstance, what else could be expected?

Questions

1. Is it really fair to the rest of the class to treat a student in this situation differently and let some of the classroom rules slide?
2. Should the other students have been told about Wally's mother so that they would understand why Wally was receiving different treatment? If they had known, is it possible that they could have helped Wally cope with the situation?
3. Was there anything that I could have done to help Wally that I didn't already do? Was there something I did that maybe I shouldn't have done?

Concluding Questions and Activities

1. The teacher makes the statement, "I tried to make him feel that I was concerned about him," but there is no mention of a conver-

sation with Wally about the impending death of his mother. Do you think the teacher was wise in avoiding mentioning Wally's mother's condition?

2. The teacher also says, "During the last few weeks of school, Wally got away with an awful lot. If other students had tried some of the things he did, they would have been strongly reprimanded." Is this fair to Wally or does he need more structure in his life?

3. Do you think the teacher's approach to Wally might have changed if Wally's mother had been dying from AIDS rather than cancer? Should it have been different? If so, how?

4. Talk to a school counselor to find out what techniques can be used with students like Wally. You may want to share the case of Wally with the counselor and together evaluate the teacher's actions.

5. Develop a series of lessons to use to teach death education. What are some of the social, religious, and political issues that you will need to consider as you develop these plans?

Suggested Readings

Arena, C., et al. (1984). Helping children deal with the death of a classmate: A crisis intervention model. *Elementary School Guidance and Counseling, 19*(2), 107–115.

Auten, A. (1982). ERIC/RCS: Why teach death education? *Journal of Reading, 25*(5), 682–685.

Birenbaum, L. K., et al. (1990). The response of children to the dying and death of a sibling. *Omega: Journal of Death and Dying, 20*(3), 213–228.

Christ, G. H., et al. (1991). A prevention intervention program for bereaved children: Problems of implementation. *American Journal of Orthopsychiatry, 61*(2), 168–178.

Crase, D. (1989). Development opportunities for teachers of death education. *The Clearing House, 62*(9), 387–390.

Davis, G. L. (1986). A content analysis of fifty-seven children's books with death themes. *Child Study Journal, 16*(1), 39–54.

Justin, R. G. (1988, Summer). Adult and adolescent attitudes toward death. *Adolescence, 23*(90), 429–436.

Kubler-Ross, E. (1969). *On death and dying.* New York: Macmillan.

Lester, D. (1993). The stigma against dying and suicidal parents: A replication of Richard Kaliph's study twenty-five years later. *Omega: Journal of Death and Dying, 25*(1), 71, 75.

Lidstone, S. S. (1992). Coping by caring. *Principal, 72*(2), 43–45.

Masterman, S. H., & Reams, R. (1988). Support groups for bereaved preschool and school-age children. *American Journal of Orthopsychiatry, 58*(4), 562–570.

Olowu, A. A. (1990). Helping children cope with death. *Early Child Development and Care, 61,* 119–123.

Spruce, M. (1991). When a student grieves. *Teacher Magazine, 2*(5), 30, 32.

Wellhousen, K., & Downey, J. (1992). Helping young children cope with death. *Dimensions of Early Childhood, 21*(1), 23–25.

Wilson, L. W. (1984). Helping adolescents understand death and dying through literature. *English Journal, 73*(7), 78–82.

Wiszinckas, E. (1982). Preparing children for situational crises. *Journal of Children in Contemporary Society, 14*(2–3), 21–25.

Wrenn, R. L. (1982). The concept of death and loss education. *High School Journal, 65*(6), 180–188.

Score One for the System

Background

Steven Smith is the older of two children. He was born when his mother was 15 years old. His mother and father are divorced, but the father lives across the street from the family. Steven's father is an alcoholic and his mother lives on Aid to Dependent Children (ADC) payments. His mother's boyfriend lives with her and is also their landlord.

Steven is a very sweet, bright, talkative child. He especially likes to talk about his problems. Last year, he was on the medication Ritalin because he had been diagnosed as having Attention Deficit Disorder (ADD). His third-grade teacher (he is now in fourth grade) said that before he was on the medication, he was very hyperactive and that taking the medication allowed him to concentrate on his studies. Steven was still a little "antsy" but there was a big improvement in his behavior when compared to how he acted before taking the medication. His mother took him off the medicine over the summer and told him she didn't want him to get addicted to it. According to her, Ritalin was a drug and drugs are bad. She didn't put him back on medication in the fall because she was hoping he wouldn't need it. I told Mrs. Smith we could monitor his behavior to see if the medication was working and that she could work closely with Steven's doctor, so that the medication would be safe for Steven. She responded by saying that she couldn't get Steven into the clinic until January because it was booked until then. Meanwhile, Steven believes that the drug is bad for him and doesn't want to take it.

Steven's third-grade records showed that he received Bs and Cs the first marking period, and Ds and Fs the second marking period. He was "placed" in fourth grade, meaning that if he did not do well within six weeks, he would be brought back into the third grade. I wondered how long he had been on the medication during the school year and why there was such an extreme change in progress between the two semesters. His third-grade teacher told me that he missed a lot of school last year and was often late when he did attend. Steven continued to miss a lot of school in the fall also. I asked him why he was missing so much school and he told me it was because he woke up late and it was too late to come to school. I told him that I didn't care how late it was, I'd rather have him here for an hour than not at all. I asked why he didn't set his alarm clock but he said he didn't have one. He also said that his mother sleeps until one o'clock in the afternoon. After our discussion, he came to school every day—he was almost always late—but he came.

One day I asked Steven why he didn't do his homework. We had recently had a discussion about the importance of his schoolwork and I had talked with his mother about it just the day before. Steven replied that he had to babysit his little brother and he didn't have time to do his schoolwork. He also said that was another reason why he was late every-day for school—he had to walk his little brother to the bus stop.

Incident

Steven stayed to talk with me after school on several occasions. Steven likes to talk so much, I sometimes wondered if what he said was just a story he made up to get attention. He revealed to me that Jim, his mother's boyfriend, does drugs with his (Jim's) friends at their house. He makes it very plain that he doesn't like Jim. He said he saw a razor blade that was used by Jim and his friends to separate the drugs and that he would bring it to school to show me. I told Steven that he should talk to the DARE officer about all of this and that he shouldn't bring the razor blade to school because it was dangerous and he could get into trouble. He spoke to the DARE officer the next day and then conveyed to me that the officer was going to go to Steven's house to have a talk with Steven's mother. I spoke with the DARE Officer, but he told me that he decided not to go to the house to talk with Steven's mother because he speculated that it might get Steven into trouble with his mother's boyfriend.

One day, shortly after Steven had talked to the DARE officer, I noticed that Steven wasn't doing his work. When I asked him why, he told me that he was worried about his mother. I instructed him to stay after school and we'd have another talk. I wondered if he was using his family problems as an excuse not to do his work. Later that day, Steven showed me the razor blade he had in a plastic bag in his pocket. He said, "This is the razor blade I was telling you about."

Steven then told me that his mother was taking drugs but he didn't want to say anything to the DARE officer because he didn't want to get his mom in trouble. He also reported that Jim yelled at him all the time, called him names, and swore all the time. He told me that one time he spilled jelly on his pants and Jim made him stand in the corner for two hours. During this time, according to Steven, he had to keep his coat and hat on and was forced to hold a heavy book behind his back. Another time, he told me he was concerned because his mother was being "beat-up on" by Jim.

I showed the razor blade to the DARE officer, but he didn't say much about it. I also showed my principal and other teachers the razor blade and told them a little about the situation to see what they thought. The secretary advised me to call Protective Services and my principal agreed.

I called Protective Services and told them everything I could remember. I also told Steven I was going to get some help for him. Protective Services took my call very seriously and acted quickly. A day or two later, they sent someone to talk to Steven at school and later visited the home to talk to his mother. But that was it, as far as I know. I called them back to see what happened and I never got through. Meanwhile, I put the paperwork through to make sure Steven could get school counseling and testing.

A few weeks later, Steven told me that he knew something but his mom made him promise not to tell. Then a few days after that, he told me he was moving and that was what he was not supposed to tell me. He said they were moving because his mother's ADC payments had stopped and she couldn't pay the rent. The following day, Steven came in and reported that the night before, Jim had been strangling his mother and Jim hit her in the face and now she bad a black eye. That same day, his mother came in to tell me it was Steven's last day and I saw her black eye. Steven started telling me about the fight right in front of her. She was very embarrassed and she told Steven to stop talking. I pulled her aside and informed her that she didn't deserve to be treated that way and that there are people who could help her. She said they were just wrestling and Jim got too rough. I gave her a list of clinics where she could get free counseling. I advised her if she didn't want to go for counseling (which she said she didn't), she ought to consider going anyway for Steven's sake. I even suggested that she could have Steven go by himself. I said that Steven was very worried about her and couldn't concentrate on his studies because of this. I explained that I felt he needed to talk to someone about his problems.

The following day, no more Steven. I worked so hard to help him, and where did I get? I felt terrible, and I couldn't help but wonder if there was something more I could have done for Steven and his mother.

Discussion

I think the system stinks! First of all, Protective Services should care enough to follow up with the people who contact them to keep them informed and to get further information from them. Second, I had reported Steven's absences and tardiness to the truancy officer, but if he did anything, I didn't hear about it. Third, how can a parent be allowed to take a child in and out of a school system with no notice and not tell the school where they are going? I don't know what really went on at Steven's home, but I know it was a bad situation. How can a child be allowed to live under those conditions?

I think parents get too many chances these days and I think the laws should change and become more strict. Was Steven's mother running away from Protective Services when she moved, or was it just because she was broke? Being a first-year teacher at the time, I did all that I knew how to do. I listened to my heart and even discussed adoption with my husband if things didn't work out for Steven. I feel so hopeless. How can we help students like Steven?

Questions

1. Should I have handled the situation differently? What other approaches could I have taken?
2. Is a child like Steven, who loves his mother very much, better off without her if Protective Services did take him away? What would keep him from being shifted from foster home to foster home?
3. Did Protective Services act correctly? Should I have kept trying to reach them and forced them to tell me what actions they had taken?
4. Could Steven's academic problems be a result of his Attention Deficit Disorder, or is it more likely due to the psychological problems related to his home life?

Concluding Questions and Activities

1. The author titles this case report "Score One for the System." Do you think that is an appropriate title? Why or why not?
2. Given the information in this case report, do you think an experienced teacher or counselor should be able to answer the

teacher's question: "Could Steven's academic problems be a result of his Attention Deficit Disorder, or is it more likely due to
the psychological problems related to his home life?" What is the
normal procedure for diagnosing a student with ADD?

3. The teacher makes the comment, "Being a first-year teacher at the
time, I did all that I knew how to do." How do you think a more
experienced teacher might have responded to this situation?

4. The teacher seems to have become very attached to Steven, even
to the point where she "even discussed adoption with my husband if things didn't work out for Steven." Do you think this
may have influenced the way she handled the situation? Is there
anything in the case report that might indicate that this has
happened?

5. Does the literature on ADD, Ritalin use, or children of drug and
alcohol dependent parents give you any insights that you could
apply when dealing with a student such as Steven?

6. Contact someone from Protective Services in your area and find
out the procedure for reporting suspected child abuse. Also, find
out what the procedure is for follow-up.

7. Find out if there is an ADD support group in your area, and, if
so, make a brief report on what services they offer for either the
family of an ADD student and/or for professional educators.

Suggested Readings

Barkley, R. A., et al. (1984). Effects of age and Ritalin dosage on the
mother-child interactions of hyperactive children. *Journal of Consulting and Clinical Psychology, 52*(5), 750–758.

Birke, S. (1993). COAs: Behind the masks. *Momentum, 24*(20), 54–60.

Derrington, M. L., & Mendonsa, C. (1992). K–3 support: Blending teaching, counseling, and social services. *ERS Spectrum, 10*(1), 35–39.

Divoky, D. (1989). Ritalin: Education's fix-it drug? *Phi Delta Kappan, 70*(8),
599–605.

Emery, R. E. (1989). Family violence. *American Psychologist, 44*(2), 321–328.

Gomez, K. M., & Cole, C. L. (1991). Attention Deficit Hyperactivity Disorder: A review of treatment alternatives. *Elementary School Guidance
and Counseling, 26*(2), 106–114.

Hawkins, J., et al. (1991). Teacher perceptions, beliefs, and interventions
regarding children with Attention Deficit Disorders. *Action in
Teacher Education, 13*(2), 52–59.

Hinchey, F. S., & Gavelek, J. R. (1982). Empathic responding in children of
battered mothers. *Child Abuse and Neglect: The International Journal,
6*(4), 395–401.

Jaffe, P., Wolfe, D., Wilson, S., & Zak, L. (1985). Critical issues in the assessment of children's adjustment to witnessing family violence. *Canada's Mental Health, 33*(4), 15–19.

Jaffe, P. G., Hastings, E., & Reitzel, D. (1991). Child witness of woman abuse: How can schools respond? *Response to the Victimization of Women and Children, 14*(2), 12–15.

Kirst, M. W. (1991). Improving children's services. *Phi Delta Kappan, 72*(8), 615–618.

MacAulay, D. J., et al. (1991). Attention deficits in hyperactive children: Connecting psychological theory with classroom practice. *Canadian Journal of Special Education, 7*(2), 132–142.

Mick, L. B. (1991). The nature of Ritalin: A response to Cooter. *Intervention in School and Clinic, 26*(5), 302–303.

Silvern, L., & Kaersvang, L. (1989). The traumatized children of violent marriages. *Child Welfare, 68*(4), 421–436.

Stein, J. A., et al. (1993). Differential effects of parent and grandparent drug use on behavior problems of male and female children. *Developmental Psychology, 29*(1), 31–34.

Whalen, C. K. (1981). Teacher response to the Methylphenidate (Ritalin) versus placebo status of hyperactive boys in the classroom. *Child Development, 52*(3), 105–114.

Response of
Jan Collins-Eaglin, Professor

As the world becomes more complicated, as children are faced with increasing challenges, and as teachers are confronted with dilemmas and difficulties not covered in traditional teacher training programs, teachers of today must rethink the role of teaching and student learning. In the past, teachers viewed students from an academic perspective. They analyzed learning problems from the perspective of academic ability and often assumed that if a child was not learning, there were deficits in the child's ability or motivation. Even though numerous theories and books have explored the socioemotional realm of the child as it relates to learning and achievement, it is not in the usual frame of reference of teachers to explore the home life and socioemotional effects on the child's learning. The questions become: How often can the teacher directly apply the theories and speculations in everyday practice? How does one intervene in the life of the child when the signals and the child's behavior clearly indicate that for various reasons not connected with ability or motivation, the child is not learning from the teacher?

The preceding cases illustrate how frustrating it is for teachers to break through the walls of "not learning" and begin to intervene and truly help the child. The case reports exemplify children in crisis. Things are not working in their lives, their homes, their families. Life is too painful, too challenging, too threatening for them to learn and achieve freely.

Each case report poses critical issues that the teacher needs to reflect on in order to intervene and assist in the crisis. Jerry questions the value of his own learning style and wonders about his future in the educational system. Eventually, something goes desperately wrong and he dies. His tutor questions the quality of their interaction and, in a tormenting way, wonders, "What could I have done differently?" Wally's mother was dying and the teacher was faced with the dilemma of how to help Wally through this difficult time. In the end, however, the teacher feels helpless and concludes that all of the attempts to help Wally were futile. Steven's mother and boyfriend are on drugs. How should the teacher respond? There are no right or wrong answers, special techniques, or tested formulas to deal with these children. Each teacher tried to make the classroom a safe and conducive place but, unfortunately, these efforts were not adequate to fill in the gaps in the children's lives.

Each of the cases has common elements: (1) the child was in crisis and had some sort of abusive or traumatic situation in the family, (2) the teacher understood that there were socioemotional factors wreaking havoc in the child's life, and (3) the teacher felt alone and frustrated in trying to help the child. The behaviors described in the cases are symptomatic of chaotic households and traumatic relationships. These behaviors include withdrawal, fear, immaturity, antisocial behavior, a drop in classroom achievement, pathological aggression, and/or hyperactivity. Children who are victims of trauma often feel as though they are merely going through the motions of living—they are numb, they avoid showing their feelings, and they limit their relations with other people because they trust practically no one.

Jerry seems to be a child who had experienced some sort of trauma. He was withdrawn, afraid to open up to the tutor, and untrusting of his own innate intellectual ability. The tutor valiantly tried to establish a relationship with him, to create a safe place in the school environment, and to help him experience success. Jerry was able to respond only minimally to the efforts. Yet the tutor felt that there was always "that underlying current of despair." Jerry shared what he chose to, but his withholding of information and prevention of contact hindered any sort of bonding and working alliance. The tutor suspected that Jerry's depression literally killed him. He was asleep on train tracks, under the influence of drugs or alcohol, when a train hit him. Alcohol or drug abuse is typical of adolescents who have experienced trauma. Adolescents will often use alcohol and other drugs to counteract and anesthetize emotional pain. Paradoxically, the alcohol is used to make one feel alive and to feel some sense of control. Jerry's withdrawal behavior is not uncommon for teenagers because, in their quest for an identity, they feel that no one else has gone through what they are feeling. As a result, they may become quite depressed and even suicidal.

The next case presented illustrates not a child victimized by some type of abuse but rather by the trauma of having to cope with the death of his mother. In this case, Wally's trauma could have been eased with a more systemic approach from the teacher and staff. Wally, watching his mother die of cancer, came to school disinterested, unorganized, and withdrawn. The teacher initially responded to Wally's poor performance by expecting less from him without further probing for more information about the reason for his low performance and/or trying to ascertain his true academic potential.

It was not until December that the teacher discovered that Wally's mother was dying and that he was uncertain about where he would live and of who his caregivers would be. The teacher tried to make school a place where Wally would want to be, but ignored the real education issue at hand—how to help Wally cope with the impending death of his mother. Death education would be very appropriate in this situation. The teacher should examine his or her own feelings and ideas about death and then help Wally explore his. The work of Elizabeth Kubler-Ross could guide this discussion. Wally was probably struggling with feelings of guilt, anger, and abandonment. Often, children feel they are the cause of family catastrophes such as death and divorce. Talking and communicating help children clarify and temper their concerns.

In this case, Wally must have been worried about what would happen to him. He must have wondered where he would live and if he would end up living with people who would be good to him. He probably was furious that his mother was leaving and concurrently feeling guilty for having these thoughts. It is normal to feel angry when someone is dying, but children don't have the cognitive ability to understand these thoughts and feelings. A teacher or caring adult can help children sort through their feelings, dispel their feelings of guilt, and understand their anger. Openly talking about death and stages of grief could greatly alleviate the pain and truly make school a good place for Wally to be—a place where he knows someone cares.

It is important to note that Wally cries out not only for a caring person but for a caring curriculum. Teachers typically complain that they are not qualified to teach death education. Many feel that their jobs are already too complex or that they do not have the time to address the curriculum at hand, much less add another component to the curriculum. I have often had teachers state that they are not social workers and do not feel competent to engage in such personal matters. My response is, "I understand."

Because the world of a child is becoming unprotected and dangerous, the world of the teacher is changing rapidly. In this new world, teachers are expected to accept roles that they have not been trained for. In the best of all situations, it would be wonderful to teach a child who is ready to learn all the math, science, and reading that can be taught and ignore the world, social environment, and negative influences on the outside. Unfortunately, we do not have that luxury in reality. Children in the classroom bring their worlds with them. Today, the ecosystem of children is endangered by the economic demands on parents, television images that promote violence, neighborhoods full of drugs and guns, and parents who are not capable of being parents due to their drug and alcohol abuse and/or to their immaturity.

In the story of Steven, we see the destructive power that alcohol and drugs have on the lives of children. Steven's mother and boyfriend are heavy drug users. The behavior patterns of children of alcoholics or substance abusers are similar to that of abuse victims. These children live in an unpredictable and chaotic environment. When the parent is drunk or high, it is not unusual for some sort of physical, sexual, or psychological abuse to occur. Furthermore, there is a code of silence enforced in these households that forces children to remain silent about what occurs in their homes. In addition, when the parent becomes dysfunctional, children are often left to take care of themselves, of other children in the household, and of the nonfunctioning parent.

The teacher in Steven's case illustrates how the act of caring, although not alleviating the situation, may help a child know that someone hears and cares. Steven exhibited hyperactive behavior in school, was unable to concentrate, and his grades reflected his inability to perform. As a result of bizarre logic by his mother, Steven was a victim caught between a rock and a hard place. Children caught in conflict at home compensate for lack of parenting by using their energy for basic survival, and often cannot concentrate in school.

In the third grade, Steven's hyperactivity was lessened by Ritalin, so he was able to concentrate better. The teacher and Steven saw the improvement and this was reflected in his grades. However, sometime between third and fourth grade, the mother takes him off the medicine because she believes that "drugs are bad." As a result, Steven's behavior, attention span, and grades all plummet. Even though Steven had trouble in the fourth grade, his mother refused to give him the medicine, did not cooperate with the teacher, and allowed her son to fail at an endeavor that was critical to his development. In addition, Steven began to miss school more and more often. However, the times when Steven did attend class demonstrate that he was motivated, even though his performance was way below normal. Steven reported to the teacher that his mother and her boyfriend were using drugs. What is ironic in this case is that the mother took Steven off medication ("drugs") that was helpful to him while she herself was on drugs that were destructive and destroying herself and family life. As Steven's situation deteriorated, the teacher correctly called the DARE officer, but with little success. In response to Steven's reports of physical abuse, the teacher brought in Protective Services, but the results were still ineffective.

The teacher probably did all that could be done on an individual basis. The crux of the problem appears to be that the teacher was forced to act alone in analyzing and determining what the best course of action was for assisting Steven. The teacher didn't have the means, time, or expertise necessary to intervene on a level that was required. Both Steven and the teacher were, to some extent, victims of the system's lack of response. Just as Steven was alienated when trying to make sense of his environment, the teacher was alienated from a cohesive, systematic approach for dealing with these crises. As long as teachers are autonomous and have to rely on wits, bits of information, and isolated bureaucratic services, the results will probably be the same. The child will be lucky if help is given. Unfortunately, because of the burden carried by so many individual service agencies, it is likely that, more often than not, the parent, child, and/or teacher will fall through the cracks. There is a need for broader communication and cooperation between services to help children and families like Steven's.

True teaching and learning will not occur until educators can address the needs of the whole child, not just the academic (math or reading) side. What happens when you try to work with children in an isolated, compartmentalized manner? They tune you out or give you a message that states, "I won't learn from you because my world is in turmoil." This may happen because the child's nurturance needs are far greater than his or her learning needs. If you think back to the most effective teacher you had, or the teacher that had the greatest impact on you, my guess is it would be one who cared and saw you as more than just a student in a classroom.

But truly, who has the time, expertise, and energy to do all of this? The solution lies not in one individual learning and implementing all this information but rather in a collaborative, interdisciplinary approach to working with children in crisis in the schools. It is an ironic note that collaborative and cooperative learning is being heavily stressed as an important strategy for academic achievement. Yet teachers, and even educational systems, do not adequately practice what they preach, as illustrated by the case reports.

In order to help identify the critical pieces that matter in the child's world and to help identify the resources available to help the child, the teacher and a helping team could use the metaphor of an ecosystem in the shape of a concentric circle. The child is the center of his or her world (the ecosystem). The child's self-concept, worth, and esteem are part of the inner circle. Moving outward, parents, siblings, and immediate family would be the next circle of influence. Friends, social networks, and schools would be in the next circle, and the outside circle would include the child's community, state, and country. Those people who are closest to the child's inner circle have the most impact on the child. When the members of this circle are under stress, one has to move to the other circles to find the resources and help for the child.

Schools, because they are in the circle next to those who have the greatest influence on the child, are often in a position to offer special help. Unfortunately, they are not always ready or prepared to respond, intervene, and assist. Another great resource that can assist in these situations is the concerned adults in the neighborhood or community. There are individuals who may or may not have children in the school but who have survived similar situations. These individuals may be willing to serve as mentors, providing some support and stability for the children. If the resources in all of the circles could be pooled together, teachers would not feel so frustrated when dealing with children in crisis. It is critical to think beyond tried and true solutions and to discover creative ways to connect with others in solving these problems. The higher-order, critical thinking skills that are being taught in schools today need to be employed for problem-solving cases like these presented.

A good example of bringing resources together and creatively intervening in a desperate situation is provided by Lois Timnicka's description of a school in south central Los Angeles (Timnick, 1989). On an almost daily basis, someone in the school neighborhood dies from a gunshot wound. Often, the victims are members of a student's family. The principal became alarmed when she saw some children regress to bedwetting, others become overly withdrawn or hostile, and even the best of students struggle to concentrate. She called in a mental health team and had the members develop a way to help the children cope with their experiences. The school now has a weekly grief class, where children have the chance to cry as they express their feelings and concerns. The children talk about life and death and discuss ways to stay safe in an unsafe world. As a result of this class, the principal has been able to see an improvement in the children's behavior and an increase in their learning.

This school's experience provides just one example of how professional educators can creatively join forces and solve problems. Unfortunately, until cooperative teams become the norm rather than the example, teachers will continue to feel frustrated, discouraged, and confused because children who so clearly need help cannot get it. Viewing the child as a whole and within the social context of his or her learning readiness means a reevaluation of the system. I believe the team approach is one way to begin to address the issue of children in crisis.

Reference

Timnick, L. (1989, September 3). Children of violence. *Los Angeles Times Magazine*, pp. 6–12, 14–15.

QUESTIONS, EXERCISES, AND ACTIVITIES

1. Compare and contrast the ways in which the adults responded to a child in crisis. You will want to examine the initial reaction of the adults to the child's behavior. Look for the things the adults did that they felt should have helped, and identify their concerns about the children and their family situations.

2. Collins-Eaglin asked the question, "How often can the teacher directly apply the theories and speculations in everyday practice?" Argue the position that teachers apply theory more often than is recognized and support the argument with specific examples.

3. Do you agree with Collins-Eaglin's statement that "it is not in the usual frame of reference of teachers to explore the home life and socioemotional effects on the child's learning" or lack of learning? Defend your position.

4. In all three cases, there were outside agencies that, according to the teachers and the tutor, should have been more responsive to the calls for help. Does the lack of support from these agencies in any way diminish the school's responsibility? Are there times when these agencies could be in conflict with the school? Can there be too many agencies intervening? What happens when services are well coordinated?

5. Select one of the three students (Jerry, Wally, or Steven) and write the case report from his point of view. Present the background and the incident from the student's perspective.

6. Of the three cases, which are you most prepared to handle? Which do you feel you are least prepared to handle? Why? Describe some things that you might do so that you are better prepared to help the children in your classroom who may be facing one type of crisis or another.

SUGGESTED READINGS

Adrian, C., & Hammen, C. (1993). Stress exposure and stress generation in children of depressed mothers. *Journal of Consulting and Clinical Psychology, 61*(2), 354–359.

Ayers, W. (1989). Childhood at risk. *Educational Leadership, 46*(8), 70–72.

Brodkin, A. M., & Terr, L. (1992). Childhood trauma: How teachers can help. *Instructor, 101*(8), 23–24.

Butte, M. P. (1993). Developing curriculum to reduce emotional stress in middle schoolers. *Middle School Journal, 24*(4), 41–46.

Dickerson, V. (1985). Children at risk. *Teacher Educational Quarterly, 12*(2), 68–75.

Exline, J. (1993). Children in crisis in the classroom. *Momentum, 24*(2), 12–16.

Feldman, S. (1992). Children in crisis: The tragedy of underfunded schools and the students they serve. *American Educator: The Professional Journal of the American Federation of Teachers, 16*(1), 8–17, 46.

Glenn, J. (1990, Fall). Training teachers for troubled times. *School Safety,* 20–21.

Locke, D. C., & Ciechalski, J. C. (1985). *Psychological techniques for teachers.* Muncie, IN: Accelerated Development, Inc.

Murphy, L., & Ella-Corte, S. (1990). School-related stress and the special child. *Special Parent/Special Child, 6*(1).

Scaps, E., & Solomon, D. (1990). Schools and classrooms as caring communities. *Educational Leadership 48*(3), 38–42.

SECTION 7

EVALUATION
OF STUDENTS

The three case reports in this section deal with some aspect of the evaluation of students. In "Special Kids, Special Grades?" the teacher ponders about the best way to evaluate students who have special needs. She discusses some of the techniques, but it is obvious she feels that she lacks the skills to evaluate special education students.

In "To Pass or Not to Pass," a high school quarterback is about to fail Algebra II. The teacher realizes a failing grade will mean that the student will lose a full college scholarship. To make matters worse, the student is being tutored by the vice-principal, who is also responsible for evaluating the teacher who must assign the grade.

"Change of Teachers, Change of Requirements" presents a situation in which a new teacher is assigned to a class two weeks into the semester. The new teacher, after going over the course syllabus, decides the class needs to be more rigorous, and so changes the student requirements. At first, the students rebel, but they finally accept the changes. The teacher, however, begins to question his own motives.

High school students are involved in two of the cases and junior high students are involved in the third. Because the topics address issues related to setting standards and evaluating students with special needs, these case reports easily generalize to all grade levels.

This section is different from the sections that have preceded it in that *all* the case reports are left open ended; that is, no commentaries are included. Professional opinions on the topics of standards and student evaluation are plentiful. If you doubt this, just check your favorite professional source, be it written or human, and you will soon be convinced. After checking with some of these sources, you should be able to write your own commentary for each of the cases.

Special Kids, Special Grades?

Background

During my second year of teaching at a middle school, I was confronted with four special education students in my prealgebra/science block. All four students happened to be boys. One was bilingual and was very low academically, two were diagnosed as having Attention Deficit Disorder (ADD) and were considered learning disabled, and the fourth was extremely emotionally impaired and this was his first time attending a regular class for academic subjects.

In September, the special education teacher discussed each of the students with me. I admitted to her that I had no prior experience dealing with these types of students, either academically or behaviorally. She told me that these four students had been chosen out of her caseload of 15 because of my classroom management techniques, and that she was confident that I could "handle them." She also assured me that she would visit the classroom and help me in any way she could.

Each of the four students posed unique problems. I tried to handle each problem individually, either by myself or with the help of the counselors, the special education department, and/or the administration, depending on the demands of the situation. But one problem was never resolved to my satisfaction. It was the problem of testing the special education students and assigning grades to them. In college, educators are taught different methods of adapting tests for students. I employed many of these strategies, including giving fewer problems on a math test, deleting a choice on a multiple-choice test, providing a word bank for fill-in-the-blank questions, and allowing students to skip certain sections altogether. I also had students orally tested, had a test read to them, and allowed them to take a test either before or after school.

Both of the boys who had a learning disability did very well that year, especially after we discovered which strategies worked for each of them. One preferred before-school testing so that other students would not be around to distract him (he had also just taken his medication), and we found that fill-in-the-blank tests worked best for him. The second boy took the same test that was given to the other students and needed no special assistance from me. He was, however, seeing a tutor regularly. The other two boys didn't fare as well. My bilingual student would stay in class for the explanation of assignments, then go to the bilingual tutor for assistance. He could speak English clearly and could also read in English, albeit slowly. I rarely heard him use his native tongue and I often wondered if the extra assistance he was receiving was even necessary. Assignments would come back complete, but his level of understanding never changed after seeing the aide. Tests were never a positive experience for him. Likewise, tests were not a positive experience for the student with emotional impairments. He told me that he has never been able to take a test and he never will, even though he "knows his stuff." I never found him to "know his stuff" in any way, shape, or form.

Incident

I discussed my concerns with the special education teacher frequently throughout the semester. She visited the class, as promised, and assisted in the altering of tests. Unfortunately, I was the one who always came up with ways of changing a test to meet the needs of the students. The special education teacher rarely had any suggestions at all. Unhappy with the results of her help, I spoke with the coordinator for bilingual students. The coordinator suggested that I have the student work with the building's bilingual aide, which I was already doing. Outside of this suggestion, I was given no useful information. The counselor remarked, however, that some students will always fail and that I would come to realize this with more teaching experience. I spoke with the building principal, but she sent me back to the special education teacher.

Discussion

In my opinion, teachers are being put in an awkward position when it comes to assessing the learning of special education students. Most of my colleagues suggest being fair to all students and treating them all the same. Some even go so far as to say that special education students don't expect to pass and their parents don't expect them to pass either. Other teachers advocate grading special education students on what you, as the teacher, think they can accomplish. It appears that even the specialists in the field have limited ideas on how to tell if students are learning. If administrators and specialists can't agree, how can classroom teachers be held accountable for the grades of special education students?

Questions

1. With more emphasis being placed on total inclusion of special education students, should the classroom teacher have the sole responsibility for assigning grades to these students?
2. Is testing the best method for evaluating the learning of special education students?
3. Does being fair mean treating all students the same, or giving each child only what he or she needs?
4. Should general education teachers be required to take special education courses in order to accommodate all learners?
5. I spent a lot of time developing special materials for my "special learners." But my other 25 students are special too! How can I, as a teacher, justify spending so much additional time with the special education students in my class?

Concluding Questions and Activities

1. What were some of the alternative strategies the teacher used to test the boys who had learning disabilities? What are some other strategies she might have used?
2. The teacher was unhappy with the help she received from the special education teacher, the coordinator of bilingual students, and the counselor. Why do you think these individuals were unwilling or unable to help this teacher?
3. Respond to the teacher's comment, "If administrators and specialists can't agree, how can classroom teachers be held accountable for the grades of special education students?"
4. The teacher states, "But one problem was never resolved to my satisfaction. It was the problem of testing the special education students and assigning grades to them." Some of the reasons she may not have been able to resolve this issue include:
   a. The teacher lacked the skills and knowledge necessary to evaluate special education students accurately.
   b. The teacher lacked confidence in her ability to evaluate special education students.

    c. The teacher has not resolved in her own mind what role grades should play in the education of special education students and how their grades should relate to the grades of other students (i.e., does a "special" student's C in math mean the same thing as a "regular" student's C in math? If not, how is the difference communicated on the report card?).

Take each possible cause and explain some strategies that you might use to help this teacher.

5. It is possible that the professionals in this case (the teacher, the special education teacher, the coordinator of bilingual students, and the counselor) each had a different understanding of the other's role. For instance, the classroom teacher may believe that the special education teacher should be responsible for evaluating the students, either directly or by providing ways to evaluate them. The special education teacher, on the other hand, may believe that her role is to empower the classroom teacher to take on these responsibilities. Do some research to find out what some of the most common roles are for these different professionals. Then tell how you, as a beginning teacher or a new teacher in a district, would go about defining and clarifying the roles in your building.

Suggested Readings

Barnett, D. W., & Macmann, G. M. (1992). Decision reliability and validity: Contributions and limitations of alternative assessment strategies. *The Journal of Special Education, 25*(4), 431–452.

Carpenter, D., et al. (1983). Grading mainstreamed handicapped pupils: What are the issues? *Journal of Special Education, 17*(2), 183–188.

Evans, C. S. (1993). When teachers look at student work. *Educational Leadership, 50*(5), 71–72.

Fuchs, D., et al. (1990). Mainstream assistance teams: A scientific basis for the art of consultation. *Exceptional Children, 57*(2), 128–139.

Hilliard, A. G., III. (1992). The pitfalls and promises of special education practice. *Exceptional Children, 59*(2), 168–171.

Kiraly, J., Jr., & Bedell, J. J. (1984). Grading the mainstreamed handicapped student. *NASSP Bulletin, 68*(472), 111–115.

Mercer, C. D. (1991). *Students with learning disabilities.* New York: Merrill.

To Pass or Not to Pass

Background

Chris was planning on going to college. On the advice of the high school counselor, he signed up to take Algebra II. He had taken Elementary Algebra in the ninth grade and received high enough grades that he continued with Algebra I in the tenth grade. By his own admission, Chris struggled to receive a C– in Algebra I each semester. He took Geometry in the eleventh grade and his teacher told me that Chris had a great deal of difficulty with that class as well. He was given the "gift" of a C– for the first semester and a D for the second semester. Needless to say, Chris was not starting off in my Algebra II class with a very solid foundation in the abstracts of higher-level math.

Chris played football and he had to maintain his grades in order to play every Friday night during the football season. This was a good motivator for Chris, and since the team was having a winning season, there was a lot of motivation for him to keep his grades up. Chris had attracted the attention of several talent scouts from small colleges. Several of the colleges even mentioned a possible full-ride scholarship if Chris would come play football on their campus.

During the football season, Chris worked hard to keep his grades up. Because he was the type of student who did not catch on to concepts very quickly, he needed to come in for extra help on the daily lessons. He came in for help almost every day during his study hall, which was also my conference hour, and he was able to maintain a C average the first nine weeks.

The football team ended the season undefeated. This meant that the team would continue in the state play-offs. The team won their first game but lost the second. Even though the football squad had gone further in the state play-offs than any previous team from our school, the players felt as if they had let the students down. For a few weeks after the football season ended, the whole football team was very depressed about the results of their last game.

Chris' depression had a drastic effect on his grade. He had been maintaining a low C– up until the time of the play-offs, but he lost all interest in continuing with his studies after the loss. I called his mother to let her know that Chris was having difficulty with his work. She knew I was willing to help Chris and indicated she would talk to him about his attitude.

Just before Christmas break, Chris's grade slipped into the D range. His friends and I tried to encourage him to come in to get further help. Exams were coming up after Christmas and it was a school policy to count them as 20 percent of the final grade. I was very concerned that Chris was going to fail unless he started to put more time in on his studies. Chris told me that he was going to study over the break and that he was counting on this extra time. However, Chris left for Christmas and his books stayed in school.

When Chris returned in January, the push was really on to study for the exams. He did devote some extra time to the class, but it quickly became obvious that he had let too much time go by. It was impossible for Chris to catch up on what he had missed during the previous weeks. He ended up receiving a D for the semester.

When I made a point of talking to him about his grade and the problems that I thought he would encounter in the second semester based on this semester's grade, Chris indicated to me that he found the material very difficult. He felt he was in way over his head. I told Chris I would be willing to work with him to try to get him back to an acceptable grade, but that he would have to put a lot of extra effort into the class. That meant he would have to come in every day and follow up by finishing his homework completely. There would be no senior "skip days" or slack time. I also wanted Chris to be honest with himself. Unless he was willing to make the commitment, he had to realize his grade could possibly drop. I also pointed out that all the second-semester material would be new. I told him to discuss his choice with his parents and I would support whatever decision they made.

Chris decided to stay in my Algebra II class for the second semester. I think the most influential factor in his decision was that his best friend, who was a football player, was also in the same Algebra II class. They both decided to turn over a new leaf, especially in their study habits.

There were some positive changes in Chris's behavior at the start of the second semester. He and his friend both came in for extra help and this helped Chris raise his grade up into the C range.

As the semester evolved, however, Chris's interest began to fade fast. He stopped coming in for extra help and was not working on his homework. I tried to help him, but he showed very little interest. His friend continued to come in for extra help and he indicated that Chris did still study with him on some occasions.

Sometimes right before a quiz or test, Chris would appear at my door for help on material that the class had been working on for at least a week. We would sit down and work together for a couple of hours, but it was usually too late. I always offered Chris the option of retaking the quizzes and tests, but only after we reviewed the material he had not mastered. Chris ended up with a D for the nine weeks.

The start of the second nine weeks was also the start of spring sports and Chris was going out for track. All of a sudden, grades were taking on a new meaning for Chris. I did find it rather strange, however, that somehow he wasn't as interested in getting help from me as he had been during the football season.

Incident

Shortly after the start of the spring sports season, I began to notice that the assistant principal was coming into my room a little more often than usual. He would check out what I was teaching and what was happening in the classroom. It also seemed he appeared more often on the days I was giving a quiz or a test and he always made it a point to look over the questions. I found out later that Chris had been going to him for some extra help. I thought this was great. Chris was getting some extra help from somebody and I was glad. It also explained why Chris had stopped coming to me for help. However, in spite of this extra help, Chris's grades continued to slip and finally dropped into the failure range.

Near the end of the year, the assistant principal informed me that he had been giving Chris extra help with his math. He also made the statement that it wasn't my fault that Chris was getting such a poor grade. This struck me as odd because I didn't feel that I was to "blame" for Chris's grade.

Later that week, I went into the office and the principal was by my mailbox. He initiated some small talk, which led to a conversation about Chris's grade. I indicated that unless Chris passed the remaining quizzes and tests, it looked like he could fail. The principal's reply was, "Do you realize that Chris has a scholarship to college? Who will care about this grade a year from now?" The bottom line was that the principal was asking me to change Chris's failing grade to a passing one. I was totally floored that the principal would imply that I should give a grade that was unearned. This would not be a favor to Chris or the college he planned to attend. What would I be setting myself up for by giving him the failing grade in class? I knew I couldn't pass Chris if he was failing, because that would violate my belief system.

As it turns out, it was the principal who had asked the assistant principal to see if I was the deterrent to Chris's grade. The assistant principal had been asked to help Chris because Chris was one of the principal's favorite students. The assistant principal assured the principal that I had gone out of my way to help Chris and that it wasn't my fault that Chris was failing. It was at this point that the principal suggested that I change Chris's grade, since it wouldn't make any difference a year from now.

Discussion

Chris did manage to pass the remaining quizzes and the final exam. I also allowed him to turn in some missing homework. He ended up with a barely passing grade of D– for the semester. I felt relieved that I was not put in the situation of failing Chris, but I couldn't help but notice that the principal treated me differently after this incident and he was not nearly as friendly or as supportive as he had been in the past.

Questions

1. Was there more that I could have done for Chris when he gave up in early December?
2. Chris just barely made the cutoff for the D–. If he had missed the cutoff by a point or two, should I have given him the D– anyway? After all, a failing grade would have cost him his scholarship and "who would care about the grade a year from now?"
3. Was it right for the principal to ask the assistant principal to help Chris without telling me he was doing so?
4. How should I have responded to the principal when he subtly asked me to "change" Chris's grade?
5. This incident has affected the working relationship between myself and the principal. What can, or should, I do about this?

Concluding Questions and Activities

1. The teacher implies that Chris came into Algebra II with a very weak background in math and that Chris was able to maintain a

passing grade during the football and track seasons but not at other times. How might you explain this, considering the fact that Chris wouldn't have as much time to study during the sports seasons as he would at other times? The teacher credits it to sports as a motivator, but can a motivator help to make up for lack of basic knowledge in math?

2. Chris was getting a lot of extra help from the teacher and the assistant principal. We know Chris was motivated by football, but do you think perhaps the teacher and assistant principal were as well? Is this fair to the other students who don't do well in sports or academics?

3. Some schools have established "no pass, no play" rules, which means that if a student doesn't pass a class with a C or better, he or she cannot participate in sports for the next six weeks. Is this fair? What about students like Chris who may stay in school only so that they can participate in sports?

4. How would you, as a classroom teacher, have reacted when you found out that the principal had asked the assistant principal to find out if you "were the deterrent to Chris's grade"? (Remember that assistant principals are often asked to play a key role in teacher evaluations.)

5. Do you think the assistant principal and principal acted unethically in this case? Is there a set of ethics that teachers and administrators should follow?

6. Do some investigating and find out what the requirements are for high school students to participate in sports in your community.

7. Prepare a survey that you might administer to students, teachers, and administrators to evaluate what they think about the relationship of academics and sports at the high school level. Before you develop the survey, you should consult the professional literature in this area.

Suggested Readings

Amen, J., & Reglin, G. (1992). Stress and the high school senior: Implications for instruction. *NASSP Bulletin, 76*(548), 78–84.

Andrews, A. (1983). Grade inflation—How great? What are the concerns of parents, educators? *NASSP Bulletin, 67*(466), 81–88.

Carter-Wells, J. (1989). Academic preparation for college: What we know, where we need to go. *Research in Developmental Education, 7*(2).

D'Onofrio, J. (1992). Communicating with style. *Principal, 71*(3), 40–41.

Durbin, B. B. (1986). High school athletics: A valuable educational experience. *NASSP Bulletin, 70*(492), 32–34.

Goldman, L. (1985). The betrayal of the gatekeepers: Grade inflation. *Journal of General Education, 37*(2), 97–121.

Herlihy, B., & Herlihy, D. (1985). Improving principal-teacher relationships by understanding the concept of power. *NASSP Bulletin, 69*(485), 95–102.

Keith, T. Z. (1982). Time spent on homework and high school grades: A large simple path analysis. *Journal of Educational Psychology, 74*(2), 248–253.

Majesky, D. (1993). Grading should go. *Educational Leadership, 50*(7), 88, 90.

Purdy, D. A., et al. (1982). Are athletes also students? The educational attainment of college athletes. *Social Problems, 29*(4), 39–48.

Soltz, D. F. (1986). Athletics and academic achievement: What is the relationship? *NASSP Bulletin, 70*(492), 20, 22–24.

Weldy, G. R. (1984). Coping with twelfth-grade letdown: A solution to senioritis. *NASSP Bulletin, 68*(460), 89–93.

Zirkel, P. A., & Gluckman, I. B. (1993). It's the law: "No pass, no play" rules. *Principal, 72*(3), 62–63.

Change of Teachers, Change of Requirements

Background

I had taught in a private high school for three years before I was unexpectedly laid off. The next fall, I began substituting in the high school near my home. Within a short time, I was asked to fill in for an English composition teacher who was to be on an extended leave. The outgoing teacher, Mrs. Lambert, left two weeks into the semester. The students liked Mrs. Lambert and they were unhappy whenever I did anything differently than she did.

In spite of this, after about a week, I decided that Mrs. Lambert had been too easy on the students and that it was time to change the course requirements. I gave the students a new list of assignments and let them know that my requirements were going to be tougher than Mrs. Lambert's requirements. Not only were my requirements tougher but also my teaching style was completely different. In Mrs. Lambert's class, the students were given the first 15 minutes of the class to finish their homework from the night before. In my class, the students were expected to have their homework done before the class began, and it was assumed that they had read the material to be discussed in class each day. In addition, Mrs. Lambert reduced the workload of the students if something special, such as homecoming, was going on. I let the students know right away that this practice was going to stop.

Incident

One of the students made it very clear that she resented the changes that I was making. She questioned the new assignments and repeatedly asked why the class had to do "new things." It wasn't long until the class took up the war cry and rallied behind her. The students echoed her sentiments with similar objections, and she would boisterously defend their verbal onslaughts. Even though the tensions were rising in the room, I stuck to my guns. I asked the students to keep a journal, which meant additional work for them because they had to write in the journal each day. Additionally, they were required to write one short paper per week. Mrs. Lambert had assigned only three papers for the entire semester.

The students became more and more upset with the assignments and I was losing control of the situation. I felt that there was very little learning going on during class because so much energy was being spent on discussing the appropriateness of the new assignments. I understood why the students were so angry and I decided that the best way to defuse their hostility was to be honest with them. I answered all of their objections to the assignments and explained to them why I thought each of the assignments was necessary. For instance, I told them the journal was necessary because it would get them writing every day. By doing this, they would be better students and perhaps they might find that they actually liked to write. Next, I tried to make certain that I did not return anger for anger. I responded to their questions and not to their hostility. Finally, I did everything that I could to be the best teacher I could possibly be. Student papers were returned promptly, I commented on each journal entry, and I gave them little reason to criticize my work. If they did a great deal of work, then so did I.

My strategy worked. The class stopped objecting after they saw that I could address their objections calmly and could offer rational explanations for the change in course requirements. The student who was initially such a vocal opponent became a charming proponent, and the class and I seemed to be functioning as a team. It took a while, but eventually the students and I developed a sense of *esprit de corps*. The class and I were working toward the same goal—to make them better writers.

Discussion

Even while explaining to the students why I was such a "tough grader" and why I required so much work from them, I was questioning my own motives. I wasn't certain if the real reason I was being so hard on them was because I wanted them to learn or because I wanted to prove that I was a good teacher. I was upset when the private school let me go. They told me that it was due to a lack of funds, but it still embarrassed me that I had been fired. If I could show that my students learned just as much in public school as they would if they were in private school, everyone would know that I was an excellent teacher.

Questions

1. Should a teacher consider the students' input regarding the amount of work to be done?
2. It seemed to me that Mrs. Lambert required very little work from her students. Doesn't the public school administration have some control over this? Wasn't she being unfair to the students by expecting so little?
3. What is the best response when a teacher feels a growing resentment from class members?
4. What should I have done if my strategy of being honest hadn't worked?
5. If my motivation turned out to be that I wanted to be an excellent teacher, is that bad? Is student learning always more important that excellent teaching? Can the two be separated?

Concluding Questions and Activities

1. What were some of the strategies that the teacher used to help make the change in requirements easier for the students to accept?
2. Do you agree that a syllabus is a contract between the teacher and the students and shouldn't be changed unless both agree?
3. Why do you think the teacher began to question his own motivation for changing the grading practices for the class? Is this a sign of reflective thinking or does this demonstrate a lack of self-confidence?
4. When you teach a class for the first time, you must decide how you will evaluate the students. How should you go about doing this?
5. The teacher talks about his feelings toward being fired by the private school. Do you think this is a normal reaction to being laid off, even when you know the layoff has nothing to do with you but rather with the school's budget?

Suggested Readings

Montmarquette, C., & Mahseredjian, S. (1989). Could teacher grading practices account for unexplained variation in school achievement? *Economics of Education Review, 8*(4), 335–343.

Nottingham, M. (1988). Grading practices: Watching out for land mines. *NASSP Bulletin, 72*(507), 24–28.

Orstein, A. C. (1990). The evolving accountability movement. *Peabody Journal of Education, 65*(3), 12–20.

Pine, P. (1985). *Raising standards in schools: Problems and solutions. AASA critical issues report.* Arlington, VA: American Association of School Administrators.

Prakash, M. D. (1985). *Minimum competency testing: Grading or evaluation?* New York: Ford Foundation.

Reavis, C. A. (1988). *Extraordinary educators: Lessons in leadership.* Bloomington, IN: Phi Delta Kappa.

Stathem, R. L. (1990). I remember Jennie. *Phi Delta Kappan, 71*(9), 728–729.

Stiggins, R. J., et al. (1989). Inside high school grading practices: Building a research agenda. *Educational Measurement: Issues and Practice, 8*(2), 5–14.

Terwilliger, J. S. (1989). Classroom standard setting and grading practices. *Educational Measurement: Issues and Practice, 8*(2), 5–14.

Thomas, W. C. (1986). Grading: Why are school policies necessary? What are the issues? *NASSP Bulletin, 70*(487), 23–26.

Section 7

Questions, Exercises, and Activities

1. Evaluate each of the case reports based on the information provided in "Decision Reliability and Validity: Contributions and Limitations of Alternative Assessment Strategies" by Barnett and Macmann (see the Suggested Readings that follow).
2. What are the similarities and differences among these three cases?
3. How were the decisions of each of the classroom teachers affected by the actions of another educator (teacher, counselor, administrator, etc.)?
4. Select a curriculum area and develop a portfolio of alternative assessment techniques. You may want to refer to the articles written by Perrone, Valencia, and Wolf (see the Suggested Readings that follow) for suggestions.
5. After reading Frisbie's and Waltman's article, "Developing a Personal Grading Plan" (see the Suggested Readings that follow), develop a grading plan that could be used to assess the students in these three case reports.

Section 7

Suggested Readings

Austin, S., & McCann, R. (1992). *Here's another arbitrary grade for your collection: A statewide study of grading policies.* Philadelphia, PA: Research for Better Schools.

Barnett, D. W., & Macmann, G. M. (1992). Decision reliability and validity: Contributions and limitations of alternative assessment strategies. *The Journal of Special Education, 25*(4) 431–452.

Ediger, M. (1993). Approaches to measurement and evaluation. *Studies in Educational Evaluation, 19*(1), 41–50.

Evans, C. S. (1993). When teachers look at student work. *Educational Leadership, 50*(5), 71–72.

Frisbie, D. A., & Waltman, K. K. (1993). Developing a personal grading plan. In K. M. Cauley, F. Linder, & J. H. McMillan (Eds.). *Educational psychology: Annual Editions Series* (pp. 216–224). Guilford, CT: Dushkin Publishing Group.

Gallini, J. (1982). Evidence of an adaptive level grading practice through a causal approach. *Journal of Experimental Education, 50*(4), 188–194.

Orstein, A.C. (1990). The evolving accountability movement. *Peabody Journal of Education, 65*(3), 12–20.

Perrone, V. (Ed.). (1991). *Expanding student assessment.* Alexandria, VA: Association for Supervision and Curriculum Development.

Pine, P. (1985). *Raising standards in schools: Problems and solutions. AASA critical issues report.* Arlington, VA: American Association of School Administrators.

Purkey, W. W., & Novak, J. M. (1984). *Inviting school success: A self-concept approach to teaching and learning* (2nd ed.). Belmont, CA: Wadsworth.

Robinson, G. E., & Craver, J. M. (1989). Assessing and grading student achievement. *ERS Report.* Arlington, VA: Educational Research Service.

Stiggins, R. (1987). Design and development of performance assessments. *Educational Measurement: Issues and Practices, 6*(3), 33–42.

Stiggins, R. (1988). Revitalizing classroom assessment. *Phi Delta Kappan, 69,* 5.

Valencia, S. (1990, January). A portfolio approach to classroom reading assessment: The whys, whats, and hows. *The Reading Teacher,* 338–340.

Wiggins, G. (1988). Rational numbers: Scoring and grading that helps rather than hurts learning. *American Educator, 12,* 4.

Wolf, D. P. (1989). Portfolio assessment: Sampling student work. *Educational Leadership, 46,* 35–59.

Section 8

Challenge Cases

The cases in this section are offered as a challenge to your ability to identify the key issues in a case when given only the case report and the authors' questions. The cases are all untitled, they contain no commentary, and there are no concluding questions, activities, or readings. You are on your own! You must decide what the main issue is for each case, analyze what is troubling the teacher, evaluate the teacher's level of reflective thinking, and then synthesize the material so that you can develop a set of strategies to help you deal with similar situations in your own classroom. One word of caution: The last case may prove to be the most challenging of all. The case demonstrates just how difficult it can be to sort out the real issues when human bias is involved. Good Luck!

Challenge Case 1

Background

I teach at an "alternative" high school. The program is designed to give students a second chance. The students come to our school for many different reasons. Some come because they choose to and because they did not do well in the regular high school setting; others are forced to attend either by their parents or, in some cases, by the courts.

Many people are surprised that, in this state, the law does not require that teachers in alternative high school programs be certified. In many cases, it's hard to find people who are willing to work with these students because of the students' "past histories"; therefore, a number of programs in other districts do not always use certified teachers for their classrooms. In my district, however, you must have a teaching certificate in order to teach in the program. I am a certified teacher, but in all honesty, my college training did not prepare me for this kind of program.

As you might imagine, I was a little worried going to my class the first day of school. I kept wondering: What was I in for? Will the students listen? What will I do if . . . ? It took a while for me to adjust to the situation and feel comfortable with the job, but during my past two years, I have managed to gain the respect of many students. I have come to enjoy talking to the students and working with them, and I find teaching in this program to be very rewarding.

Incident

I have encountered many interesting problems in the alternative education program. The most recent one occurred only a few weeks ago, just
after the students received their report cards. Mitch, a student at our
school, is highly thought of by many of the other students. He is quite
bright and is in our program because he is on probation and not allowed
to attend his regular high school. He must maintain passing grades or he
will be sent to juvenile jail.

Our school gives three progress reports every semester and the
grades are cumulative. In order to get any credit for a class, students
cannot miss more than 10 days of school and they must receive passing
grades on two progress reports. After looking over the grades on his
progress report, Mitch asked me the following, "I have a B– and a C+ on
my report cards. That means I've gotten passing grades on two of the
three progress reports. If I don't do anymore work for the rest of the
semester, will I pass if I just come to class?" I was on the spot. I knew
technically the answer was yes, but if I told him so, I knew he would
come in every day and just put his head down and sleep. Also, there were
several other students who would probably do the same. On the other
hand, if I told him no, I would be lying—and I have a policy of never
lying to my students because I believe this is important if I am to establish
a level of trust with them.

Discussion

Choosing my words carefully, and using our course description as a
reference, I told Mitch something to the effect that many important topics
have not been covered yet and overall he has not met all of the requirements. Later, I met with my co-workers and our boss and raised the issue.
No one knew why the policy was written the way it was, but technically
Mitch was correct. However, everyone agreed we cannot give credit to a
student for simply being a "warm body" for 6 of the 19 weeks.

Questions

1. Did I handle this situation in the best way possible?
2. Mitch is no fool—he had to know he was right. Fortunately, he
   didn't push it, but he could have. What should I have done if he
   had pushed the issue?
3. Is there ever a time when a teacher can withhold the truth from
   a student? Is there ever a time when it is okay to lie to a student?

4. What message are we sending to the students if we allow them to do just enough to pass the class? We have to set standards, but once the standards are met, are the students free to slough off the rest of the year?
5. Knowing that the policy isn't going to be changed any time in the near future, what can I do to make certain that this situation doesn't occur again?

Challenge Case 2

Background

Every classroom teacher has children with special needs. Some children have social difficulties and others have academic difficulties. One of my students, Jack, had previously been tested and labeled as learning disabled (LD), which makes him a special education student. In order to have a full understanding of Jack's difficulty and my dilemma, I must first explain our special education program.

After a child is tested and observed by a team of school staff, the team decides whether the student is in need of special education assistance. The team then determines the amount of time that a student is to spend with both the special education and regular classroom teachers. This time issue depends on how many subject areas require assistance and how many grade levels behind the child is. All of the special education children are mainstreamed into a regular education setting. They are spread evenly among the teachers so they are not set in a "tracked" classroom with low achievers. Our school policy also evenly spreads out high and middle achievers.

In Jack's class, I have two children who are mainstreamed from special education. Jack's main area of difficulty is reading. In my fourth-grade room, the lack of reading ability affects almost all of the other subject areas. Jack has been in the special reading program for two years and little progress has been reported.

At the start of the year, Jack was with me for math only. He received all other instruction from Mrs. Mitchell, the special education teacher.

Mrs. Mitchell approached me midyear and suggested that I teach Jack in science and social studies so he would not be behind the other children in fifth grade. After some discussion, I decided to teach him in these areas. During the time that I taught Jack these two subjects, he experienced some success and some failure. He had lots of teacher and peer help and he truly seemed to enjoy being part of the class for the additional time. He would sometimes volunteer to read aloud and, even though he did a poor job of reading the material, he had a very positive attitude. Mrs. Mitchell and I were pleased with our arrangement.

Incident

Parent-teacher conferences occurred about six weeks after Jack had made the switch to my room. Jack's mom attended the conferences and was quite reserved while Mrs. Mitchell and I were discussing Jack's strengths and weaknesses. It was not until we stopped speaking that I could sense the trouble in Jack's mother's eyes. She attempted to speak in an unemotional tone, but it was obvious that she was quite upset.

Her main concern was that Jack was not receiving the intense help that he needed in reading. She felt that by having me teach science and social studies to Jack, he was losing out on reading instruction. I explained that the time in question was never spent on reading. The only difference was that he received more individualized instruction in science and social studies with Mrs. Mitchell than he did in my classroom. I also discussed how I teach reading through the use of subject area material. Jack's mother's main concern at this point was that she felt Jack should receive increased instruction in reading and decreased instructional time in other areas. She expressed concern that she, as a parent, thought of this when it was really the responsibility of professional educators. After this meeting, Mrs. Mitchell and I decided to keep Jack in my classroom for science and math and that Mrs. Mitchell would provide reading instruction during the time that he previously spent on social studies.

Discussion

The development of an individual educational plan is an integral part of the special education program. The instructional plan for Jack was designed to include the same subject areas as all other fourth-grade students. This is our school policy with all special education students because we believe that it helps them succeed once they exit the special education program. It is apparent that the school policy was not successful for Jack. He had been in the program for two years with little progress. Something needed to change so that Jack could be more successful in reading and in his future educational career.

Questions

1. Should a child with special needs leave the regular classroom for individual instruction? What are the social implications of this action?
2. Should all children, no matter what their ability level, be expected to study all subjects?
3. Once a child enters a special education program, do teachers tend to accept the child's lower ability level or do they expect the child to achieve and eventually exit the program?
4. I think Jack's mother was correct when she said that Jack needed reading instruction more than he needed social studies, and it bothers me that I didn't recognize this before the mother brought it to my attention. How can I, as a teacher, learn to be more proactive so that I can provide a better educational opportunity for my students?
5. Jack took the extra instruction from Mrs. Mitchell to mean that he didn't do very well in my class. We both tried to reassure him that this wasn't true, but it took a lot of convincing before he began to accept it. How do you find the right placement for the child without causing the child some emotional trauma?
6. Which is more important for a child at this age: the curriculum, the development of reading skills, or the development of social skills?

Challenge Case 3

Background

In my second year of teaching, I started a seventh-grade foreign language program integrated with social studies and language arts curriculum. The goal of the program was to introduce students to three languages—Spanish, French, and German—and to stimulate the students' interest in foreign languages. One of the girls in my class, Stephanie, made me doubt the fact that I could persuade students to enjoy learning foreign languages.

Stephanie was a paraplegic from birth. I didn't know what caused this paralysis and I was not sure if I wanted to know. I was afraid if I knew the reason for her paralysis, it might cause me to pity her, so I did not seek out the information. I did know that Stephanie was a B student in her other classes and she seemed to be a good student. This was my first experience in dealing with a child in a wheelchair. I decided that, as far as possible, I would not treat her any differently than I did the other students in my class. She would be like all the other students to me and she would receive no special favors as far as the work expected in class.

In the second week of the class, I found Stephanie's paper to be identical to the paper of the girl who sat next to her. They both had three wrong answers and the answers to these questions were exactly the same. I approached both girls together outside of class. I told them that their papers were identical and that I considered that cheating. They were both going to receive zeros on their papers. Stephanie and the other girl both denied cheating. I told them I was still going to give them zeros and that

I expected each of them to do her own work. After this incident, Stephanie developed a really bad attitude. I tried very hard to be low keyed with her and not react to her negative attitude, however. I joked with her and her neighbor but it didn't change their attitude toward me.

About this time, Stephanie was beginning to develop a friendship with the girl who sat next to her. I was now starting to see them together outside of class. Stephanie seemed to be trying very hard to make friends with this girl—almost too hard. Stephanie was at the age where one of the most important things is how many friends you have and how popular you are. In middle school, the last thing you want to be is different, but for Stephanie there was no way she could avoid this. To be part of the "in crowd," she would have had to be part of the sports teams. Stephanie could not be a part of the girls basketball team, the marching band, or cheerleading. I think she was having a very hard time dealing with this. It seemed that the anger at being in a wheelchair was being changed to a negative attitude against the world. I became very concerned and asked some of her teachers if they noticed this same attitude. They said that they did and that Stephanie's mother knew and understood that Stephanie was going through a very tough time.

Incident

As part of my class, the students use their foreign language phrases to develop skits that they perform in front of the class. I told the students they would be able to pick their own groups the first time, but if there were problems, I would pick the groups the next time. I expected Stephanie to be with her new friend but this did not happen. Usually, if a student does not have a group, I just ask the nearest group to add a student. In the past, this had never created a problem, but Stephanie refused to be a part of any group. She refused to do the assignment. When I told her that if she was not a part of a group, she would receive an F on the assignment, she still didn't change her mind. After the event, I let Stephanie's mother know what had happened and she said she would talk to Stephanie about it.

About two weeks later, I assigned the same skit in another language. Since there had been a problem with Stephanie and another group, I decided to assign students to groups this time. Stephanie still refused to do the assignment. I kept Stephanie after class so that we could talk in private. When I asked Stephanie why she refused to do the assignment, she simply replied that she did not want to do it or to be a part of any group. She said none of the people in class were her friends and she could not work with them. I explained to her that we do not always get to work with people we like. Her response was that she really could not work with these people. I made a judgment call and told her that I would make an exception in this case. She would have to develop a skit and then read it in front of me alone. She agreed to this and followed through with the assignment.

When I made my judgment, I had the feeling that Stephanie was too embarrassed to be involved in something that she would have to do in front of the class. I am not sure if Stephanie was too embarrassed to be a part of the group or if she felt as if she did not belong. My belief is that it was a combination of both of these that caused her to refuse to be a part of a group.

Discussion

Even though I took the time to talk to Stephanie and I made an exception for her, her attitude did not change. By the end of the 10-week class, she was not studying or doing her work. She received a D in the class, not just because of the skits, but because she was not putting any effort into the class. She had no enthusiasm for foreign language at all. I made several attempts to warm up to Stephanie and to get her involved in the class, but her negative attitude continued. Stephanie was still trying hard to be her neighbor's friend. The girl seemed to like Stephanie a lot, but sometimes I had the feeling that she also felt burdened by her. When I say "burdened," I mean that Stephanie wanted to be the girl's only friend. Stephanie became very jealous when the girl spoke to anyone else. If was almost as if the girl felt required to be Stephanie's friend. I did not get involved because I felt that Stephanie needed to learn about friendship on her own. I also felt that Stephanie did not like me, so what I would have to say would be disregarded anyway.

Questions

1. Did I do Stephanie a kindness by making an exception for her, or did I do more harm than good?
2. Are you really able to treat a child with a disability the same as other students, with no exceptions?
3. Should I have pushed Stephanie to be the same as the other children, or should I have let her develop an interest in the project on her own?
4. Can a teacher expect to create an interest in his or her class for every student? Are there some students that a teacher just will not be able to get through to?
5. Should I have found out all of the information on Stephanie's case before she entered my class, or should I have waited to develop my own opinion of her?

Challenge Case 4

Background

Paul Smith entered our school this fall as a freshman. He came to us from a small, private school where he was in a classroom of approximately eight students and where, according to his mother, he received a lot of individual attention. His mother told us that Paul had previously been diagnosed as having Attention Deficit Disorder (ADD), although this information was not included in his school records. He was scheduled to be tested by the school psychologist for our county, but, as of February 1, the testing had not been done.

Incident

Paul transferred into my Typing/Word Processing class about halfway through the first nine-week marking period. At that time, I had no information about him and handled him as I would any student coming into my class. We had already covered the introduction to the keyboard, two chapters on the word-processing program, and some background information on computers. Nothing he had missed up to that point, however, would prevent him from achieving success on the work that was currently being assigned.

Paul's typing speed was slower than most of the students in the class, but I figured that this would pick up as he acquired more experience on the computer. Since assignments were graded according to accuracy, not speed, I didn't have any reservations about his ability to succeed in my class. Most of the other students were typing about 20 words a minute at that point, having had at least nine weeks of typing in seventh and eighth grades. Paul had no previous experience in a typing class. I told him my expectations were that he would increase his speed every week by 1 word a minute (which was my expectation for the rest of the class as well). I told him to ask for help whenever he needed it, and I checked on him periodically.

It soon became apparent that Paul was getting behind. I would discover halfway through the class period that he was having difficulty loading a program on his computer, but he wouldn't ask for help. He had different problems every day, but the results were the same—he wasn't getting his work done. I started paying more attention to him during class. Often, I would observe him sitting at his computer doing nothing. When I would ask him if he had a problem, sometimes he would say "Yes" and I would work with him to solve the problem. At other times, he wouldn't have a problem—he just hadn't been on task.

I assigned another student to work with Paul, but this didn't produce the desired results either. When Paul did manage to complete his work and turn it in, it was always full of typing and/or formatting errors. My policy was to allow students to correct any assignments with a grade below C, so I would return his work to him and ask him to redo it. This created another problem. Since he had other work to do, he just got further behind, and often his corrected copies were not any better than his original copies. I asked Paul to come in during his study hall to try to catch up, but he often stated that he had work to do for his other classes. At this point, I spoke to our school counselor to get some background information on Paul. I was told he was going to be evaluated by the school psychologist and that he was thought to have ADD. He was experiencing difficulty in all his classes. I was reluctant to take him from his study hall to do work for my class if he needed the time for his basic, academic classes.

I asked Paul to come in after school so I could work with him one on one. He did arrange to stay after school but chose a day that I was unavailable to stay. This was right before Christmas vacation. When school resumed after Christmas break, I spoke to his mother by phone and asked her if she had any suggestions. She did not. I told her I had some other ideas, but that it was more than likely that Paul would fail this grading period.

Discussion

I felt frustrated because I was not really sure how to help Paul. He was not what one would think of as a typical ADD student. Other students I have had with ADD have been extremely hyperactive—demanding attention by their behavior. Paul was a quiet student who could easily get overlooked because he never caused a disturbance. He just didn't focus on the task. I suspect he got distracted or just daydreamed. This was compounded by the fact that he wasn't a fast typist. His speed had not improved much since his first day in class.

One weekend, I decided to develop a plan for helping Paul. The plan looked something like this:

1. Make contact with Paul at least twice during each class to be sure that he is on task and not having any computer problems.
2. Continue to have another student beside him who can help him when necessary.
3. During my free period, meet with Paul during his study hall on a regular basis so I can give him one-on-one attention. On these days, he will go to study hall during his usual time in my class. This way, I will not be "robbing" him of his study hall, but I will have time to work with him individually.
4. Have Paul proofread his own work to determine if he can really "see" his errors. It may be that he has a reading-related problem that causes him difficulty in this area.
5. Focus on having Paul turn in quality work (i.e., work with few or no errors) rather than having him turn in quantity (i.e., keeping pace with the rest of the class).
6. Continue to work with the counseling office and wait for results of the psychological testing.

That Monday, as I walked into the building, I was explaining to another teacher my plan for Paul. Suddenly, Paul appeared—with his right arm in a cast. He had broken his arm over the weekend and would be in the cast for at least the rest of this grading period.

Questions

1. Since Paul has learned the rudiments of typing, would he be better off dropping this class now (since we just began a new semester)—especially since he has broken his arm?
2. Is my solution of working with him during my free period really a good solution? I can do this because I teach only half time, but I would be teaching him individually—in essence adding another "class" to my schedule.
3. I have the option of grading Paul on a pass/fail basis. If I chose this option, what minimum standards would be acceptable for passing?

4. Even if I don't put him on pass/fail, I will have to give him an ability grade because I'm requiring less work from him than the other students (lower typing speed, less work in terms of quantity). Is this a good alternative? What minimum standards should be considered acceptable? (An ability grade is a grade our school allows us to give based on a student's efforts to work to his or her potential. It is noted on the student's permanent record as such.)

Challenge Case 5

Background

There are many situations that occur during a school year that require teacher intervention. Some are of a larger scale than others, but often the smaller-scale incidents linger in a teacher's mind. The situation I will discuss is one of these smaller, yet significant, occasions.

Becky's mother came to see me at the beginning of the school year to inform me that Becky had very low self-esteem. Becky, a fourth-grader, was extremely overweight for her age and was often teased because of her physical appearance. The previous year, she had attended group counseling sessions that were designed to help her and the other participants develop a higher confidence level. As a result of these sessions, her mother was confident that Becky had overcome the problems associated with her low self-image and now accepted herself as she was.

Becky was very quiet at the beginning of the year and she seemed to have no friends. However, she warmed up to me very quickly and she didn't act quite as shy when she was around me. I noticed that she tended to have a better rapport with adults than with her peers. This is probably due to the fact that adults are not as critical of her physical appearance as her peers are.

Early in the school year, I spoke with Becky's teacher from the previous year. She inquired as to how Becky was progressing and, in the course of our conversation, mentioned that she suspected that Becky had cheated on assignments and tests, although she was unable to confirm her suspicions.

Throughout the school year, Becky appeared to be doing well. The classroom was organized in cooperative groups, so many social and academic interactions between students occurred all day long. Students learned how to participate as a cooperative group member in a process that was learned and experienced throughout the year. Normally, problems with the group process decrease the longer the group works together. With Becky's group, however, the problems had continued and, instead of lessening, they grew. I met with the groups whenever they had a problem, which was a fairly regular occurrence with Becky's group. The source of the conflict was usually Becky. The other group members always seemed to have the same two complaints—either Becky was copying off their work or she was taking charge of a group assignment rather than acting as a participating member of the group. I tried to implement strategies that would help the group solve their own problems and, on several occasions, I had a private chat with Becky about her behavior.

I came to realize that Becky could be a bit bossy and that she had difficulty compromising. If there was an assignment that required a partner, Becky usually was left without one. A few times, I paired her up with Katelyn. Katelyn was an easy-going girl and I thought she would be able to work with Becky. This worked only for a short time. A couple of days after the two girls had handed in a report that they had worked on together, Katelyn came to me to complain. She told me that she had done all the work for the report and Becky had not done what they had agreed she would do. I talked to Becky about this. She seemed flustered and I had a hard time getting a straight answer from her. Again, I discussed the rules for working as a team member. I also told Katelyn that she should have discussed the situation with me prior to handing in the report so that we could have worked out a solution. I did not change Becky's grade for the report.

Both of Becky's parents attended the spring parent-teacher conferences. After we had discussed Becky's academic progress, I mentioned that Becky was having difficulty participating as a team member. Becky's mother became very upset and she verbally lambasted me with such statements as, "Don't you know that children at this age don't work together well?" I informed her that this was not my experience and that I had my students work in cooperative groups for the last three years. She continued to make excuses for Becky's "bossy" (her words) personality and her weight problem. The conference ended when the next set of parents arrived. The strange part was that Becky's parents left saying that this was the best year that Becky had ever had and that they were pleased with her progress. My impression of the conference was that the father knew exactly what I was talking about and that the mother made excuses for Becky instead of helping Becky address and deal with her problems. This seemed to be especially true of Becky's weight problem, which the mother thought was the cause of all of Becky's problems.

Incident

Occasionally, if I got bogged down in correcting math papers, I would ask if a student would like to come in after lunch and help me out. I would then randomly select an interested student. Becky was chosen to correct papers shortly after the spring parent-teacher conferences. Before she came to correct the papers, I scanned her paper for errors. She had at least five errors on her paper, but I did not mark or correct her paper. After Becky corrected the papers, I leafed through to see what grade she received. Becky had given herself 100 percent on her paper. It was evident that she had erased and changed her answers. I told Becky that I had checked her paper before giving her the stack and saw that she had several answers incorrect. I pointed out how I could see where she had erased and changed her answers. She stood silent, with an expression of being caught in a situation in which there was no way out. I discussed with her the fact that if I thought she was doing 100 percent work, I would know she understood the concepts, but if she got several incorrect answers, then I would know that she needed extra help and I would be able to help her. I tried to stress that by not letting me know she didn't understand something, she was cheating herself.

Discussion

Becky continued to be quite bossy with the other children and they continued to complain about her copying their work but, because school was almost out and I was exasperated with the situation, I let Becky's behavior slide near the end of the year. I knew she was cheating and that she was having trouble working in groups, but I just didn't say anything. Unfortunately, the possibility exists that I will have Becky next year for fifth grade. I had enough trouble dealing with Becky this year—I don't know how I will be able to deal with her next year.

Questions

1. Should I have contacted the parents after I caught Becky cheating the first time?
2. Was there a better way for me to deal with Becky when it was so obvious that she had cheated?

3. Did I unfairly set Becky up for the incident? After all, I did look at her paper before I left it for her to grade. Should I have gone ahead and marked it so that she wouldn't have been tempted to cheat?

4. What do you do with a child who the other students won't accept as a member of their group, especially when using cooperative learning as an instructional technique?

5. If I have Becky in my class next year, how can I more effectively deal with her and her parents?

6. If Becky's problems do stem from her low self-esteem, what can I do to help her deal with the problem more effectively?

Challenge Case 6

Background

Every teacher must develop his or her own way of managing student assignments and paperwork. A highly organized system makes it easier to retrieve completed work, to correct the papers in a timely fashion, and to provide feedback to both students and parents. I believe that it is important to be consistent in the way in which students' work and notes to parents are sent home. My system is not fancy, but it usually does the job. There was one time, however, when my system caused problems rather than prevented them.

At the Open House in early fall, I explained to the parents that student folders would be sent home on Mondays. "These folders will contain all corrected work, notices, and notes from me" was what my parents heard me say in September. I continued by saying, "If your child has any missing work, I will make note of it in the folder. Please sign the folder and have your child return it on Tuesday morning. There is also a spot on the form for any comments that you might like to make." I began this system because of the districtwide policy that all school notices are to be sent home on Mondays. This consistency of communications has proven to be an excellent way to keep parents informed of school activities and of their children's progress.

For most of the year, I followed this procedure routinely and it worked well. Communications between home and school were greatly improved by the system. The students knew that if they didn't complete their work throughout the week, their parents would know about it. This fact provided extra motivation for the students to complete their seat-work.

To allow for individual differences in time needed to complete assignments, I collected all assignments the day after they were given. I had all the students turn in their work at the same time. I then attempted to grade their work that night and put it in their mailboxes the next morning. This usually provided quick feedback. Some children checked their boxes regularly and others did not. At the fourth-grade level, I preferred this method over the common one where students put their work in a specific basket.

Incident

At the time of the incident, my system was to grade an individual's assignment and then immediately record it in my gradebook. This seemed to expedite paperwork because I did two tasks at once and handled the work only once. This was the specific spot of the "system failure." On Monday, I recorded missing assignments in the comments column of each folder, along with other comments that I might have about the child's work for that week. If, on Tuesday, a student returned the missing work along with the Monday folder, there was no late penalty. For each day that the paperwork was late, I would mark the grade down 10 points. I provided rewards for children who were not missing paperwork and other rewards for those who turned in missing work on Tuesday.

Tommy, a student in my class, often had missing work recorded in his Monday folder. When he took his folder home on the second Monday in April, it indicated that he was missing an assignment and a test. On Tuesday, I asked Tommy for his folder. He informed me that his mother would be bringing it in after school. My curiosity was piqued because his mother is not a frequent visitor to the classroom.

At 3:30, when I returned from taking my students to their buses, Tommy's mother was waiting. She had Tommy's missing test in her hand. I glanced at the test and could see that I had already graded it. Tommy's mother was anything but pleased. I attempted to handle the situation by explaining that I had made a mistake and I was sorry. I also told her that I always ask the students to check through their folders as I hand them out to see if I have made the very mistake that I did in Tommy's case. She was too upset to let it go at that, and then she let it slip that she was considering going to the principal to complain. My blood pressure rose but I commented very calmly, "We can go discuss this with him now if you wish." She declined but insisted that most of Tommy's missing assignments throughout the year might not be his fault at all but rather be a result of my disorganization. I informed my principal of the incident as soon as Tommy's mother left.

I thought about what Tommy's mother said and, although I knew that Tommy's other assignments had not been turned in, I did set up a new system to organize Tommy's work so that there would be no doubt in the future. Tommy was given a clipboard with a sheet for his daily assignments. I insisted that Tommy must take some responsibility and that he was to write down each assignment in every subject. I would then initial the correct spot when I collected the completed work. His mom was to sign the sheet if she saw Tommy complete the work at home. This system made all of us a little bit more accountable for our work.

Discussion

Tommy's work habits improved immediately. He still had missing assignments from time to time, but the assignment chart worked wonders for him. His attitude about school improved and his self-esteem soared. I did not return a corrected paper to him without first recording it. I handled each paper twice. The first time around, I checked all papers. The second handling was reserved for recording all grades. I goofed with a few other students after that, but never Tommy. My new management system required a bit more time, but it was more effective. Tommy's mother was supportive of the system and never complained again.

Questions

1. Was it fair to my other 30 students that I gave Tommy's assignments much more individual attention? By doing so, did I communicate to the children that they needed to have a problem before they could get individual attention from me?
2. Is there a better way to collect, record, and return students' work, and communicate the results to the parents weekly?
3. Did I overreact by changing my whole system when there was only one parent who complained?
4. It is possible that more than one assignment was misrecorded, although I doubt it. If I had found that I had misrecorded several assignments, how should I have corrected my mistake?
5. Why would Tommy's attitude toward school improve and his self-confidence increase simply because of the new system?

Challenge Case 7

Background

George was a 12-year-old seventh-grade student when he entered our small, rural public school. The school district consisted of approximately 1,000 students between kindergarten and twelfth grade. This traditional school district had very limited resources for educational purposes. Monies needed for special education or remedial classes were scarce.

George had very limited abilities and consistently received very low marks (Ds and D–s). He seemed socially immature and was occasionally ostracized by other students. His very quiet, introverted personality led to social isolation. However, his social and academic inabilities never caused behavioral problems in the classroom. The county school psychologist tested George when he was in the third grade. It was found that he had an IQ of 74. In this state, a student with an IQ of 70 or lower is considered Emotionally/Mentally Impaired (EMI) and is eligible for a special education placement. Because George's score was 74, he remained in the regular classroom. George's parents were contacted several times regarding George's lack of ability and progress, but they denied that their child needed any special education and they remained uninvolved.

Incident

In the classroom, George exhibited low self-esteem and nervousness. His body language suggested that he was very introverted and evasive.

When he was having trouble with the instructional material, George had a very difficult time approaching his teacher for clarification or help.

As George's English teacher, I immediately began to notice his exceptionally low academic and mental abilities. It was evident that, regardless of how much effort George put into a task, his reading and writing skills were extremely limited. His written work was always turned in on time but it was very difficult to read or interpret. He seemed to be trying, but he just didn't possess the reading and writing skills of the average seventh-grader. Throughout this period, I tried to contact George's parents, but they apparently did not perceive his inabilities as severe and they remained uninvolved and unconcerned.

I finally brought the matter to the attention of the principal. I made a list of the various problems that George was experiencing and showed examples of his work to the principal. The principal proceeded with an analysis of George's academic history and test results. Because George's IQ score was above the cutoff of 70 and because George was not a behavioral problem, the principal determined that George could not be considered EMI or receive special education. The principal then decided that it would be best for George to continue in the regular classroom. I questioned whether this was the best decision, since it was so obvious that George needed special help. I told the principal that there must be a way that the school could make an exception in this case and I pleaded with him to help me find a way to get the extra help that George needed. He stated very bluntly, "There is nothing we can do. The school district has very limited funds and resources and we can service only so many special education students." It was evident to me that the principals's final decision was influenced more by the school's limited funds than by the needs of the student.

Although I did not agree with the decision, I felt that I had to abide by it. As a nontenured teacher, I did what I could for a student who no one else saw as a problem. I tried to give George as much individual help as possible, but, because of my large class load, the amount of individual instruction I was able to provide was very limited.

Discussion

Several factors must be taken into account when determining a student's need for special education. The state has said that students with an IQ of 70 or less are eligible for special education. However, in George's case, it is highly evident that he is in need of special education. In his situation, another IQ test should have been administered to determine his current status. Results taken from a test administered three or four years ago may not be representative of his current ability. When there are limited resources, are the ethics of education being compromised? If so, there must be alternative ways of giving academically needy children the attention and help they deserve. If George had received individual instruction, his reading and writing skills might have improved.

It is obvious that George's inabilities should have been recognized and dealt with when he was much younger. I recognized George's needs early and acted quickly in what I thought was an appropriate manner in an effort to meet his instructional needs. However, in my opinion, the principal made a grave error in not pursuing the matter further (i.e., having the child retested). This child has been, and probably will continue to be, passed along year after year without receiving the necessary attention.

Questions

1. What are some recommended alternatives that may be implemented to help the children whose needs are not met due to limited resources?
2. What are some suggested guidelines for determining the need for special education for a particular child?
3. What can a teacher do to respond to the needs of a child who does not test low enough on the IQ test to be eligible for special education but who obviously needs a lot of extra attention?
4. When a child who has special needs has been assigned to a classroom, what should the teacher do when he or she does not have the skills or knowledge to deal with the special need?
5. I believe that George's previous teachers gave him a passing grade just because he tried hard. This allowed him to proceed to the next grade level with little reading and writing skills. What else might they have done? Would it be fair to fail George when he doesn't have the ability to do the work? Is it fair to give him passing grades when he hasn't met the basic requirements?

Challenge Case 8

Background

Approximately 300 of the 940 students in my K–6 school are ESL (English as a Second Language) children. Nine languages are represented in the school. In my class of 34 fifth-graders, 15 are ESL. Spanish, Vietnamese, Lao, Afghan, and Navajo are the non-English languages spoken in my classroom. My class is considered a "regular" classroom and I am not a certified ESL teacher. Of my 15 ESL students, 6 go to the ESL teacher for reading; 4 also go to the ESL teacher during the last period of the day for additional English instruction. An aide, shared by all of the fifth- and sixth-grade teachers, assists the other ESL students while they are in my class. Dealing with limited-English-proficient children is nothing new at our school.

A Vietnamese boy named Vinh presented a special problem for me. Vinh came to my room as a new student in October. I had three other Vietnamese students in my class, but Vinh was different because he was not even literate in his own language and had practically no formal education whatsoever. I learned from his mother during parent-teacher conferences that Vinh had been to what was the equivalent of second grade for three months in Vietnam. That was the only time he had been to school. Through a translator, Vinh's mother explained that Vinh did not like school in Vietnam, so she didn't force him to attend. When he came to my class, Vinh didn't know how to hold a pencil, open a book, or speak or understand a word of English. It was apparent that he had never before sat at a desk.

Incident

I could see right away that Vinh was not fitting in socially or academically. He was not familiar with the letters of the alphabet or with numbers. My students are used to new students from other countries and they are always happy to "Americanize" these students, but they soon saw that Vinh was different. His unpredictable scratching made them uncomfortable. He had no idea of what was appropriate and inappropriate behavior in the classroom—or in any public setting. Although I rarely heard any rude remarks directed at Vinh, I did see some patronizing behavior toward him—most of it was probably unintentional, however. Some students would pat him on his head as if he were a puppy or talk to him in a voice appropriate for speaking to babies or pets.

I came up with three options for how to help Vinh. One choice was to move him down to first or second grade. Vinh's mother had confirmed that he was 10 years old, but he was much smaller than all of my students, even the other Asian children. He could easily pass for a first- or second-grader. Our (unwritten) district policy on this matter is to place the student at an age-appropriate level. This is designed to help build the student's self-concept. It is permissible to have students receive special instruction at their ability level for individual subjects. In other words, I could keep Vinh in my fifth-grade class but send him to a lower grade for math and language instruction.

Another choice would be to place Vinh in the self-contained learning disabled (LD) class. Because Vinh was definitely two years below grade level, he would easily qualify for placement in the fifth-grade special education class. However, Vinh would then most likely be labeled LD—a label he would carry with him throughout his education, even though he may not be LD. Vinh would also need to be tested before he could be enrolled in the LD class. The district recommends that formal assessment for ESL students be given after some progress is made—at least one year after enrollment.

A third choice was to keep Vinh in my room but try to increase his amount of ESL instruction, thus helping him to catch up faster. Initially, he would follow a separate curriculum. Eventually, he might be able to do the work the class is doing, with some adaptations.

My initial choice was to move him to first grade. Socially, he did not fit in with the fifth-graders. He looked, acted, and performed academically like a first-grader. Which was worse—to be in a class with younger students doing what they were doing or to be in a class of similar-age students put in a corner somewhere doing completely different work? Those were my thoughts during those first frustrating weeks. The more I thought about it, the more I realized that if Vinh moved to first or second grade, he would be 15 to 16 years old in the sixth grade. He could probably progress more quickly through the curriculum in a fifth-grade class than in a first-grade room. I also learned that Vinh had another brother who was in third grade. If Vinh were moved down, his brother would need to be moved down also.

Having Vinh go to a language or math class at the second-grade level was considered, but those rooms are quite a distance across campus. Vinh was just adjusting to school and to my class. Trying to get him to understand to go to a different room with different students and a different teacher at certain times of the day would have been confusing for him, to say the least.

I next ruled out the option of moving Vinh to the LD room. Sure, Vinh would no longer be my problem, but would he be better off in a class made up mostly of students who had social or behavioral problems? He most likely would not be accepted by them. There were no other Asian students in that class. At least in my class, there were other Vietnamese students who could explain things to him in his own language.

So, I chose the third option. Vinh stayed in my class and received extra pull-out help. He went to the ESL class for reading during one other period, as four of my other ESL students did. The ESL teacher was able to work with Vinh two days out of five during the time my students went to music class. In addition, a volunteer from a community group that works with our school happily agreed to work with Vinh every Tuesday for an additional hour.

Vinh stayed in my class for three 50-minute periods: math, language, and spelling/oral reading. At first, I gave him completely different work from what the rest of my students were given. He could not even write or understand the numbers 1 through 10, so there was no way he could do double-digit multiplication, which was what my students were doing in math. In language, I had him practice printing the alphabet. In spelling, he just copied the words for that week. I would often assign a student to help him.

The ESL teacher and I developed a list of objectives for Vinh to work on during the first month. He learned his numbers and alphabet and mastered addition and subtraction with regrouping. He began to read and write short, simple words. After four months, he began working on multiplication and writing simple sentences to make a story. He became more culturally aware and was able to get along with other students.

Discussion

Anytime a teacher feels that he or she is taking a substantial amount of time for just one student, there is frustration—especially when that extra time does not seem to solve the problem. I felt that since I wasn't an ESL teacher or a primary teacher, I really did not know how to deal with Vinh's deficiencies.

The regular classroom setting just did not seem to be the place for him, yet I could come up with no other viable alternative. Our district has no program for completely monolingual students new to this country. Vinh would have benefited greatly from a bilingual program that focused on basic survival English and cultural awareness. Unfortunately, with budget cuts, this will never happen—not in the near future anyway. The district obviously does not see this as a need. It does not even have a written set of guidelines for what to do in this instance—nor does the state.

If I ever have another student similar to Vinh in my classroom, I will know that I should develop a set of learning objectives right away. This way, all the teachers working with the new student will be working on the same things. I would also talk with my homeroom students more about the new student. They need to discuss their feelings. It wouldn't be difficult to turn the "new-student" challenge into a learning opportunity for everyone.

Questions

1. Is the regular classroom the best placement for non-English-speaking students new to this country?
2. What policies or procedures can schools or districts establish to assist teachers when they receive these students?
3. How can teachers deal sensitively yet firmly with cultural differences that may be disruptive to the classroom?
4. How can teachers establish a classroom environment that is open to different cultures?

Challenge Case 9

Background

It was late in the school year and the attention of the teachers on our elementary staff had turned to placing students in new classes for the next year. I had just received the list of children who were to be in my room and I was surprised to find two students with the same last name. When my inquiry about the matter reached the third-grade teachers who had written the list, they were dismayed about the placements. They told me that the father had requested that the girls, who were fraternal twins, be placed in the same classroom for fourth grade. The girls' present teachers were both adamantly against this.

The principal told me that the father had indeed pressed the point with her. His reasoning was that the girls had never before been placed together and he wanted them to share a classroom now. He had been making this request for a number of years and this year, with an impending divorce in the family, he wanted the girls to be together to provide a support system of sorts for each other. The principal told me that she had "run out of reasons for telling him no" and so fourth grade was to be the grade that the girls would be together.

Incident

From the outset of the first day of school, it was obvious that both girls had problems. In my classroom, the children are allowed to sit where they choose and both girls opted to sit by each other. Later, as I was to discover, this would prove very difficult in fully integrating the girls with the other students in the room.

One of the twins, Lynne, was overweight and always dressed in a masculine manner. Her greasy hair was unstyled and contrasted sharply with the intricate hairstyles of many of the other girls in the room. Her sister Linda was not as heavy, but she was extremely sensitive and often perceived the other children as being mean to her. Upon close examination, it was determined that Linda was often the one who would cause an incident, but she would refuse to admit it.

Both girls had the ability to do well in the classroom, but Linda showed little interest in the class activities. The one exception was spelling, where she took pride in spelling words of great difficulty. Linda had trouble meeting deadlines for assignments, particularly long-range ones. In addition, because she had not developed any peer-group relationships, she did not mind spending recess time inside completing work that was due.

Lynne, on the other hand, blossomed. She was an excellent writer and a hard worker. She displayed a keen sense of humor and seemed to thoroughly enjoy the creative activities in the classroom. What concerned me was that, even though at times her sister obviously annoyed her and she would physically separate her desk a few inches from Linda's, she would never choose to move her seat to another area in the classroom. Despite my encouragement and the many opportunities she had to move her seat, Lynne never voluntarily chose to do so and I didn't wish to push her. It also concerned me that, when Linda was absent from school, Lynne wouldn't make any special effort to make sure her sister knew what work was due. I always had to ask her to tell her sister. Even when Linda was present in class, Lynne would come in unprepared and offer excuses for not knowing what to do. This was in spite of the fact that Lynne had completed her homework and she had the books and other materials that Linda might have needed at home.

As Linda slipped further behind, I became increasingly concerned. Efforts to work with the father (the mother no longer lived at home) were not successful. During the conferences, the father came across as wanting to help and agreeing with my concerns, but when left to deal with his daughter's problem at home, he seemed incapable of helping resolve the problem.

Linda also was straining our student/teacher relationship. It was difficult for me to go through her assignments with her every afternoon before she went home and then have her either "pick and choose" what she felt like doing or, worse yet, produce nothing at all.

Slowly, Lynne began to take on Linda's attitude. Sometimes she would have her work done, but other times she would have done nothing and could offer no explanation for her lack of work. The final straw came when we had a major research project due on the rain forest. Lynne was unprepared and was sullen when questioned about her report. It wasn't until she realized that she would not be able to participate in the video our class was making on the rain forest that she showed any kind of remorse.

Throughout the semester, I had been filing paperwork with the Child Study Team in our school. We had a new social worker assigned to the girls' case and it was discovered that this particular family had been investigated for suspected child abuse on at least one occasion. Nothing concrete was uncovered. Despite interviews with personnel from the Department of Human Services, our school social worker, and the school psychologist, the girls would not admit to anything abnormal going on at home. Lynne did draw some pictures that aroused suspicion at the social worker's interview, but, because the girls would not reveal anything about their family life, the investigation came to a dead end.

My principal was aware of the situation with the girls and had been kept informed throughout the year, but she was not especially involved or supportive. She seemed to adopt a "What can we do?" posture and, while she acknowledged that there was a problem, she didn't feel that, given the circumstances, there was much more we could do to help. I continued to feel frustrated. I wished that there was some kind of evidence of abuse so that the girls could truly be helped out of what I felt was a difficult home situation, yet I knew there was little we could do in the absence of such evidence. We continued to provide support for the girls in the school.

Discussion

It is my opinion that placing the twins in the same classroom was a grave mistake. Our fourth-grade classes are self-contained and the students in the class do not interact with other fourth-graders except at recess, lunch, and before school while lining up. Although the father may have envisioned a support system for the girls, I felt Lynne was inhibited by her sister's actions and many times even embarrassed by them. I also felt that Lynne didn't try as hard as she could to fit in because her sister Linda would have appeared even more isolated. I think that by placing the twins together, we made a bad situation worse.

In our school, parent requests for specific teachers and placements with other students are often granted, even against the professional judgments of the educators involved. It is not uncommon for us to submit a class list in June and find that changes have been made in the finalized class list distributed in August. Often, students who do not work well together will be separated by the teachers but will end up in the same class because of the changes that were made over the summer. By honoring parents' requests without strong educational reasons, the principal is in danger of making poor decisions, as I believe she did in this case. I truly feel that final class placement decisions should best be left to the teachers directly involved with the students and that, although parental input can certainly be welcomed, the parents need to understand that their every wish will not necessarily be granted.

Looking at this situation, I do not feel that siblings should be placed in the same classroom because it can place large amounts of pressure on the children and teacher involved. I also feel that our principal should have been more assertive in explaining to the father why it would not be a good idea for his daughters to be placed together in the same classroom. Although I should have spoken up and more strongly objected to the twins being placed in the same room, I did not know the girls when the decision was made and I needed the principal to serve as an advocate. By acquiescing to the father's request, she did nothing to support the decision of her teachers.

Questions

1. What factors should be considered in choosing class placement for children for the following school year? Which factors would you rank as being the most important and why?
2. How could I have served as an intermediary to help integrate the twins into the activities in the classroom?
3. Should I have made the girls sit in different parts of the room, even though I allowed the other children to sit where they wanted?
4. Do you feel that Linda's academic program should have been modified and her requirements lessened to help her cope with possible stresses at home during this time? How might this have been accomplished without sending Linda the wrong message about not completing assignments? How might this have affected Lynne's work?
5. When I was informed that there was a possibility of child abuse, was there something more I should have done to help the girls?
6. If there was child abuse in the home, would the fact that the girls had been placed in the same room at school helped or hindered them in dealing with the abusive situation?

Challenge Case 10

Background

The high school in which I teach is considered to be the premier high school in our area. Although most of the parents can afford to send their children to private school, they elect to send them to public school because of our reputation as an outstanding academic institution. As teachers, we often form a close bond with our students that extends beyond an interest in their academic achievement to an interest in their social development as well. We feel that this is especially important since our high school is so competitive and many of our students are under great stress as a result of the high expectations that everyone holds for them. Occasionally, our compassion for a pupil will conflict with our need to uphold principles and standards that all students should learn to respect. The incident I am about to relate is one such case.

The incident involves Nadine, a senior, who served as a role model for many of the girls in the school. She was a member of the National Honor Society, had been nominated for membership in the Quill and Scroll Honorary Society for Scholastic Journalism, and held a position in the student government. Nadine was respected by the faculty for the positive role she played and was recognized as a bright, academically oriented young woman who was always willing to help in any way she could.

Incident

A couple of days prior to spring break, Nadine told me that Michelle, a student in her advanced placement English class, had accused her of stealing her paper. Both Michelle and Nadine had been working in the computer lab on their analyses of *Wuthering Heights,* which was due to Mr. Sharp, the English teacher, before they left for spring break. Nadine had looked over Michelle's shoulder to see how she was coming along. Michelle immediately began to rant furiously, accusing Nadine of copying her paper. Knowing that both Nadine and Michelle were strong students, I attributed the outbreak to stress, since students had a great deal of work to complete before the end of the semester. The idea that Nadine had copied Michelle's paper never crossed my mind. Mr. Sharp, whom Michelle approached, similarly dismissed the incident and also attributed it to adolescent stress.

However, after the students left for spring break, the issue became more complicated. Mr. Sharp realized he was unable to assign midterm grades to either Michelle or Nadine because not one, but two, of their papers, *Macbeth* and *Wuthering Heights,* were almost identical. The *Macbeth* paper had been due several weeks prior to the spring break, but Mr. Sharp had been unable to find the time to correct it until after the students had left for vacation. Although he felt guilty about not grading the papers earlier, he realized that the only thing to do was to take the matter up with the principal.

As soon as the girls returned, each was summoned to the principal's office to be confronted by the principal and Mr. Sharp. Michelle was able to produce rough drafts with handwritten corrections for both papers. Nadine said that she had made all her revisions directly on her computer disk and steadfastly maintained that the papers were her own work. The principal tried logic, reason, and even staring Nadine down to try to make her confess. At one point, Nadine remarked, "Maybe I'm psychic," to explain the similarity between the papers that had been laid before her. Finally, the girls were dismissed with the directive "to think about it" because the matter was not closed.

Shortly after this, Nadine complained to me that she was being persecuted and, although I did not say it to Nadine, I agreed with her. I approached the principal, arguing on Nadine's behalf, saying that perhaps the two girls were merely reiterating the presentation Mr. Sharp had given in class; after all, Nadine was a strong student and did not need to copy to get a good grade. The principal then asked me and another member of the English department, Mrs. Coleman, to take a look at the papers to determine if *only* plagiarism could account for the similarity between the papers. The evidence was shockingly clear; we both immediately agreed, without a shadow of a doubt, that Nadine had plagiarized.

Mrs. Coleman called Nadine into her room and related a personal experience that she hoped would convince her to confess. Nadine maintained her innocence. Mr. Magner, her advisor, spoke to her, asking her to confess. She maintained her innocence. I spoke to her and told her that it was all right to make a mistake, and encouraged her to confess. She maintained her innocence.

The principal talked to both Nadine and Michelle several more times, both individually and together. The more evidence that was gathered, the clearer it became that Nadine had copied, but she adamantly denied this. Finally, the principal and all of the teachers involved agreed that the only thing left to do was to give Nadine until the end of the week to think it over. If she did not confess by the end of the day on Friday, she would be expelled. After school on Thursday, I tried once more to get Nadine to tell the truth. I went through the papers line by line with Nadine and told her that if she did not confess she would be expelled, and I explained how that might affect her scholarship and maybe even her acceptance into college. In tears, she finally admitted that she had indeed copied the papers from Michelle's disk to her own.

Nadine apologized to Michelle and to all teachers involved, attributing her uncharacteristic behavior to extreme stress. As her punishment, she had to rewrite one of the papers and received a zero on the other, she was expelled from the Honor Society, and she was not allowed to go on the much anticipated week-long Senior Trip. In addition, she served a week of in-house suspension, was disqualified from receiving any awards at the end of the year, and was not allowed to be publicly inducted into Quill and Scroll with the other students from the yearbook staff who qualified.

Discussion

The thing that bothers me most about this incident is the fact that I took it upon myself to talk to Nadine on Thursday and to go through the paper line by line, telling her she would be expelled if she did not confess. We had all agreed that we would give Nadine an extra day to think it over, giving her a chance to come forward voluntarily. I thought that I was helping Nadine, but now I realize that the pressure I put on her left her no choice but to admit her guilt, and as a result, we will never know if she would have done so of her own accord. Furthermore, Nadine was denied the ethical experience of taking responsibility for her actions. Her motivation to confess was pure self-preservation—being expelled from school in the last semester of her senior year was a greater evil than admitting to cheating.

There are two other things that bother me about this incident. The first one is that the issue underwent an interesting transformation as events unfolded. Nadine's cheating was overshadowed by her refusal to acknowledge it. The administrator and teachers involved shifted their focus from what Nadine did wrong and instead concentrated on her moral development.

Finally, it bothers me that there were two incidents of plagiarism, but, since the first paper wasn't graded in a timely fashion, Nadine may have believed that copying someone else's paper wasn't really that serious an offense. If this is true, then it seems to me that Mr. Sharp is partially to blame because he may have inadvertently encouraged the view that Nadine had gotten away with it the first time and could do so again.

Questions

1. Did I act correctly when I told Nadine she would be expelled if she did not confess? Did I prevent her from making the decision on her own?
2. Was the incident blown out of proportion and the punishment too extreme, or should Nadine have been expelled?
3. Is it possible that the fact that Nadine was a good student, a role model for other students, and was well liked by the faculty colored the issue?
4. Should the school develop a policy on plagiarism that leaves room for weighing extenuating circumstances, or should it be made cut and dried, especially in light of their cosmopolitan student body?
5. Should Nadine have been disqualified from Quill and Scroll? (Although she was not publicly inducted, she was allowed to retain her membership, which had been registered months before.)
6. Is there some way to ensure the security of students' work when they are composing at the computer?

Challenge Case 11

Background

It is the custom at our school to have parent-teacher conferences early in the year. We believe that the conferences help to encourage communication between teacher, parent, and child. I enjoy the conferences because they give me added insights into the needs of each individual child.

When Rick's parents arrived for their conference, Rick's aunt (his mom's sister) was also present. Throughout the conference, the dad responded very few times, the mom talked some, Rick was reserved, and the aunt talked nonstop. Although most of the comments added little to my understanding of Rick, I did find out that Rick had a new baby brother. I knew this might affect Rick's behavior since he had been an only child for eight years and now the baby was the center of everyone's attention. In fact, during the conference the family wanted to talk more about the new baby than about Rick.

As the school year began, I noticed Rick was not readily accepted by the other students. He was not an outcast, but he did have problems socializing. He seemed to manipulate a friendship with two other boys in the class: Mitch and Milton. M and M (as I called them) were always together. You could tell that they were uneasy whenever Rick would approach them, but they always allowed him to join them in their activities.

Near the end of September, Mitch's mom came to me very concerned. Mitch had told her that while he was urinating, Rick had grabbed Mitch's private parts. She wasn't sure how often this occurred, but she did know that Rick had displayed "odd" behavior since first grade. I thanked her for making me aware of the incident.

Two weeks later, Milton's mom came to me with the same complaint—that while Milton was urinating, Rick had grabbed Milton's private parts. She also confided in me that she had been concerned about Rick's influence on Milton since first grade. Milton would come home singing obscene songs that Rick had reportedly taught him. I discussed the parental concerns and reports with my principal and we began to analyze the situation and tried to decide how to handle this problem. We tried to contact the social worker right after Mitch's mom reported the incident but were told that we wouldn't be able to meet with her until sometime in December.

I began watching Rick more closely. I noticed certain body language in Rick that was uncommon to third-grade boys. Whenever he talked to someone, he leaned in close and low. He was a tall child, though, and I thought perhaps his height contributed to this strange behavior. Whenever I came close to him and he was talking to someone, he would quit talking. I conferred with his first- and second-grade teachers. They didn't know of any unusual incidents concerning Rick but they both noted that he was "different." So far, nothing concrete had developed with Rick, but I continued to monitor and observe him. As November neared, Rick seemed to associate more with M and M, and only M and M. No other incidents were reported by the mothers, however.

Incident

Just before Christmas vacation, the class had a gift exchange. On the day of the Christmas party, the students brought in their gifts. As the children arrived, I placed a numbered sticker on each gift and the children placed the gift under the tree. I placed all the corresponding numbers in a container and then during the party each child drew a number. I made sure no one drew the number on the gift he or she brought. As the children eagerly unwrapped their presents, the room filled with excitement and happiness. One of the boys, Karl, received a very nice gift—a model airplane. I noticed that Rick was very intrigued with this gift and, seemingly, disgruntled with his gift of a sports mug.

At the close of the day, the room mothers and I sent each child home for the vacation with wishes for a happy holiday. I thought I was able to see each individual leave, but, with the hustle and bustle, a few children did get by without me seeing them leave the room. A few lingered on. Karl came to me with tears in his eyes and told me that his gift was missing! We scoured the room, retraced his steps, and spoke with remaining students, but no one had seen the gift. Karl was crushed.

All during the holidays, I kept going over the party in my mind. I kept thinking of how Rick had been eyeing the model all afternoon. Shortly after Christmas, I ran into Rick's mom in the grocery store and tried causally to mention the gift, thinking that if Rick had brought it home his mom would have seen it. As soon as I mentioned the model, however, she said she was in a big hurry and left.

Discussion

After the holidays, I decided to pursue the incident further and spent part of the first class period talking to the children about why it was wrong to steal. No one admitted to stealing the gift, but during the discussion Rick did seem uneasy. Shortly after this discussion, there was another reported incident of Rick grabbing a student's private parts. The principal and I decided that we needed to meet with Rick's parents and make them aware of his unusual behavior. It was also decided that the social worker should be present at the meeting.

Before I could set up the meeting, however, I entered the hospital. I underwent surgery, which resulted in my going on disability leave. My class had three different substitute teachers during February, March, and April. The last substitute teacher told the principal that Rick's behavior didn't seem "normal." She had nothing concrete—just "gut feelings" that something was not right. In spite of this, the principal did not follow up on the decision to meet with Rick's parents and the social worker.

When I returned to school at the beginning of May, I noticed that Rick's behavior had gotten worse since I had been away. He was pushing children on the playground, not doing his work during the day, and talking back to me. By the middle of May, it was reported that Rick had grabbed another child's private parts. I talked to the principal about this and we immediately called for a conference with the parents. It was once again agreed that the social worker would attend. I prayed for a quick and uncomplicated resolution to the problem. However, because the social worker's calendar was full, the meeting could not be held until the last day of school.

On the day of the conference, the social worker and I entered the conference room and found that Rick's parents and younger brother were already there. I immediately felt the tension in the room. The principal began by saying that we were meeting to discuss Rick's unusual behavior—mainly the accusations of the reported sexual incidents throughout the year. The father was furious and defensive. Every time his wife spoke, he told her to "shut up!" Before I knew it, the mom verbally attacked me, saying that I had accused her child of stealing. The parents continued to get more and more angry and finally just got up and left the meeting. As they were leaving, the dad turned to me and said, "My son may be capable of stealing, but we never saw the model in our house."

The principal, social worker, and I went over the meeting and we all agreed that I had not accused Rick of stealing and that it was the mother who brought up the missing gift. We also noted that the missing gift seemed more important to the parents than did Rick's behavior. The meeting resolved nothing. Rick went home for the summer with all of his problems intact. In all honesty, I was thankful it was the last day of school! I had summer vacation in which to recuperate and new beginnings to anticipate. Rick, his unusual behavior, and the missing gift were now part of my past.

Questions

1. I don't know if Rick stole the model airplane, but I had a hunch that he did. Does this mean that I did not remain as objective in my observations as I should have?
2. Should my principal have followed up and held the meeting earlier as planned, even though I was in the hospital and unable to attend?
3. Should Rick's parents have been notified immediately after the reports from Mitch and Milton's moms—even though I had no concrete evidence?
4. Were there other procedures that could have been followed that would have defused the meeting with the parents?
5. Was Rick's behavior really that unusual or was I seeing more than was actually present?
6. What are the best ways to handle stealing and finding the "culprit"? And is it worth the effort and aggravation?

Closing Remarks

The case reports in this book serve to demonstrate just how complex the school environment truly is. Within the cases are examples of the effects that classroom characteristics and/or school environment can have on both students and teachers. Walter Doyle, an educational researcher who studies the organization and management of classrooms, has found that the "intrinsic features of the classroom environment create constant pressures that shape the task of teaching. Although their intensity varies with particular conditions, these pressures operate in all classrooms regardless of how events are organized" (1986, p. 394).

The majority of the reports provided in this book deal with intense, negative situations. This is not to imply that teaching is an intensely negative experience. Quite the opposite is true. Most teachers find teaching to be a worthwhile, rewarding occupation. Successful teachers find ways of avoiding classroom crises and develop techniques for handling those that they cannot avoid. With experience, teachers develop their own models of teaching that work for them. Successful models incorporate findings from research, characteristics of the students in the classroom, unique properties of the school environment, and the strengths and weaknesses of the teacher. However, even the most successful of teachers will encounter difficult situations. This is true of both experienced and less experienced teachers. The cases in this book are negative because the teachers were asked to provide a report on a troubling incident. If they had been asked to provide reports on satisfying incidents, the responses would of course have been much different.

Remember—good teachers are more proactive than reactive. They constantly strive to increase their understanding of the relationships between theory and practice. They usually have highly developed reflective thinking and problem-solving skills that they employ on a daily basis. All of this is done in an effort to help their students. *Reports from the Classroom: Cases for Reflection,* is designed to help you polish your skills in these areas because, as Judith Shulman has noted, "Case-based teaching provides teachers with opportunities to analyze situations and make judgments in the messy world of practice, where principles often appear to conflict with one another and no simple solution is possible" (1992, p. xiv). It is through this analysis that teachers move from being reactive to being proactive. If this book has helped you, in even a small way, to develop your professional skills, then its purpose has been met.

References

Doyle, W. (1986). Classroom organization and management. In M. C. Whittrock (Ed.), *Handbook of research on teaching* (3rd ed., pp. 392–431). New York: Macmillan.

Shulman, J. H. (1992). *Case methods in teacher education.* New York: Teachers College Press.